THE NEW SOLUTION SELLING

THE

NEW SOLUTION SELLING

The Revolutionary Sales Process That Is Changing the Way People Sell

Keith M. Eades

McGraw·Hill

New York   Chicago   San Francisco   Lisbon   London   Madrid   Mexico City
Milan   New Delhi   San Juan   Seoul   Singapore   Sydney   Toronto

The **McGraw·Hill** Companies

This publication is designed to provide accurate and authoritative information in regard to the subject matter covered. It is sold with the understanding that neither the author nor the publisher is engaged in rendering legal, accounting, or other professional services. If legal advice or other expert assistance is required, the services of a competent professional person should be sought.

— From a Declaration of Principles jointly adopted by a Committee of the American Bar Association and a Committee of Publishers

Library of Congress Cataloging-in-Publication Data
Eades, Keith M.
    The new solution selling/by Keith M. Eades.
            p. cm.
    Includes index.
    ISBN 0-07-143539-5 (alk. paper)
  1. Selling. 2. Sales Management. I. Title.
HF5438.25 .E18 2003
658.85—dc22
                                    2003016376

5 6 7 8 9 0   DOC/DOC   0 9 8 7 6 5

ISBN 0-07-143539-5

McGraw-Hill books are available at special quantity discounts to use as premiums and sales promotions, or for use in corporate training programs. For more information, please write to the Director of Special Sales, Professional Publishing, McGraw-Hill, Two Penn Plaza, New York, NY 10121-2298. Or contact your local bookstore.

This book is printed on recycled, acid-free paper containing a minimum of 50% recycled de-inked fiber.

Dedicated to the 500,000 salespeople
that utilize Solution Selling daily to improve
their performance and contribute to their
customers' success. They bring reality
to the words honorable selling.

To Margie—the love of my life, and to
Michael, John, and David, the best sons
a father could wish for.

To my dad for giving me my first sales job,
and to my mother for her encouragement and
belief that I could do anything.

Contents

Foreword

Over the past few years, global economic pressure and competition have influenced the way customers across the world evaluate and adopt technology. Customers are seeking to reduce their ongoing operating costs to fund investments in new solutions targeted at specific opportunities in their businesses. In our engagement with partners and customers we recognize that solutions become relevant when they solve real business issues and help people and businesses become more efficient and agile.

The key to success is connection. And I believe very strongly in the importance of working to strengthen the interaction between Microsoft and our customers. It is through connection that we accomplish our goal of delivering solutions that provide customer value and satisfaction.

Our customers have asked for more predictability and consistency in their relationships with us. Towards this goal, we have established a consistent selling method for each and every one of us at Microsoft that enables us to act upon strengthening our connection and being more consistent with and predictable to our customers.

In our journey of working together, we have put the principles of Solution Selling at the core of our selling process, helping all of our 5,000 sales professionals and thousands of Microsoft's business partners consistently apply proven sales principles to make a real difference to our customers and meet expectations.

Customer satisfaction is derived from exceeding expectations. Through the use of Solution Selling we can become more predictable to our customers in how we listen to their challenges and concerns, how we provide a vision of a solution, and how we deliver on that vision.

It is my hope that by embracing the tenets of Solution Selling at the heart of our sales process, we will improve the value we deliver to customers.

This book is all about how to create and sustain a high-performance sales culture that maintains the customer as its central focus. *The New Solution Selling* describes how top-performing salespeople behave, and how this behavior fosters success—for both the customer and the seller. In this book, Keith Eades shows how our salespeople can become a key differentiator in the selection of Microsoft from all other alternatives in the market.

By adopting Solution Selling as our standard sales method, we can provide more value to our customers, while at the same time, improving our own effectiveness and efficiency. As you read *The New Solution Selling*, I would encourage you to apply these ideas for improving your own sales approach as well as for developing a high-performance sales culture within your organization to reach your mutual goal of customer value and satisfaction.

KEVIN JOHNSON,
Microsoft Group Vice President,
Worldwide Sales, Marketing, and Services

Preface

Solution Selling is the industry standard for sales execution process. Used by more than 500,000 sales professionals worldwide, Solution Selling provides the foundation of process and practices that can make "eagles" out of average sales performers.

Solution Selling has evolved to keep pace with the latest economic trends, business conditions, and the rapidly changing world of selling. In general, the pace of decision making in customers' buying cycles has accelerated, driven by improved communications and global competition. Since the original Solution Selling book was first published, the world has seen the introduction of the Internet, the World Wide Web, advanced multichannel sales strategies, greatly improved telecommunications and computing productivity tools, and emerging international markets.

Especially since the onset of the global recession, the behaviors required for sales professionals' success have changed. *The New Solution Selling* incorporates these changes while never losing the essential models that make the Solution Selling sales execution process work. *The New Solution Selling* contains the following important enhancements:

- *Strengthened process orientation: The New Solution Selling* emphasizes the value of a repeatable, integrated sales execution process. In particular, this book integrates pipeline milestones throughout each phase of the selling process. The result is sales behavior that is more consistent, that is coachable, and which produces improved sales results and higher-quality forecasts.

- *Tighter process integration*: *The New Solution Selling* contains new sales tools and job aids that help both salespeople and managers to propel the sales process forward. The integration and dependencies of the entire Solution Selling process have been streamlined and enhanced, eliminating any redundant or unnecessary step, depending on the complexity of the sales opportunity.
- *Improved precall planning*: In today's economy, no sales call can be taken for granted. *The New Solution Selling* includes new content for improving precall planning and research with supporting job aids (for example, Account Profiles, Initial Pain Chains, Key Players List, and quantifiable Value Propositions).
- *Improved focus on value*: *The New Solution Selling* includes models for communicating the consistent and convincing concept of value in each step of the selling process. Specifically, the Solution Selling Value Cycle job aids provide practical tools for identifying and expressing quantifiable and measurable value to the customer—an essential differentiator in today's sales environment.
- *New tools for managing active opportunities*: The original Solution Selling book emphasized the value of finding latent sales opportunities; *The New Solution Selling* retains this important concept, but also includes new job aids for competing effectively in active opportunities that are highly competitive. The new job aids include Opportunity Assessment and Competitive Strategy selection.
- *Linking sales to implementation/customer service*: *The New Solution Selling* includes enhancements to the Evaluation Plan sales tool to incorporate the implementation of the solution adopted by the customer, thus providing a smooth transition between the close of the sale and the delivery of the solution's value.

- *Improved scalability*: *The New Solution Selling* provides an excellent process for managing sophisticated sales campaigns as well as simpler sales transactions. *The New Solution Selling* has been tailored for midmarket and small-business opportunities, as well as for integrated telemarketing and telesales processes, with great success. For example, the 9 Block Vision Processing Model has been simplified for less complicated sales. All other job aids contained in *The New Solution Selling* are designed with scalability in mind, making *The New Solution Selling* much more relevant and adaptable to multiple sales situations.
- *Improved linkage to sales management process*: *The New Solution Selling* is completely integrated with the supporting Solution Selling Sales Management program. This enables field sales managers to effectively assess and coach their sales teams, using the common framework of Solution Selling principles.

Solution Selling has revolutionized the world of selling for salespeople. *The New Solution Selling* takes the process to the next level and makes the process relevant to everyone that engages with customers.

Acknowledgments

The New Solution Selling grew out of our work with customers who have taken our sales process seriously and implemented it and then, to my delight, realized significant increases in their sales results. To all of my customers I say, "thank you." To the many people who have helped make Solution Selling and my company—Sales Performance International (SPI) successful—I will let this book stand as a symbol of my gratitude and thanks as well.

A few people helped me start my company from the beginning and are still with me today: Sean DesNoyer, Ed Ryan, and Doug Belcher. They helped develop much of the content and most of the customer relationships that we enjoy today. I often say that God sent an angel into my life the day that I met Sean DesNoyer. Sean, I will forever be grateful for your friendship and your contributions to our business. To my mentor for more than twenty years, Jeff Fisher, I will always be grateful.

I would be remiss not to acknowledge the contributions of all of the Solution Selling Business Partners and Affiliates that have contributed to the development of our Solution Selling products, services, and intellectual properties to the levels they are at today: capability rich and scalable. Solution Selling is a constant, never-ending, and improving sales process.

I also owe special thanks for the book's improved and new intellectual property to C. J. Warstler, Jimmy Touchstone, Mike "Mac" McLoughlin, John Rossmeissl, Tracy Peck, Don Perry, Bob McGarrah and Bill Reed, who tirelessly developed courses, tools, and exercises. Their work was tested and purchased by the likes of IBM, Microsoft,

GE, Bank of America, PNC, and many other customers in a variety of vertical markets.

Drafts of my manuscript were worked on by Howard Eaton, Bob Nishi, C. J. Warstler, Bob McGarrah, Bill Reed, Jeff Fisher, Tim Sullivan, Sallie Jarosz, Margie (my wife), and Karen Langford, my patient and savvy assistant. Special thanks to Jimmy Touchstone who helped me with the book's graphics, manuscript drafts, and organization. His untiring efforts are appreciated. Grateful thanks to Jeffrey Krames at McGraw-Hill, the acquisition and book editor. Jeffrey is a passionate person who stayed with the project, worked patiently, and brought it to market.

Finally, two people deserve special gratitude. First, my wife, Margie Eades, who persevered through the long effort, always supporting me, working on drafts, and helping to inspire me. Second, Howard Eaton, my colleague in Solution Selling, also a writer, who from our first meeting at Grandfather Mountain in North Carolina, where the bones of this book were first shaped, kept me at it—through all six or so drafts of the manuscript.

Thank you all.

THE NEW SOLUTION SELLING

PART ONE

Solution Selling
Concepts

CHAPTER ONE

Solutions

When I ask salespeople and sales executives whether their company provides solutions, they answer yes—virtually every time. Yet when I ask these same salespeople what solution they provided for their last customer, their answers tell a different story. I hear all about their products and services, complete with dazzling brand names and mind-boggling acronyms.

My point is that everybody claims they're in the solutions business, but for the most part it's just empty words. The word *solution* is used so much that no one knows what it means anymore. So, when salespeople say they are in the solutions business, buyers ignore these words, because to them it's just more sales and marketing hype. It is important for individuals and companies to recognize this problem and change their approaches.

Most companies and salespeople who claim to provide solutions are unconsciously engaging in selling products—not solutions. This leads me to conclude that people do not understand what a solution is.

So what is the definition of the word *solution*? The typical response is, "An answer to a problem." I agree with this response but feel it's important to expand the definition. Not only does the problem need to be acknowledged by the buyer, but both the buyer and salesperson must also agree on the answer. So a solution is a mutually agreed-upon answer to a recognized problem.

In addition, a solution must also provide some measurable improvement. By measurable improvement, I mean there is a before (a baseline) and an after (the baseline plus a delta). Now we have a more complete definition of a solution: It's a mutually shared answer to a recognized problem, and the answer provides measurable improvement.

Recently, an executive of a $13 billion company came to me and said, "We want to be in the solutions business and deliver what we've been promising for years. One of our marketing messages is, 'We sell and deliver solutions,' but we really don't do that. Just because all our promotional literature, advertising, and messaging has been saying this for years doesn't make it true."

He went on to say they wanted to find a way to transform—notice the key word *transform*—their company from product selling to solution selling. When I asked why, the answer came back emphatically, "Because our customers are demanding it."

I helped him realize that the transformation he was after takes time and has to occur simultaneously from the top down and the bottom up. It takes a total commitment from everyone in the company to develop, sell, market, and deliver solutions. The entire organization has to adopt a new philosophy, a new discipline—a new culture. It means that everyone involved with the customer needs to be onboard and do some things differently than they did in the past. I helped him realize that the company's new hires and its existing salespeople need to improve their customer-interfacing skills. Specifically, the salespeople need to be able to define and diagnose customer problems and create visions biased to his company's unique offerings and capabilities. I told him that being in the solutions business means that the company has to commit to actually solving problems and be willing to stay engaged until its customers realize measurable, positive change.

The executive convinced me that his peers could reach their transformation goal and make the difficult shift from product selling to solution selling. This is currently a work in progress, and the early results indicate very good progress on a journey that will take longer than they expected.

WHAT IS SOLUTION SELLING?

It's a sales process. (I'll develop this more fully throughout this book.) According to research conducted by Phillip G. Ryan Associates, it's the most widely used sales process focused on executable selling in the world today. More than 500,000 individuals have been trained in Solution Selling.

Executable selling activities involve direct contact with the buyer. For many individuals and companies, Solution Selling is their total end-to-end sales process. For others with more complex sales situations, it's the executable portion of their selling process. Solution Selling not only helps with what to do, but it specifically focuses on how to do it.

Solution Selling's sales process consists of the following components: a philosophy, a map, a methodology, and a sales management system. Solution Selling does not become another thing to do (on the list of mounting chores). It becomes *the* thing to do for salespeople, marketers, and managers.

It's a Philosophy

The customer is the focal point. Helping customers solve their business problems and achieve positive, measurable results is the basis of all actions, therefore the steps within the Solution Selling sales process are aligned with how buyers buy.

It's a Map

Solution Selling provides a map of how to get from where you are to where you want to be. Solution Selling provides an end-to-end series of next steps to follow. End-to-end means from the beginning of a sale right through to winning it. This includes precall planning, creating interest, diagnosing the problem, vision processing, controlling the sale, closing, and postsale tracking. It includes the ability to identify, analyze, report on, manage, and coach individual opportunities using the process. In addition, it provides the ability to predict sales success or failure.

It's a Methodology

Solution Selling is a system of methods that includes tools, job aids, techniques, and procedures that help salespeople and sales teams navigate the selling steps that close more sales faster. It results in higher levels of customer satisfaction and increased sales productivity.

It's a Sales Management System

Solution Selling provides sales and executive management with a process to analyze pipelines, qualify opportunities, and coach skills, thus increasing productivity and predictability. It results in a high-performance sales culture.

WHY SALES PROCESS?

Not all salespeople are created equal. You've heard the cliché "Some people are natural born salespeople"? They have that amazing talent that is hard to describe. We look at this group of intuitive and talented individuals, approximately 20 percent of the sales talent pool, and we call them *Eagles*. Sometimes these intuitive salespeople are called unconscious competents. They're good, but if you ask them why they're good, they'd have a hard time telling you why. That's the classic response of the unconscious competent.

We call the second category of sales talent *Journeypeople*. This group makes up the balance of the talent pool, or about 80 percent of the sales talent in the marketplace today. These people are ready, willing, and able to sell, but they do it quite differently than the Eagles. Journeypeople can, and many of them do, become good salespeople. However, the real key to their success is having a process to follow and knowing what to do next.

Eagles are the high flyers, the rainmakers. They are the ones who do things independently and who generate business. But they can't be expected to deliver all the business we need; there aren't enough of them. The 20 percent of the revenues that the Eagles don't deliver has to come from somewhere, and it must come from the Journeypeople. A company's overall sales success depends on the success of its Journeypeople. We need to help them become successful. Figure 1.1 shows the differences.

EAGLES (20 percent):
- Are Intuitive
- Have conversations
- Ask questions

JOURNEYPEOPLE (80 percent):
- Make presentations
- Make statements
- Process is key to success

Figure 1.1
Talent Assessment

What is the typical career path of Eagles? What do most companies do with their best salespeople? If you answered, "They promote them to managers," you'd be correct. But this creates a problem. Usually, when you promote Eagles (who don't consciously know how or why they excel) to sales management, they can't help the Journeypeople they now manage. Often they simply tell their salespeople, "Just watch me and do what I do." Eagles resort to this tactic because they don't have a sales process to follow. After all, a sales process provides both what to do and how to do it. To compound the problem, when an Eagle is promoted to management, a good revenue producer is lost from the sales force.

In the end, both management and the new sales manager become frustrated because of the lack of results. If management doesn't end up firing them, these people usually quit and go to work for another company doing what they're good at: selling. If you're party to something like this in your company, stop it. The key to stop promoting the wrong kind of people to sales management is to implement a good sales process.

Eagles are an important reason why I'm so passionate about sales process. When you convince an Eagle to use an effective sales process, you have the best of all worlds—he or she is unstoppable. On the other hand, I'm equally passionate about Journeypeople and their need for sales process. Journeypeople using a proven sales process can win most of the time when competing against an Eagle without a process. A good sales process allows Journeypeople to emulate Eagle selling behavior, maximize their individual sales performance, and learn how to become tomorrow's sales managers.

THE 64 PERCENT DILEMMA

Would you consciously assign your least-capable salespeople to your most difficult prospects? Probably not, but I find a number of companies doing exactly that. We call this challenge the "64 percent dilemma" (see Figure 1.2).

The concept is based, in part, on Geoffrey Moore's analysis as explained in his book *Crossing the Chasm*. In Moore's book, buyers are separated into market segments based on their behavior.

Depicted on the vertical axis of Figure 1.2 is a group of buyers called innovators, or early adopters. This group makes up about 20 percent of the market. As a group, they typically want to be the first to have new things, and they're the easiest group to sell to.

Also depicted on the vertical axis is a category of buyers called pragmatists, conservatives, or laggards They make up about 80 percent of the marketplace. These are slow-to-act, conservative buyers. They demand things such as references, proof, and ROI (return on investment) analysis before they will make a decision. As a group, they're the most difficult to sell to.

On the horizontal axis, you have Eagles (20 percent) and Journeypeople (80 percent). When you combine the two categories of buyers with the two categories of sales talent, you have a classic matrix with some interesting findings.

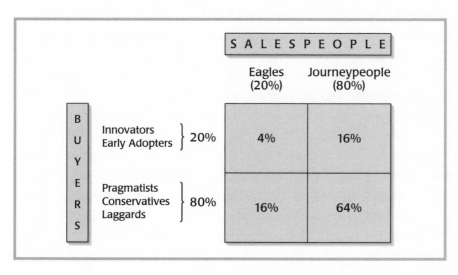

Figure 1.2 Why Sales Process?

Look at the 64 percent quadrant. This is the challenge, and it's why we call it the 64 percent dilemma. This is where companies have Journeypeople selling to the most challenging and difficult-to-sell-to buyer segment. In other words, 64 percent of the time you've got less than your very best salespeople selling to the toughest buyer segment. Why do that? The solution is a no-brainer. Companies and individuals should stop kidding themselves and stop the insanity by putting a sales process in place to help solve this dilemma. I hope that by now you're convinced of the importance of sales process. Just in case you aren't, keep reading.

SITUATIONAL FLUENCY

Buyers want to do business with salespeople who understand them— their jobs and their problems. They want to do business with someone who has situational fluency—in other words, a person who has a good understanding of their situation as well as a good working knowledge of the capabilities necessary to help them solve their problems. What buyers don't want are pushy salespeople interested only in selling their products and services. Buyers want a consultant who is going to add value to their situations. Otherwise, buyers would just go to your Web site for product information and price quotes. Salespeople must add value to the situation or they won't survive.

Figure 1.3 illustrates the elements that help salespeople develop situational fluency and gain credibility with their buyers.

If situational fluency is what buyers are looking for in salespeople, what are sales managers looking for when they hire salespeople? What I hear them say is that they want salespeople with great selling skills; they want "great closers." They look for closing skills and people with successful selling track records. Granted, success in the past is important, but I try to get them to see that success in the past doesn't ensure success in the future. This is particularly true if it involves selling into a new industry and dealing with new products, new technologies, or

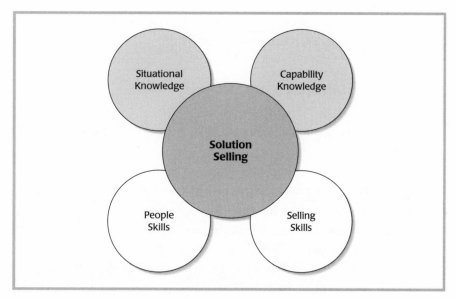

Figure 1.3 Solution Selling Situational Fluency

new services. The good ole boy, backslapping, tongue-wagging sales-person doesn't get the job done anymore.

I am not minimizing the importance of good people skills and good selling skills. In fact, in Solution Selling we incorporate key selling skills as a part of the overall process. Solution Selling develops situational fluency by integrating the knowledge competencies (situational knowledge and capability knowledge) with people skills and selling skills. Solution Selling is the only sales process that integrates all four of these components.

DIFFICULTIES IN SELLING
SALES MANAGEMENT, AND EXECUTIVE MANAGEMENT

In addition to integrating both knowledge and skills, Solution Selling addresses specific selling, sales management, and executive management difficulties. What follows are some of the challenges we often see and hear as we begin to work with our clients. See how many of these issues resonate with you.

Typical Selling Difficulties

- "I'm having a hard time meeting, much less exceeding, my sales quota."
- "Our product isn't competitive anymore."
- "Buyers say our services are too costly and can't justify them."
- "They wouldn't let me in at the right level."
- "If only my manager would have discounted."
- "The consultant didn't do a good job."
- "I lose control of our prospects at the end of the sell cycle."
- "We got in too late."
- "The prospect didn't know what she wanted."
- "We missed the needs of certain committee members."
- "I get an opportunity started and our resellers drop the ball."
- "My manager tells me what to do, not how to do it."
- "My competition's Web site is great, and we get outsold before we even get started."
- "My managers demand detailed sales forecasts—do they want me to sell or enter data into a system?"
- "Prospects can buy the same capabilities from someone else, so I have to outsell my competition to win the business."

Typical Sales Management Difficulties

- "It's becoming increasingly difficult to predict revenue."
- "My salespeople are comfortable calling on technical and end users but are ineffective with executive management."
- "Many of our salespeople wing it."
- "We lose more to no decision than to any single competitor."

- "Only a few of our new hires develop into top producers. There must be something wrong with our hiring model."
- "Salespeople take sales support or technical people with them on too many calls."
- "Marketing efforts are out of sync with our sales efforts."
- "Salespeople blame losses on the product."
- "As soon as the pipeline looks good, prospecting stops."
- "We're making our numbers but it's too tough. Life is too short to work this hard!"
- "It's difficult to find new opportunities, so we end up responding to RFPs or tenders wired for our competition."
- "By the time I'm asked to get involved, it's usually too late."
- "Qualifying out of opportunities isn't in our vocabulary."
- Quarter-end fire drills have become a way of life."

Typical Executive Management Difficulties

- "Getting accurate revenue forecast is a nightmare."
- "All our strategic initiatives are dependent on making our revenue goals."
- "The sales group is a mystery. Other groups in the company are much easier to hold accountable."
- "We make great products in this company. Why can't we sell them?"
- "Growing cost is not the problem; growing revenues is."
- "We missed our quarterly revenue number. Fortunately, it was on the plus side. What would have happened if it had been on the negative side?"

In the next chapter, we explore the underlying principles of the Solution Selling sales process, which will serve as a springboard to each step in the process and the rest of the book.

CHAPTER TWO

Principles

The New Solution Selling was developed in response to today's highly competitive global economy and draws on years of research and selling experiences. The principles covered in this chapter are the foundation of Solution Selling. After reading this chapter, please begin to apply the principles immediately. You don't have to wait to finish the entire book before you start.

SOLUTION SELLING PRINCIPLES

A partial list of Solution Selling's underlying principles include:

- No pain, no change.
- Pain flows throughout the entire organization.
- Diagnose before you prescribe.
- There are three levels of buyer need.
- There are two types of opportunities—Looking and Not Looking.

- Get there first, set the requirements, and make yourself Column A.
- You can't sell to someone who can't buy.
- Buyers' concerns shift over time.
- Pain × Power × Vision × Value × Control = Sale

Solution Selling Principle—No Pain, No Change

The foundation principle of Solution Selling is: No pain, no change. We define pain as a problem, a critical business issue, or a potential missed opportunity. If a person or a company doesn't have a problem, critical business issue, or pending missed opportunity, why should he change? We use the word *pain* in Solution Selling to emphasize the concept. We don't encourage salespeople to use this term with buyers.

I believe this concept holds true for virtually everything sold today. I remember making this statement in a Solution Selling workshop and being challenged by one of the attendees. She asked, "How can that be? What are the so-called pains associated with luxury items?" Unknowingly, she began to answer her own question with her next statement: "After all, people buy luxury items because they want to, not because they have to." I simply looked at her and asked, "Have you ever wanted something so much that not having it was painful?" In other words, the desire to have, to achieve, or to experience something may itself become the pain or the reason that will cause you to change the way you're currently doing things.

Pain gives people a reason to change. Pain causes people to take action, to change a negative situation, or to act on their wants and desires for a better situation. People and companies don't typically do things or buy things without a compelling reason. When pain is admitted and the value of the resolution of the pain is quantified, it provides buyers with a compelling reason to act.

Solution Selling Principle—
Pain Flows Throughout the Entire Organization

How dependent are football, hockey, and basketball teams on their players to be in sync in order to perform well? Everyone knows that team sports require players to be in sync in order to play well and win championships. Companies and organizations are no different. Simply put, people within functional groups are dependent on each other. This concept—interdependence—is the structure upon which companies are built. Although the level of interdependence within companies may vary, it's always there.

Interdependence has a great deal to do with selling, particularly for solutions that are implemented throughout a company. In today's world of complex decision making, more than ever we need to understand the problems and challenges of our prospective buyers more holistically. Only then can we address the root causes of problems and provide solutions rather than simply treat the symptoms.

One individual's problems link to other people within the same organization. In selling, it's important not only to identify and quantify the pain of the individual whom you're talking to but also to link that problem to others. The enabling solution means greater value for the customer and a companywide selling opportunity for salespeople.

In Chapter Four, I graphically map these links into a sales aid called a Pain Chain. The Pain Chain illustrates problems and their reasons and how they are manifested throughout an organization.

Solution Selling Principle—Diagnose Before You Prescribe

When you diagnose before you prescribe, you have an understanding of the customer's problem before you discuss the solution. The reverse of this, prescribe before you diagnose, means that you will be proposing a solution without understanding the problem. Even if your prescription turns out to be correct, the customer may feel uncomfortable and bring the sale to a halt. This principle is described in more detail in Chapter Seven.

Solution Selling Principle—Three Levels of Need

There are three levels of need, and you'll find people, buyers, and organizations at all three levels. The key is for salespeople, and anyone else involved with buyers, to be aware of this and adjust their approaches accordingly. The approaches differ, depending on the level of need at which you find people (see Figure 2.1).

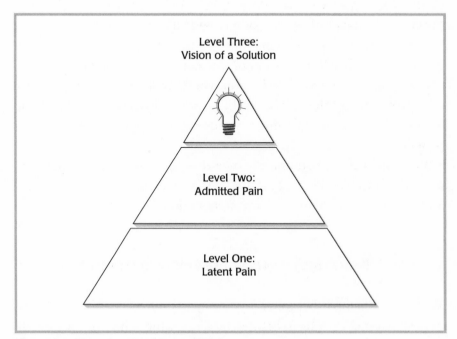

Figure 2.1 Three Levels of Buyer Need

Level 1: Latent Pain Buyers who are not looking and not actively trying to solve a problem are in latent pain. There are two primary reasons for buyers being at this level of need: ignorance or rationalization. Ignorance means they're unaware of the problem, and rationalization means they know about the problem, but they may not believe a solution exists or they may have failed at previous attempts to solve the problem. Buyers at this level frequently rationalize the potential solutions as too expensive, complicated, or risky. Whether because of ignorance or rationalization, buyers at this level of need are living with problems that in most cases can be solved.

Key salesperson action at this level is to help the buyer become aware of and admit his or her problems. I often tell salespeople that if buyers aren't aware they have problems that the salesperson's products or services can solve, selling the problem is the first thing they have to do.

Level 2: Admitted Pain The buyer is willing to discuss problems, difficulties, or dissatisfaction with the existing situation. The buyer admits the problem but doesn't know how to solve it. At this level, buyers tell us their problems but aren't taking action. An example of this is e-business. People know they should be doing something in this area, but they're still on the sidelines. Why? They don't have a clear vision of what to do or how to get started.

Salespeople at this level should fully diagnose the problem and create a vision of a solution that buyers can see themselves implementing.

Level 3: Vision of a Solution The buyer accepts responsibility for solving his or her problems and can visualize what is needed to address them. This is the action stage.

Key salesperson actions at this level are to support the buyer's vision if you created that vision or to reengineer the buyer's vision if you didn't. The biggest mistake salespeople make with buyers at this level is to assume they have a good chance of winning because the buyers are in a ready-to-buy frame of mind.

In summary, you'll find buyers at all three levels. In the first level of latent pain, your job as the salesperson is to make buyers aware that a problem exists. In the second level, admitted pain, your job is to confirm the pain that they're having and lead them to a vision of a solution. At the third level, vision of a solution, the approach is to develop or re-create a vision of what the buyer will be able to do differently after implementing your capabilities.

Solution Selling Principle—Looking and Not Looking

If you look at Figure 2.2, you'll see that potential opportunities are divided into two primary categories: Looking and Not Looking. *Looking* means

Figure 2.2 Looking and Not Looking

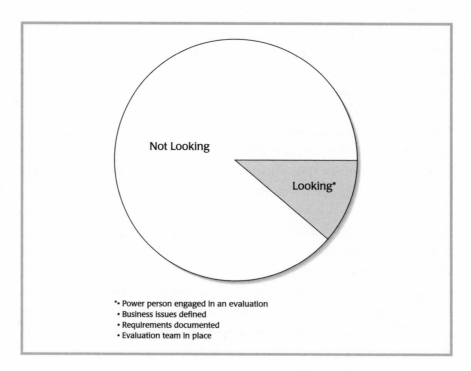

Not Looking

Looking*

*• Power person engaged in an evaluation
• Business issues defined
• Requirements documented
• Evaluation team in place

the buyer has made a commitment to buy something. The buyer has defined his or her requirements and is engaging salespeople in an evaluation process. What percentage is actively looking to buy? The answer varies, but in most cases only 5 or 10 percent are actually looking. That means that over 90 percent of the potential customers are Not Looking. Why is this? Is it because that 90 percent have no problems? No. Either through ignorance or rationalization, these potential buyers are living with their problems; their pain is latent. The greatest opportunities lie with these people who have problems but who are not actively engaged in looking for a solution. Why does the Not Looking category of buyers provide such great potential? The answer lies in the next principle.

Solution Selling Principle—Get There First, Set the Requirements, and Make Yourself Column A

The main goal in this competitive world of selling is to win the business and help our customers. The probability of winning is much greater when you get there first, set the requirements, and put yourself in the most favored position, Column A. Look at Figure 2.3.

The chart illustrates how organizations typically evaluate and buy things. Most companies and individuals, either consciously or unconsciously, use some type of evaluation matrix to help them decide. People rank competing companies into first, second, or third choice, and so on. The key task is for the salesperson to control Column A because of the high probability of winning the business. When a salesperson sells in the latent (Not Looking) area, that salesperson has an excellent opportunity to set or define the buyer's buying requirements—and claim the Column A position. If the salesperson does a good job during this definition phase, the buyer's vision (buying requirements) becomes aligned with the salesperson's products and services and becomes the buyer's first choice.

Figure 2.3 Make
Yourself Column A

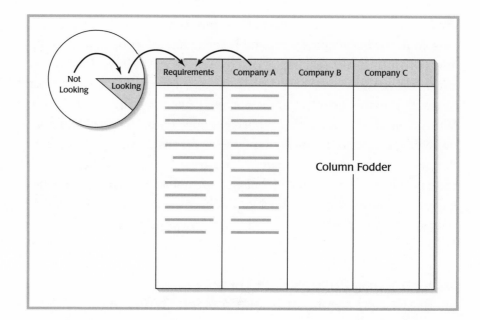

Experience has proven that salespeople who become Column A stand an overwhelming chance of winning the sale. Our experience and research indicate that companies that find opportunities in latent pain, bring them to the active state of evaluation, and become Column A win more than 90 percent of the time.

The question many salespeople ask is, "Can I still win if I didn't define the problems, create the vision, and put myself in Column A?" The answer is yes, but the odds of winning are lower. There are some very specific things you must do to increase the odds of winning. I'll cover those topics in Part Three, "Engaging in Active Opportunities."

Solution Selling Principle— You Can't Sell to Someone Who Can't Buy

You can't sell to someone who can't buy; however, you can spend a great deal of time, money, and effort with people who can't make a purchasing decision—and a lot of salespeople do. You can take people to lunch and engage in a lot of social activities in an attempt to influence them, but sooner or later you need to interact with people who have real power. These are people with the influence to get what they want or the absolute authority to make a buying decision. If the person you're dealing with doesn't have power, then he or she must provide you with access to someone who does.

I encourage sales and telesales people to target and call on people as high up in an organization as possible. It's better to start high and be delegated down than to be warned not to go over someone's head and get trapped inside an organization.

Many salespeople complain they have difficulty calling on and getting access to powerful people, and there are several reasons for this. For one, young salespeople typically have little experience calling on executive or high-level personnel, and they're understandably uncomfortable. Another reason is that many salespeople can't talk about the business of the person they're calling on. They lack situational knowledge. Instead, these salespeople target and call on lower-level people, who tell them what they want to hear and most likely let them buy lunch.

Solution Selling Principle—Buyers' Concerns Shift over Time

As buyers progress through their buying process, their concerns change. Their statements and actions provide feedback on where they are in the process. Ultimately, the more salespeople understand what is important to buyers as they move from one buying phase to another, the better positioned salespeople will be to respond appropriately to the buyers. Figure 2.4 illustrates this.

For example, at the beginning of the buying process, buyers are typically concerned with needs and cost—we call this Phase I (or the determining needs phase). However, once their needs are defined and budgets are established, their concern shifts to evaluating alternatives that can

Figure 2.4 Buyers'
Concerns Shift
over Time

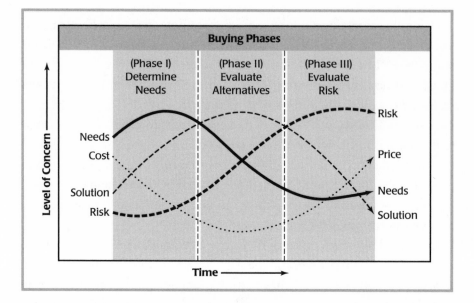

meet their needs and budget. This is Phase II. Toward the end of their buying process, after they've evaluated alternatives in Phase II, buyer concerns shift to risk and the cost of making a commitment. We call this Phase III (or evaluating risk). The buyers' shifting concerns and the level of those concerns define their particular buying phase. The more salespeople are aware of the psychological buying model and the buying phases, the better aligned they are with their buyers.

Take the example of first-time home buyers. Let's look at a young couple, Bob and Mary, and how their shared concerns shift over time as they progress through their buying process.

Buying Phase I: Determine Needs Bob and Mary have recognized a pain: they're tired of paying rent when their money could go toward owning a house.

In Phase I, Bob and Mary have to go through needs analysis. Their list of needs includes a number of vital requirements: three bedrooms, safe neighborhood, less than a forty-minute commute to and from work, two-car garage, convenient to shopping, good schools, and so on. Their annual household pretax income is $110,000, so they establish a budget figure for the price of a house as well as a monthly mortgage payment. Once these criteria have been established, they move to Phase II of their buying process, where they compare and evaluate their alternatives.

Buying Phase II: Evaluate Alternatives In Phase II, Bob and Mary are considering which house best matches their list of requirements and fits within their budget. It's normal buying behavior to evaluate alternatives, compare, and shop around. After all, smart buyers must make sure they're buying the right product or service, or in our couple's case, the right house.

It's a difficult time for our first-time home buyers. They have lots of choices with many homes meeting the majority of their needs. They get very excited while shopping because they're seeing all the possibilities. It's an emotional time, and it's very easy to lose sight of the budget that they originally set. We often hear people in Phase II say, "Yes, we have a budget, but we're going to get what we need even if we have to pay a little more." This sounds good to the salesperson at the time, but watch out—Phase III is coming. No matter what buyers tell you in Phase II about how price is not the most important factor, it almost always is in Phase III. It's part of the psychological buying process that buyers go through. (See Phase III in Figure 2.4.) In Phase II, buyers need to decide whether choice A, B, or C is the right one. It's important that the salesperson (in this example, a real estate agent) stay in alignment with the buyers (Bob and Mary). Let the buyers compare in Phase II and be prepared for vision reengineering, if necessary. Vision reengineering is described in detail in Chapter Seven.

At the end of Phase II, buyers tend to change their behavior: they start to become concerned about risk. Their body language and actions can indicate that they are entering the third buying phase.

Buying Phase III: Evaluate Risk What are the consequences of taking action? What happens after Bob and Mary buy the new house? What is their greatest concern? Risk. They begin questioning their own decision. They may ask questions such as: Will the warranties be honored? If we're unhappy during inspection or something goes wrong and it needs fixing, will we incur legal costs? How expensive could those legal costs be? Can we afford them? How secure are our jobs? Can we afford this house if something happens to either of us?

Risk causes people to slow down their decision-making process and maybe not make a decision at all. It's in this phase that salespeople lose deals without knowing why. The salesperson may have been winning the opportunity up to this point, but because he or she doesn't understand the risk phase and is not in alignment, he or she says and does the wrong things and loses the sale.

What about the price? Earlier our couple said it's important, but they were going to get what they wanted even if they had to pay a little more. What has happened to that perspective? Why are they trying to negotiate a better deal at the last minute? The answer is they have to, because they're in Phase III of their buying model, where risk and price are their major concerns.

The point of this example is that no matter what you sell, your buyers go through buying phases and their concerns shift as they go through them. It's important for salespeople to first recognize where buyers are and then align their selling activities with what is important to the buyers at the particular phase they're in.

Solution Selling Principle—Formula for Sales Success

The formula for sales success is Pain × Power × Vision × Value × Control = Sale. Each element of the formula should be monitored as a part of the sales process. Because it's a formula, if you have a zero in any variable on the left, you get a zero or no sale on the right.

- *Pain.* Has the buyer admitted pain?
- *Power.* Does the buyer have the influence and authority to make a buying decision?
- *Vision.* Does the buyer share the salesperson's vision of a solution?
- *Value.* Is there compelling value in the proposed solution? Does the buyer concur?
- *Control.* Is the salesperson able to exert elements of control over the buying process?

The sales formula can provide you with a quick way to qualify opportunities, measure the opportunities' probability of success, and help manage sales pipelines to meet revenue forecasts.

CHAPTER THREE

Sales Process

Solution Selling's research indicates that the majority of salespeople and the companies they work for do not utilize a common sales process. This truly amazes me in light of the complex and highly competitive world that we all sell into today. Our research also indicates that both individual and company-wide sales performance improves dramatically when a company-wide sales process is deployed. It is not uncommon for individuals and companies to realize a 15 percent or more increase in their productivity. The whole business generally prospers when everyone has a common language to use and a process to follow.

Like most Eagle salespeople, I was initially turned off by the term *sales process*. I thought a process was something that engineers and manufacturing people used, and it certainly didn't apply to me, a superstar salesperson. However, in 1984, I got turned on to what a sales process really is and what it can do, and my world has never been the same.

In that year, I was responsible for the training and development of 400 salespeople in the software industry. The challenge was to get our existing salespeople productive, selling the newly acquired products and services into an industry with which they were not familiar.

Previously, they had been selling financial reporting software to executives in the financial services industry. These customers knew who we were, the leader in the space, and they could readily understand the capabilities of our existing products and services. The new industry was manufacturing and the new products and services centered on automating their core business and how they manufactured their products. At the time this type of automation was generally known as a Materials Requirement and Planning System, or MRP II System. This was a big challenge because our salespeople did not know the manufacturing industry, and they certainly didn't know anything about the new products and services we had acquired to sell into this new space.

Could this be done at all was the first question, and where to start was the second. My first reaction was that it would be easier to start over with all new salespeople, but that wasn't an option. I had to use the existing sales talent we had and find a way to make it work.

Initially I started to teach all four hundred salespeople everything I thought they should know about the industry and back that up with comprehensive product training. I quickly learned that I didn't have enough time or money to make this approach work, and the salespeople didn't have the patience to endure it. Luckily, I stumbled upon a consultant who had previous experience selling into the manufacturing industry who suggested a different approach. He recommended that I start by teaching the salespeople how and why buyers buy manufacturing systems in the first place and then map or align our products and service capabilities to those issues. At first, I thought that seemed too simple, but I tried it and it worked. Thanks to the approach, we were able to quickly get the majority of our existing salespeople productive selling these newly acquired products and services into a new industry. Thankfully so, the approach helped the company grow to be the largest independent software company in the world at that time.

WHAT IS PROCESS?

By definition, a *process* is a systematic series of actions, or a series of defined, repeatable steps intended to achieve a result. When followed, these steps can consistently lead to expected outcomes.

There are many examples of process in our daily lives that we may not be aware of: Our cars are built or assembled using manufacturing processes, our clothes, our homes, and even the food we eat use process to ensure its quality and consistency.

It's the same in sales. A sale is a series of defined, repeatable steps that, if performed well and consistently, will lead to expected results. On the other hand, a sales effort without a series of well-defined steps too often leads to an unfavorable result.

A sales process defines and documents those end-to-end steps that lead to increased sales productivity. It provides a framework for each step in the process. A good sales process allows you to identify, analyze, qualify, and measure opportunities and then determine the next step in selling. A good sales process should also be aligned with how buyers buy rather than with how salespeople want to sell.

WHY HAVE A SALES PROCESS?

The simple answer is that it provides everyone involved in the sales effort with a roadmap of what to do next which leads to a higher probability of success. After all, today few sales campaigns are orchestrated by a single individual. And it doesn't matter if your sales cycles are one-event transactions or a series of events over long periods of time. Knowing what to do and when to do it is critically important to success.

A sales process allows individuals and companies to:

- Determine the next-step selling activities that lead to a higher probability of success
- Diagnose and correct sales deficiencies at individual and group levels
- Measure selling progress at an opportunity level
- Predict revenue attainment at an opportunity level
- Provide a common language that can be used by everyone who participates in any sales opportunity
- Manage customer expectations and improve overall customer satisfaction
- Enjoy life more

SALES PROCESS ELEMENTS

The five key elements included in a sales process are:

1. The customer's buying process
2. Selling steps that align with the buying process
3. Verifiable outcomes that let the salespeople know if they've been successful at each selling step
4. Job aids and tools that facilitate each processes's selling step
5. A management system that measures and reinforces the process and also determines the probability of success

Solution Selling's pyramid of sales process elements is shown in Figure 3.1.

Define the Customer's Buying Process

The cornerstone of a good sales process is in knowing how buyers buy rather than how a company or its individuals want to sell. If we haven't

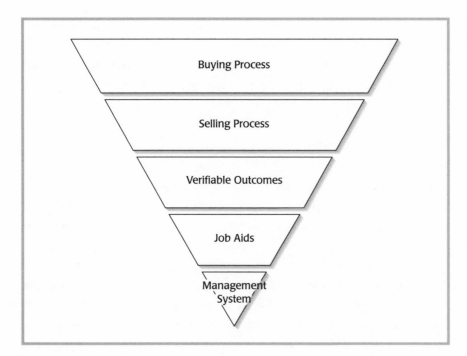

Figure 3.1 Sales
Process Elements

defined how our buyers buy, then we make assumptions that throw us out of alignment with our buyers. Misalignment with buyers is one of selling's most critical mistakes.

Another thing you have to remember is that buyers can have multiple buying processes. For example, they may buy commodities differently than they buy strategic business applications. To deal with this, sales organizations need to modify their sales processes to align with their customers' buying processes.

Define the Selling Steps

The second element in developing a sales process is to define and align the selling steps with the buyer's buying process steps. This is very important because being out of alignment with the buyer is the biggest reason for sales failure. Solution Selling's research indicates that when salespeople take action without knowing why or what the expected result should be, their failure rate is more than 50 percent.

Verifiable Outcomes

Each step in your sales process should have measurements and verifiable outcomes. There should be no question about whether or not a step has been completed. For example, when calling on a customer with the power to buy, your sales process might require the salesperson to send a letter confirming that the customer has agreed to evaluate your offering. Good sales process would measure this step and grade the salesperson's progress accordingly, using a verifiable outcome such as the letter itself—an item that can be inspected or verified and usually indicates buyer action.

Job Aids

On the basis of how buyers buy, salespeople may be required to engage in selling activities that require some specialized knowledge or skill to facilitate the sales step. When this occurs, specific job aids or sales tools can help them. For example, if the buyer's buying process requires him or her to justify the value of a purchase, then the salespeople must align themselves with this requirement and be prepared to develop a business case, ROI (return on investment), or value analysis. An automated model or spreadsheet might be provided to a salesperson as a job aid or sales tool. Many of my customers have developed online libraries of job aids and sales tools to help their salespeople facilitate their Solution Selling sales process.

Sales Management System

Initially, we didn't include sales management in the sales process elements because we didn't think of it as a salesperson's activity. But over the years, our experience and our customers have helped us see how critical effective management is to the sales process. An effective sales management system monitors, manages, and maintains the integrity of the sales process. The activities include pipeline and opportunity assessment, individual opportunity identification and analysis, opportunity and individual salesperson coaching, sales revenue forecasting, and reporting.

TWO SALES PROCESS MODELS

In Solution Selling, we use two different models to illustrate sales process. Each model represents a particular way to approach the process: the Step Process Model, which is taken from the buyer's perspective and the Process Flow Model, which is taken from the salesperson's perspective.

Either way, it's important to have a map that helps salespeople know what to do and when to do it. Without a map, staying in alignment with prospective buyers is very difficult, if not impossible. I'm including both models for your review.

Step Process Model

I use the Step Process Model when making an overview presentation or discussing an active sale, because I can see every aspect of the sale on one page (see Figure 3.2).

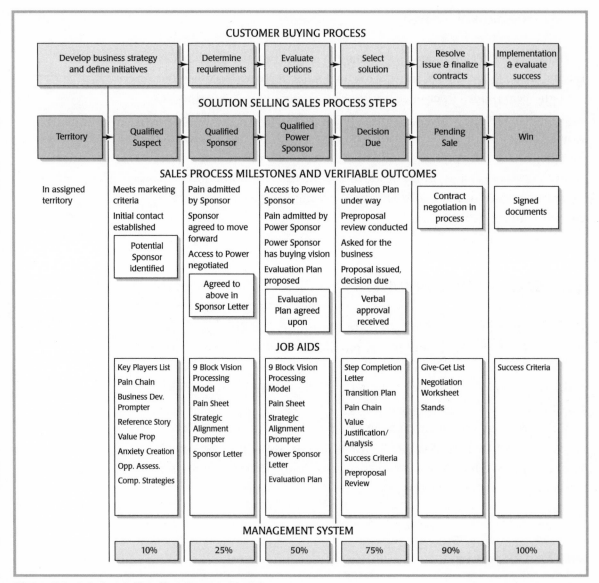

Figure 3.2 Solution Selling Step Process Model

As you can see in this example of the Step Process Model, the sales process is based on how buyers buy—the buying process. In the second row down from the top of the diagram are seven Solution Selling sales process steps. Each step marks a major progression in Solution Selling's sales process. To give this example more depth, I have included the selling activities that we typically expect at each sales process step. In Solution Selling we call these defined points in the sell cycle *Milestones*.

Now look at the area labeled *Verifiable Outcomes*. Verifiable Outcomes identify the major deliverables or results we expect to conclude each selling step. For example, if a salesperson has completed the Qualified Power Sponsor step, the Verifiable Outcome is Evaluation Plan Agreed Upon, meaning that the salesperson and buyer have agreed on a way to evaluate the solution and the evaluation process leading up to a signed agreement.

You will also notice specific Solution Selling Job Aids traditionally used during the designated step. Most of these job aids will be introduced during the course of this book.

Last but not least is the link to the management system, which allows you to track the progress of an opportunity. Each of the steps in the Solution Selling Step Process Model is measurable and assists in more accurate forecasting via the defined Milestones and the Milestones' probability (yield percentages).

Take a few minutes to examine this model and ask yourself if you could sell more if you had these elements defined for you. Most people say "yes." So why wait? Get started today.

Solution Selling's Sales Process Flow Model

The Sales Process Flow Model was developed to help salespeople learn the Solution Selling process. I personally like to work with the Sales Process Flow Model because it helps me to visualize where I am and what I have to do next with an opportunity. Look at Figure 3.3, the Sales Process Flow Model. It is a view of the Solution Selling sales process from the salesperson's perspective.

From this point forward in the book I'll use the Sales Process Flow Model (see Figure 3.3) to guide us through the Solution Selling sales process.

THE SOLUTION SELLING SALES PROCESS

A clear line of distinction can be made between opportunities that are started by salespeople in the latent pain area or, alternatively, where the opportunities find them and they are active. These are two very different starting points for sales opportunities. I will cover both starting points as well as each step in the Sales Process Flow Model in greater detail throughout the rest of the book. However, for the balance of this chapter, I will provide a brief description of each step of the model.

Starting from the top, the Sales Process Flow Model divides into two parts: to the left are latent opportunities (people not looking to buy anything from you or anyone else), and to the right are active opportunities (people who are already looking to buy and most likely have a vision of what they need—and their vision likely doesn't include you). I'll start with latent opportunities.

Latent Opportunities

In Chapters Four through Eight, I will break down each selling step that is required when dealing with latent opportunities, those opportunities where buyers aren't looking to buy anything. You'll learn how to identify opportunities through precall planning and research, and you'll

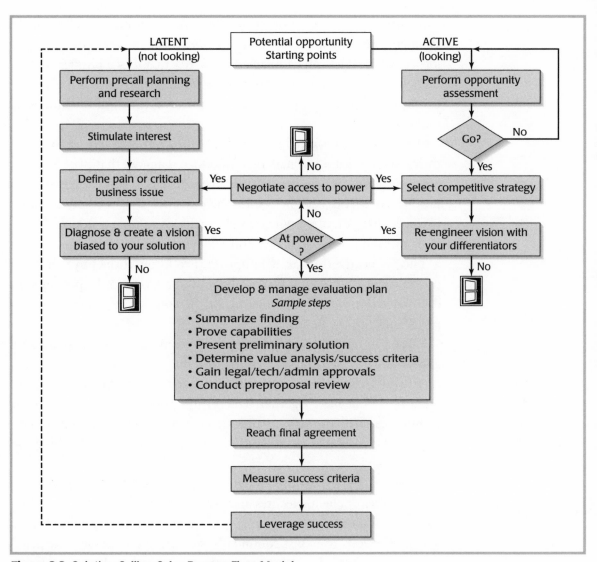

Figure 3.3 Solution Selling Sales Process Flow Model

learn how to prospect and stimulate interest in buyers who hadn't planned on buying anything, or at least not from you. Prospecting activities may take the form of an email or a letter that uses a Business Development Script, a Reference Story, or a Value Proposition. I'll give you examples of how to prospect as we proceed through the stages of the process.

After you've generated interest from your buyer, you need to define their pain or critical business issue and then diagnose that issue and create a vision in such a way that the prospect can see how your unique products or services can help solve their problems. It's a solution biased toward what you offer, which might include multiple products or services or even involve partners and alliances.

Having gotten this far, it's important to know if the buyer has the power to buy. If not, you have to bargain for access to the person who does have that power. If, however, the person can buy, then you simply advance to the next step.

Once you're at the power level, you develop an evaluation plan. This allows both parties (the salesperson and the buyer) to move in a structured way to a mutual decision to move forward and reach an agreement to do business together. This brings good project management techniques into your sales process which helps build credibility with buyers and increases the probability that you will successfully close more sales.

As you can see from the model, the sales process doesn't end when the customer or client executes an agreement. In the Sales Process Flow Model, you must measure against an agreed-upon list of criteria, called *Success Criteria*. You must continually measure and determine the delta, or the positive change, your products and services make on your customers' business. Then, with positive results, you can leverage your customers' successes and prospect for additional selling opportunities both inside and outside your customers' environment. Once you've measured the delta, then you can determine if you actually provided a solution or not. Remember our definition of a solution from Chapter One: A solution is a mutually shared answer to a recognized problem, and the answer provides measurable improvement.

Active Opportunities

In Figure 3.3 (page 39), look again at the right side of the model, the active opportunities—opportunities that you didn't create. These opportunities might have come from an incoming phone call or a formal RFP (request for proposal) or an RFI (request for information). The critical point is that the buyer has found you. In Chapters Nine and Ten, I discuss how you can decide whether you should engage and compete or disengage and look for more promising opportunities. You'll learn how to assess the opportunity, select a proper competitive strategy, and make a go or no-go decision. Not surprising, often the best thing to do is to decide not to engage, which is very hard to do, especially if you or your company is behind quota.

Assuming you believe you can win, you must reengineer the buyer's existing vision, gain access to power, exert control over the buying process, and establish the value of your unique offering to the client.

The next chapter begins Part Two, "Creating New Opportunities." We first explore the world of precall planning before moving into other chapters on stimulating interest, diagnosing pain, and creating visions.

PART TWO

Creating New Opportunities

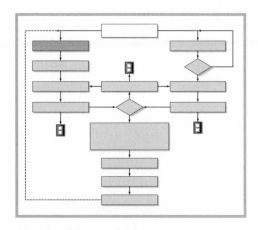

CHAPTER FOUR

Precall Planning and Research

Here's an exercise. Think of a selling opportunity on which you're currently working. Next, take a piece of paper and draw a straight horizontal line; then write "beginning" at the left edge of the line and "end" at the right edge. Now mark an **X** where you believe you are in your opportunity. Then mark where you think your manager would say you are. Do the same for your technical expert or sales support person, if you have one. If a business partner is involved, mark that too. Finally, and most important, mark a big C where you think your customer thinks he or she is.

The point is that often we're not all in sync with each other. Every person tends to have a different opinion and point of view. That makes tracking our progress through a sale or opportunity difficult. We need defined points or Milestones in the sell cycle, to enable us to track our progress or lack of progress.

Applying the Milestone principle to this book, we'll track our progress by using the graphic of the Solution Selling Sales Process Flow Model at the beginning of Chapters Four through Thirteen.

(The darkened box illustrates where we are in the sales process. This will help us navigate through the book.)

Visually, the Process Flow Model shows two starting points for potential opportunities. One entry point is for latent opportunities (left side) and the other is for active opportunities (right side).

Part Two of this book deals with buyers and opportunities in latent pain, those in the Not Looking segment. Chapters Four through Eight deal with specific activities and skills associated with creating new opportunities. Competing for active opportunities is addressed in Part Three, specifically in Chapters Nine and Ten.

For most salespeople and businesses, their greatest potential lies in latent, or Not Looking opportunities. Ironically, it's where they spend the least amount of time and effort. I'm a firm believer that creating new opportunities is the lifeblood of most companies. After all, how many companies can survive long term on the amount of business their existing accounts are generating for them now? No matter how long you've been doing business together or how good your existing relationships are, things will change. The big questions are: What can you do about developing new opportunities? Where do you start? I recommend you start with precall planning.

PRECALL PLANNING

Most salespeople have assigned territories, market segments, or industries containing specific accounts for which they are responsible. The job is to examine them and create new selling opportunities. Figure 4.1 illustrates this concept.

Salespeople with large accounts tend to have access to multiple opportunities. However, if you have small- or medium-sized business accounts, perhaps only a few opportunities exist. Regardless of the account or opportunity, the first effort is to look for specific business

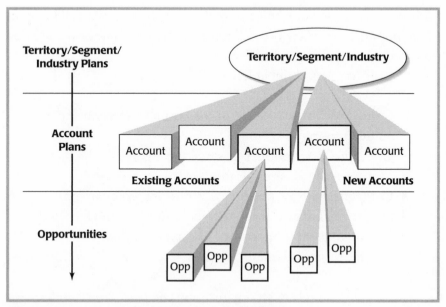

Figure 4.1 Identify Opportunities Through Planning

issues, ones you can help existing clients solve. The intent of Figure 4.1 is to show that no matter how your sales environment is structured, opportunities exist, and planning can determine where the opportunities are and how to go after them.

Keys to Management-Level Dialogue

The real key to getting good management-level meetings and having meaningful conversations is to have good situational knowledge, which is knowledge developed through personal experience, training, reading, research, and planning.

When it comes to precall planning, salespeople should try to uncover buyer data and critical issues that will be relevant to their conversations with executives. Do your homework thoroughly, and you will increase your comfort level when you call on executives. This in turn increases your success rate and productivity.

Key areas to research include:

- Company: history, nature of the business, mission statement, annual reports
- Offerings: description, types, uniqueness
- Market analysis: size, location, trends, maturity
- Competition: how positioned, strategies, comparisons
- Financials: balance sheet, income statement, track record
- Executive biographies: work history, education
- Critical business issues

Getting to high levels in an organization can help shorten sell cycles at the opportunity level. It also allows an account-level perception of credibility.

In Figure 4.2 (Account Profile, Titan Games, Inc.—Example), you will see the first reference that we will make to a fictitious company called Titan Games, Inc. (TGI). TGI will serve as our case example as I introduce you to new concepts, job aids, and situations throughout this book. The detailed information found inside this sample Account Profile will provide you with some additional background on TGI.

Guidelines for Existing Accounts

In your precall planning activities, it's important not to take existing accounts for granted, because things constantly change. Always be looking for new opportunities in the account. After all, there's no better prospect than an existing customer. On the other hand, if you've had a bad experience with one of your customers, don't fall into the trap of

Company

Titan Games, Inc. (TGI), is a twenty-year-old organization that manufactures and distributes educational and recreational games and toys throughout the world.

Offerings

TGI manufactures a line of educational and recreational games and toys that are endorsed and approved by leading experts in the field and are ergonomically designed.

Market Analysis

Loss of shelf space has created market erosion, and hence a loss of sales while lessening the company's competitive position.

Financials

Sales have declined in direct proportion to market and shelf space loss. Earnings per share have had a disproportionately high decline as margins are squeezed, and costs cannot be reduced quickly enough to protect profits.

Competition

There are five primary competitors, three of which are technologically in a position to take advantage of TGI's inefficiencies.

Executive Biographies and Likely Critical Business Issues

The CEO, Susan Brown, was hired in the past year to turn the company around because earnings per share have declined. The VP Finance, Jim Smith, has been with TGI for the past five years. He is currently unable to positively affect profits due to missed revenue targets and the increasing cost of credit write-offs. The VP Sales, Steve Jones, is chartered with increasing revenues for TGI. He has been hampered by technology limitations that cause his salespeople to spend too much time servicing existing accounts while not developing new ones. The CIO, John Watkins, has been chartered with finding a solution to the technology deficiencies.

Potential Capabilities

TGI appears to need a way during the ordering process for existing customers to place orders directly over the Internet so that salespeople can spend more time developing new customers.

Figure 4.2 Account Profile, Titan Games, Inc.–Example

thinking that that customer won't do any more business with you. Remember, problems are opportunities, and that's when your customers need you the most. Don't let an account's current perception of you or your company limit your willingness or ability to introduce new ideas.

The following are guidelines for precall planning in existing accounts:

- Complete the research as if it were a new account.
- Eliminate incorrect, inaccurate, or misleading assumptions.
- When new issues are uncovered, seek support from your previous or current Power Sponsor for your next contact.
- Ensure that your contact on the next level doesn't represent any potential conflict (company politics often is a factor you need to keep in mind).
- Don't let a customer's preconception of your organization limit your scope and penetration in that account.

Information Sources

Many sources of customer information, including the Internet, can help salespeople spot trends and opportunities. More information is available today for salespeople to use than ever before.

I've discovered that many salespeople believe that doing research is someone else's job. That's a big mistake. Assume it's your job and do your own precall planning. If you get help, great, but don't abdicate this responsibility.

A partial list of available information sources includes:

- The account's Web site. Reviewing a customer's Web site can tell you a great deal about the current events in the organization. Web sites often include press releases. If nothing else, a mere mention of a press release lets the customer know you cared enough to do research on its site.

- Hoover's Online, *Wall Street Journal,* MSN Business Online, CNN Business Online, *Barron's,* Standard & Poor's, Compass, Dun & Bradstreet
- Industry periodicals and industry associations
- Annual reports (make sure you read the chairperson's letter), press releases, and annual report cover letters can hint at initiatives for the coming year
- Archives of news and wire stories
- SEC filings—for critical, unbiased information
- The account's shareholder department (email with specific questions). Become a shareholder if it's an important account so you can obtain shareholder-only information.

What to Look for in the Information

Remember the Solution Selling principle of no pain, no change while you're gathering information. Look for pains and critical business issues that will give people reasons to change. Note the distinction between account-level and opportunity-level activities in Figure 4.3.

Account-level activities	• Identify key players
	• Identify potential areas for critical business issues (pains)
	• Match up key players with critical business issues (pains)
Opportunity-level activities	• Align your capabilities to each key player and pain
	• Create an initial pain chain for the potential opportunity
	• Target the most likely power sponsor
	• Develop a reference story/initial value proposition
	• Construct a business development strategy (letter, e-mail, phone, seminars, and so on) using specific information gathered

Figure 4.3 What to Do with the Information

Once you discover what you think are relevant and critical business issues, it's time to use the information and kick-start new opportunities. In account-level activities, you concern yourself with identifying the key players and the potential areas for critical business issues (pains) and matching up key players with critical business issues (pains). At the opportunity level, it's important that you align your capabilities to each key player and his or her pains and that you have a good set of job aids and tools. I also suggest you create a straw man before you attempt to create new opportunities.

BUILD A STRAW MAN

Straw man is a term with which you may or may not be familiar. Building a straw man means building a model or profile of your prospective buyer. It helps you work with that buyer, and it can help you recognize a good target when you come across one.

The straw man is based on past experience, research, and opportunity assessment. Though it requires work up front, it's easier to create new opportunities when you have a model of what the target opportunity looks like. You'll be more likely to recognize new opportunities and be better prepared to sell.

Building a straw man also helps you develop your situational knowledge, a key ingredient in successful selling today. Your straw man could include:

- Profile of the target opportunity
- Defined marketing criteria (for example, industry, size, revenues, employees)
- Key players
- Pains or critical business issues for the key players
- Product and services capabilities aligned to each key player and pain

- Initial Pain Chain for the potential opportunity
- Sponsor and Power Sponsor targets
- Reference Story and/or an initial Value Proposition

SOLUTION SELLING JOB AIDS AND SALES TOOLS

Precall planning creates more than its share of anxiety, which reminds me of Marshall McLuhan (1911–1980), the Canadian expert on media and communications. He said, "Our Age of Anxiety is, in great part, the result of trying to do today's jobs with yesterday's tools." Tools—the correct tools—are so crucial. The wrong tools can get you into trouble; the right tools can help you get the job done. If all you have is a hammer to work with, everything begins to look like a nail.

This applies to selling, particularly when you're attempting to create new opportunities. In specific selling situations, you need the right job aids and sales tools, applied in the right way, at the right time. Solution Selling has invested a lot of time and money developing job aids and sales tools. They're used by some of the world's largest and smallest companies to their great advantage. We're in constant touch with our global client base, working with them to determine which job aids and sales tools they need and which tools are most effective.

We introduce job aids in precall planning because we believe in starting with the end in mind. Knowing what job aids you're going to use while you create new opportunities means gathering the necessary information during the precall planning stage. Solution Selling has four job aids that are designed to assist or help you stimulate interest and create new opportunities. They are (1) the Key Players List, (2) Pain Chains, (3) Reference Stories, and (4) Value Propositions. Each job aid fulfills a specific purpose and becomes a best-practice procedure that makes your job of stimulating interest and creating new opportunities easier, less stressful, and more successful.

Key Players List

A Key Players List is a starting point for developing situational knowledge. This list identifies, connects, and leverages the pains of key players throughout a targeted industry. It also identifies the pains of people who have the influence and authority to make buying decisions. The Key Players List is useful for deciding who to call on and what to talk about.

Three steps are involved in building a Key Players List:

1. Identify the specific industry.
2. Identify the key players (by title) in the given industry.
3. Identify potential areas of pain or the likely critical business issues facing each identified key player.

Figure 4.4 is an example of a Key Players List for the manufacturing industry. You need to develop a Key Players List for the different industries and accounts or opportunities in which you're engaged.

We recommend that marketing people help build these for the vertical markets that your organization focuses on most often. In the perfect world, companies would have a database that contained Key Players Lists for all the industries they work with, and each list would be updated periodically with information on industry trends, market feedback, and salesperson input. The Key Players List should include the relevant job titles of the likely people salespeople will deal with in the course of the normal sales situation. Think about the power this kind of information and knowledge brings to salespeople. Once you've completed your research and you know the key players and their likely pains, you'll have increased confidence knowing who to call on and how a critical business issue connects C-level executives (CEOs, CFOs, COOs, CSOs, and CIOs) and managers across the company or enterprise.

After you've built a Key Players List, you're ready to link the pains of each of the key players together. As I mentioned earlier, there is inter-

KEY PLAYERS LIST	
Key Players	**Potential Pains**
Chief Executive Officer	• Not meeting investors' expectations
	• Declining stock price
	• Decreasing EPS/shareholder value
Chief Operating Officer	• Rising operational costs
	• Declining margins
	• Inability to consistently reach productivity goals
CFO/VP Finance	• Declining cash flow
	• Declining ROI and ROA
	• Eroding profits
CIO/VP IT	• Inability to meet users' technology demands
	• Trouble keeping up with technology change
	• Difficulty implementing new technologies—Lack of resources
VP Sales (and Marketing)	• Missing revenue goals/new account sales targets
	• Inability to accurately predict sales revenue
	• Declining customer satisfaction
VP Manufacturing	• Not meeting manufacturing and shipment schedules
	• Excessive inventory levels
	• Lack of capital for equipment
VP Engineering	• Inability to get new products to market on a timely basis
	• Escalating design costs
	• Inability to develop a new product plan

Figure 4.4 Manufacturing Industry Key Players List

dependence in an organization. This interdependence can be illustrated in the Pain Chain, one aimed right at your target opportunity.

The Pain Chain

W. Edwards Deming, Ph.D., was considered a "quality guru" and one of the early pioneers of total quality management (TQM) throughout the world. He developed several theories about business. One of his theories was organizational interdependence. He described how certain relationships have higher degrees of interdependence (mutual dependence) than others do. For example, a bowling team has low interdependence. Each bowler bowls independently of the others, and the team simply adds up the collective scores at the end of the game. On the other hand, an orchestra is an example of high interdependence. If one brass player is off-key, or the percussion section is off-tempo, it will affect the overall quality and sound of the orchestra.

Deming believed—and I do as well—that businesses are even more interdependent than an orchestra. For example, what happens in a business when production delays occur and shipping dates to customers are missed? Customer service gets lots of calls from unhappy customers. Market share starts to slip, revenue targets may be missed, and overall morale and profits may fall. In other words, many people and many functions in the business are adversely impacted. This is because the organization is so interdependent. Knowing this, we developed a job aid called a Pain Chain. It captures the essence of this type of interdependence and helps salespeople identify and solve problems across the company or enterprise (see Figure 4.5).

One of my favorite expressions is "A picture is worth a thousand words." In very simple terms, Pain Chains are pictures depicting the key players and their pains, the contributing reasons for their problems, and the impacts of those pains on others in an organization.

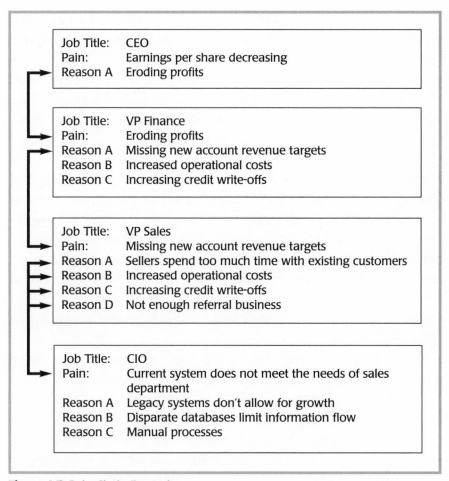

Figure 4.5 Pain Chain Example

When used, Pain Chains differentiate salespeople from their competition by giving buyers the impression that the salespeople who use Pain Chains understand their business. Can you imagine a salesperson walking into a room full of businesspeople and showing them a graphic similar to Figure 4.5 and then asking if this correctly depicts their current situation? Remember, this picture indicates each key player's pain, the reasons for the pain, and the impacts or linkages to other key people in his or her organization. I can imagine it because I see it happen on a regular basis, and the reactions and results are phenomenal. You can truly differentiate yourself and the way you sell by your approach and the job aids you use. Your ability to build and confirm a Pain Chain with a customer demonstrates an understanding of his or her business environment. The customer will respect that.

How to Use Pain Chains. Pain Chains are not organizational charts. They may look similar to organizational charts, but their purpose is very different. Pain Chains trace the flow of pain throughout an organization. Generally, the pains at one level become reasons for another pain at a higher level. Usually this correlation is exact, but it doesn't have to be. Pain Chains are living documents that should be refined over time as pertinent or more relevant information becomes available.

The Pain Chain usually manifests itself at three key points in the sell cycle.

1. Before starting an opportunity: Pain Chains are developed via precall planning analysis or from earlier account situations provided by marketing.
2. While engaged in an opportunity: Pain Chains that have been previously developed from earlier account situations and are being used as a starting point can become a map that a salesperson can use to navigate through an organization. The salesperson can validate or change information in the Pain Chain as he or she learns more about the customer's specific situation. The Pain Chain flow can provide information that is the cornerstone of the impact conversation to take place during vision processing.
3. To close an opportunity: By the end of a sell cycle, the salesperson has met with several key players. This question often

arises: Who should the salesperson focus his or her efforts on? The Pain Chain helps to answer this question. The salesperson also can begin to describe the benefits and the value to each person in the chain. This approach gives confidence to salespeople who are only comfortable talking about their products. It provides a map that links their product offerings to high-level business issues.

The Reference Story

A Reference Story is a third-party success story. It details how you were able to help another person with the same job title with a problem that the prospect may also have.

Figure 4.6 is an example of a Reference Story that could be used with Titan Games, Inc.'s VP Sales. It's about another VP Sales who works in a major manufacturing company.

Reference Stories, if designed and shared effectively, can quickly establish credibility in the mind of the prospect, stimulate interest in the prospect for working with that salesperson further, and begin the discussion of critical business issues that the prospect is faced with in his or her organization.

Reference Stories enable salespeople to give examples of how the prospect's peers solved their business problems by implementing capabilities provided by the salesperson's organization. The prospect usually has the same problem or pain or at least can relate to it.

Reference Stories are *not* lengthy reminiscences of how the salesperson's organization has helped a different customer. Reference Stories should be short, concise examples that focus on how other customers have successfully solved a business problem with the capabilities you provided.

If your prospect becomes interested, several things can happen. The prospect will either admit pain or direct the salesperson to another part

Situation	A particular situation that might interest you concerned another VP Sales of a major manufacturer.
Critical issue	His critical issue was missing new account revenue targets.
Reasons	Main reasons for this were that his customers were required to place all orders via their salesperson, so salespeople were spending all their time servicing existing customers and had no time for developing new ones.
Capabilities (when, who, and what)	He said he needed a way, when wanting to order, that existing customers could place their orders directly via the Internet, thus allowing his salespeople to have the time to develop new customers.
We provided	. . . him with those capabilities.
Result	The result was that over the last six months, the firm's existing customers placed 96 percent of all orders using the Internet. His salespeople had time to develop new customers, increasing the size of the customer base by 10 percent. Overall revenue increased by 6 percent.

Figure 4.6 Reference Story—Example

of the organization, or the salesperson will discover that the prospect already has a vision of a solution. The conversation then continues by engaging in vision processing (Vision Creation or Vision Re-engineering).

Keep Your Reference Stories in Accessible Databases. In a perfect world, companies would have a database that contained customer references for all titles and industries they work with. Those Reference Stories would have detailed account histories behind them so that the salesperson could contact the account owner for more information if necessary.

Many of our clients, most notably IBM, Lotus Development Corporation, and Microsoft have built electronic libraries of prospecting job aids. These aids include Account Profiles, Key Players Lists, Pain

Chains, and Reference Stories. Such databases are widely available to the selling organization, because one salesperson's success can be another salesperson's Reference Story.

The Value Proposition

The term *value proposition* may be one of the most overused industry phrases. It seems like everyone is using the term or claims some sort of value proposition. The problem with overused terms is that buyers become resistant to them and the intended purpose gets lost. This problem is also compounded by companies and salespeople who use valueless value propositions.

By "valueless" I mean that there are no quantifiable numbers or money associated with the so-called value statements. For example, companies make valueless value propositions when they say, "Our company can make you more efficient and help save you lots of money by using our state-of-the-art software," or "Because our company is the leading provider of electronic components in the automotive industry, that makes us the safe and reliable choice to do business with."

In Solution Selling, Value Propositions are simple, clear statements directed at a specific and targeted customer, the quantifiable benefits they can achieve by solving business problems, and the investment needed to make this possible.

For example: "We believe Titan Games, Inc., should be able to increase sales revenue by 10 percent each year (valued at $10M of potential revenue and $3.2M in profits annually) by enabling customers to place their own orders, allowing salespeople more business development time provided by our e-commerce offering for a three-year investment of $1.15M."

The Value Proposition Template This template is straightforward and presents the proposition like this:

We believe [client name] should be able to [improve what?] by [how much?] through the ability to [do what?] as a result of [what enabler, technology, service, etc.?] for an investment of [what relative cost?].

You build a Value Proposition by taking the data of a previously successful customer, overlaying those results onto another customer's situation, and projecting or extrapolating what the results would be for that customer. Figure 4.7 is an example of positioning a Value Proposition.

Some Value Propositions may even provide ranges of value and investment instead of defined numbers; for example, "increase revenue by 10 to 15 percent for an investment around $500K to $800K."

How to Use Value Propositions Value Propositions are statements (not guarantees) that attempt to project the potential quantified benefit

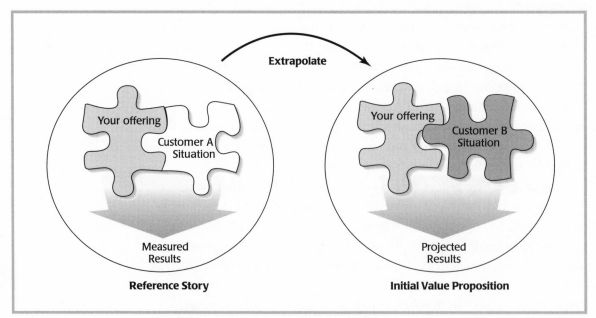

Figure 4.7 Positioning the Value Proposition

(value) to a prospect and his or her organization through the implementation of your specific capability or offering. Value Propositions are intended to create curiosity and serve as a catalyst to start a sales cycle. To create a Value Proposition, a salesperson must know about a value already achieved by a customer who has used the salesperson's products or services. Like reference stories, Value Propositions can be delivered over the phone, face-to-face, by email, or as part of a targeted direct marketing campaign.

Preliminary research usually uncovers a prospect's data such as annual sales, the number of employees, cost parameters, profitability, earnings, and so on. Then you apply the measurements based on actual results from previous customers. Please note that your initial Value Proposition starts with "We believe." In other words, it's according to your research and opinion. It's early in the sale, so you have to present it as your opinion. Only later, after diagnosis and proof, will your buyer own the Value Proposition.

If your arithmetic is correct and the proposed results are promising, the prospect has to listen to you. It's good if the prospect challenges you. He or she might ask, "How did you figure that? What have you based it on? What makes you think we could get that result?" If this is the case, you have achieved the goal of stimulating the interest of the client, and you can now engage in a more specific conversation about what is possible.

Value is a rich ingredient in selling, even at the early stage of prospecting. Value helps to stimulate curiosity and interest. Value can move prospects from little or no interest to active curiosity in what you're selling. Value is a significant commercial aphrodisiac.

Value is a key component of Solution Selling. Value is used throughout the process of selling a solution. Historically, many people have often used the word *value* in selling, but rarely has it been defined, much less quantified. People use the term often but have a hard time explaining it. In Solution Selling we give value the following definition: Value = Total

Benefits – Total Investment. This definition means that value is quantifiable. Salespeople should always quantify *value* rather than simply use the word and leave it to the prospect to figure it out.

The Value Cycle

Solution Selling's philosophy on value is that value is not just a word; it's an integral part of every step in the sales process. I want salespeople to lead with value in the beginning of the process because it helps to gain and stimulate interest. Verify the value during the diagnosis and evaluation steps of the process. Close with value during the reaching-final-agreement step, because it gives the buyer a compelling reason to act. Measure the value in the success criteria step so that you can ensure success and leverage it for future engagements. The Solution Selling Value Cycle includes the following: leading with value, verifying and confirming value, closing with value, and measuring.

Leading with Value Conduct precall planning and research so that you can deliver a confident and targeted initial Value Proposition that will stimulate the buyer's interest in your offering.

Verifying and Confirming Value Diagnose the critical issue(s) behind the initial Value Proposition and quantify how your capabilities can provide a solution. This is the process of taking the initial Value Proposition (what you think might be possible) to a Confirmed Value Proposition (what the buyer believes is possible). This can evolve into a more inclusive Value Proposition (including other customer beneficiaries) or a broader value analysis (even a formal ROI analysis).

Closing with Value Using the Confirmed Value Proposition provides a compelling reason for the buyer to act. When the buyer understands the value your solution delivers, the buyer is less likely to bargain for a discount. A thorough value analysis can help the buyer and salesperson recognize the measurable impact of not taking action—thus creating a compelling reason to act.

Measuring Make sure the customer achieves the results he or she anticipates. Measuring success allows you to leverage positive results for additional business. We defined a solution earlier as a mutually shared answer to a customer's recognized problem that must provide some measurable improvement. There's a *before* (a baseline) and an *after* (the baseline plus a delta). Quantifiable value helps you establish both the baseline and the delta to ensure that a solution was delivered.

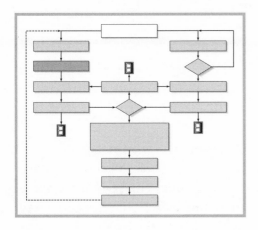

CHAPTER FIVE

Stimulating Interest

Stimulating interest is one of selling's most important skills. Yet surprisingly, it's one of the most underdeveloped and misunderstood. When asked to prospect—develop new business—our natural inclination is to find a likely buyer (preferably someone we know—it lowers the pressure) and begin selling. We sidestep stimulating interest. Selling is our real job, not stimulating interest, at least that's what too many salespeople think. Stimulating interest is someone else's job. It's marketing's job, or it belongs to telemarketers specialized in making first calls. We have sales quotas to meet.

Few would argue that when it comes to selling, it's the results—meeting or exceeding quota—that really matters. And if we miss our sales goals, sometimes we blame others.

It's not acceptable for a salesperson to blame others, saying, "I didn't make my quota this quarter because marketing didn't do a good job." That doesn't fly. It's after the fact. Face it, what counts is that you personally meet your quota, and that usually means you have to stimulate interest on your own and get the process underway—one that will fill your pipeline. I've included the necessary skills and job aids to perform the task in this chapter.

PROSPECTING BASICS

One of the key selling skills in Solution Selling is prospecting. Prospecting conjures up many negative images for people. I'm sure you have some of your own. I recently received a telemarketing call at my home at dinnertime. The person was attempting to sell encyclopedias. My reaction wasn't, "Oh, I'm so glad you called. I was just thinking about my need for encyclopedias." Nor was my reaction friendly. In fact, I was upset because the caller interrupted dinner with my family. You know the feeling. I'm sure the same thing has happened to you.

Solution Selling has a unique approach to prospecting. We define prospecting as *the ability to stimulate interest or create demand for your products or services versus finding people already looking to buy something*. How many salespeople do you know today who can actually do this?

Prospecting Versus Polling

There's an important distinction between prospecting and polling. Prospecting stimulates and creates interest where there currently is none. Polling is looking for people who are already looking. Both are important activities but require different approaches and skills, although polling can be done with little or no training.

Though polling helps find opportunities in your active or Looking territory, prospecting helps bring opportunities from the latent or Not Looking segment. Many salespeople think they're prospecting when they contact a potential customer and ask, "Are you in the market for . . . ?" or "Are you looking to buy . . . ?" In Solution Selling terminology, that's polling: conducting a survey and not really prospecting. There's nothing wrong with polling, but why use your best and brightest resources to simply gather data? The skill of prospecting, the ability to stimulate and create interest in what you sell, should be part of every salesperson's skill set.

Create Interest and Curiosity, Not Tension, with Your Approach

Solution Selling uses pain to prospect and stimulate interest. If you're a salesperson and you're not making quota and your missing your revenue targets, would you be curious to know how someone else (a peer) has solved this challenge? The same holds true for almost every other person and job function. When you try to create interest, focus on creating curiosity first, not on the immediate action you want the prospect to take. Too many times salespeople create tension by asking the prospect either to learn about their company, to hear about their products, to make an appointment, or to buy something. The salesperson hasn't earned the right to expect these requests to be granted by the prospect. First the prospect must be curious—almost asking to learn more.

Reserve Sacred Time for Prospecting

This is one of the most important disciplines in which salespeople can engage. I use the term *sacred* to stress the point that nothing is or should be more important than this activity. If two salespeople have equal sales skills and equal products or services, which one is going to win more business? The answer is the salesperson that has the most opportunities in his or her pipeline.

I have clients who have made prospecting a sacred activity for their salespeople. Wherever their salespeople work—in an office cubicle, in home-based offices, or in open work areas—time is reserved for prospecting, and it isn't violated. During that time, meetings are not held and salespeople are not disturbed. One customer's salespeople who work in cubicles hang flags, curtains; even shower curtains in the entrances to their workplaces. The clear signal is: do not interfere; salesperson prospecting—and no one does.

How much time is recommended for prospecting? The amount of time will vary based on your pipeline, your market, and how new the salesperson is to a territory. If the pipeline is reasonably filled with quality opportunities, then I counsel most salespeople to have at least 10 percent of their time devoted to prospecting, including precall planning and what we covered in the last chapter. On the other hand, if the pipeline isn't full or if the quality of the pipeline is poor, then more time is required. The 10 percent suggestion simply maintains the pipeline. However, if most salespeople spent 10 percent of their time in real prospecting, as I'm suggesting, their pipelines would be healthier. And the ability to meet quarterly and yearly quotas would be much easier.

I also recommend that salespeople block out large segments of time rather than break up prospecting into small segments. Salespeople who spread out their prospecting activities, such as one hour a day, somehow find ways to disregard their schedules. Something "important" comes up, and prospecting gets shelved. It's more difficult to disregard a reserved four-to-five-hour period of prospecting time.

Target High

I recommend that you target your prospecting activities one or two levels higher in the organization than you're willing to settle for, in case you get delegated down (in many cases you will). In that case, it also helps to be sponsored by a more senior person.

As I mentioned in Chapter Two, many salespeople complain they have difficulty contacting high-level executives. Such job levels are outside many salespeople's comfort zones. This discomfort can be helped through precall planning, use of the job aids that I introduced in Chapter Four, and practice, practice, practice.

Whether going after new accounts or recognizing new opportunities in existing accounts, prospecting C-level executives (CEOs, CFOs, COOs, CSOs, and CIOs) can decrease your sales cycle time and increase your success rate and productivity. Learn to call on top C-level executives.

Eagle salespeople make it a habit to call on these people. Thorough and professional research includes learning about these C-level executives, their responsibilities, and their pains, so when you meet them, you feel more informed. Targeting high and preparing for conversations with these high-level executives is part of the job.

Experiment with New Approaches

People tend to get into routines and habits of doing things the same way over and over. Think outside your normal prospecting methods; prospecting doesn't just mean using the phone.

If your approach isn't working, try a different one. I recently worked with a salesperson who informed me that our prospecting model didn't work. Upon inquiry, I learned the salesperson had made over one hundred phone calls using only one version of a business development script, and it wasn't working. Use common sense. It's like fly-fishing; you usually have to try several flies before you discover which lure the fish are interested in. This applies also to prospecting—try several different prospecting methods: different Business Development Prompters, Business Development Letters, initial Value Propositions, and Reference Stories.

Remember the SW Rule

The SW Rule says, "Some will. Some won't. So what? Someone else is waiting." Prospecting is a numbers game, and large numbers of people and businesses have pain. If you get rejected, don't despair; someone else is waiting. Not everyone is going to be interested in what you have to offer, so don't take it personally. It helps to have a thick skin when prospecting. If you don't have one, develop one.

I know some of these ideas sound corny, even irksome, but face it—prospecting takes mental toughness. Selling always will be subject to the laws of numbers. Some will become interested. Some won't. So what? Someone else is waiting.

PROSPECTING METHODS

One of the big hurdles salespeople have to overcome is their negative perception of prospecting and their belief that it's someone else's job. I often ask audiences that I speak to, "What's the first thing that comes to your mind when I use the term *prospecting*?" Inevitably, the first words out of their mouths are "cold calling." Not all prospecting has to be done over the phone. I happen to think that the phone is a very good way to prospect, but it's not the only way. I want to share some information and ideas on various methods and venues for prospecting, such as networking, seminars, trade shows, and other marketing-related activities.

Networking

Networking is an informal system whereby people with common interests assist each other. It's a real and very important activity for salespeople. In today's world of interconnectivity, collaboration, and a real openness to sharing, if salespeople aren't participating in networking activities, they should be.

Networking opportunities include:

1. *Existing customers*: Use your database of current customers as a resource for targeting future opportunities. You should also look for the next opportunity while still engaged in a current one. Don't be afraid to ask existing customers about additional problems they might have.
2. *Referrals*: You probably don't ask current (satisfied) customers for referrals enough. Many of our customers attend seminars, conferences, and user groups and have built up friendships and acquaintances with people in similar occupations as theirs. Assuming that there is not a conflict of interest, ask them to refer you to other people both inside and outside their organizations who might benefit from your capabilities.
3. *Industry associations*: These forums are designed to share industry trends, industry business issues, and technology-related topics, and so on among their members. To know someone or to become a member of the association can be a valuable conduit for potential opportunities. Salespeople tend to think these groups are not for them— not true. Get involved, get active, and it'll amaze you to see how much business can be generated through this avenue.
4. *Social events*: Don't disregard venues outside the working environment. People are usually more open and relaxed in a social environment. Think how often you are asked what you do for a living at social events.

Solution Seminars

One approach is to invite all like-minded people to a Solution Seminar. These seminars focus on solving business problems rather than selling or pushing products. Take attendees through the following steps:

1. Provide a short introduction of your organization.
2. Uncover a list of the most common problems or issues you believe the audience faces.
3. Ask the audience to add to the list.
4. Get the audience to prioritize issues they're curious about.
5. Use the Reference Story model to describe how you have helped others address each of the top prioritized issues (if possible).
6. If appropriate, describe or demonstrate the products or services that helped your referenced clients address those issues.
7. Share results your clients have achieved.

The objective is to stimulate interest and have your seminar attendees request additional information from you after the seminar.

Trade Shows

Consider different booths for different buying audiences. Position one booth toward buying audiences consisting of visionaries (prechasm) and another toward more conservative audiences (postchasm).

With the prechasm audience, choose a technology-oriented trade show where you can display and demonstrate your products. The real focus should be on your technology differentiators, while attempting to tie in the business line value only to those technology enthusiasts whom you feel have a tendency to appreciate the business side of the enterprise.

With the postchasm audience, choose events that are attended by executives in your market. Do something different: Limit product displays, and instead display Reference Stories, Value Propositions, and lists of clients. Have conversations about business issues that focus on specific capabilities you provide to help solve specific business problems and be ready to discuss business-level reference stories. Be prepared to offer proof.

BUSINESS DEVELOPMENT PROMPTERS

In Chapter Four, I introduced several job aids and sales tools, including the Key Players List, Reference Stories, and Value Propositions, that can be used to help stimulate interest. In Solution Selling, we also use Business Development Prompters as valuable job aids to stimulate interest.

Business Development Prompters are designed to help you create new opportunities in latent pain markets—your Not Looking territory. A Business Development Prompter can be sent by mail, fax, or email, talked about on the telephone, used in face-to-face direct sales meetings, mailed as part of a direct-mail piece, or used at a trade show virtually anywhere. This job aid is designed to create curiosity, not to sell anything. It has been designed to take the pressure off you and your buyer. Its only purpose is to create curiosity about how you've been able to help other people in similar job titles with similar critical business issues solve their problems.

THREE BUSINESS DEVELOPMENT PROMPTER FORMATS

A Business Development Prompter can be used in several ways. Here are three main ones: (1) for a new opportunity, (2) for a new opportunity with a menu approach, and (3) for a customer referral approach.

New Opportunity

Your Business Development Prompter should describe a common or high-probability problem that can be solved using your product or service. You are simply asking your prospect or buyer if he or she would be interested in hearing more about it. There is no direct pressure to buy; it's too early for that.

Figure 5.1 is an example of a Business Development Prompter for a new opportunity. Assume the prospect is the VP Sales for TGI, our fictitious manufacturing company. Based on your precall planning, you know that management just missed last quarter's earnings forecast, and no one at the prospect's company is happy—the CEO most of all. You make a first call to that sales executive.

Good Business Development Prompters are tailored toward specific people and jobs and their particular business difficulties. In other words, if you're calling doctors, talk about the critical issues of other doctors. If you're calling a bank president, talk about another bank pres-

Name	My name is Bill Hart
Company	with _____ (*selling organization*)
First-call notice	You and I haven't spoken before, but . . .
Industry expertise	I have been working with toy manufacturers for the past eighteen years.
Job title expertise	One of the chief concerns I'm hearing from other sales executives . . .
Pain	is their frustration with missing revenue targets due to poor new business development practices.
You can help	We've been able to help our customers solve this issue.
Are you curious?	Would you be interested to know how?

Figure 5.1 Business Development Prompter Format, New Opportunity

ident's difficulties and how you helped that president solve those difficulties. You must make intelligent assumptions to create a good
prompter. Here are the key elements:

Your Name. State your name, and the way you want to be addressed.
Just the facts. Of course, you would adapt to each country's culture. In
North America, just stick to the facts, build credibility.

If this is a first call and you don't know the buyer, say, "You and I
haven't spoken before . . . ," so the prospect won't be distracted won-
dering whether he or she knows you. This way the prospect won't miss
the rest of your message while he or she mentally flips through the
Rolodex trying to recall who you are.

Your Company. Tell who you work for—no product stuff. Stick to
building your credibility and demonstrate that you're a different kind
of salesperson.

Specify Your Industry and Your Company's Expertise. Establish
your industry expertise by stating how long your company has been
working in that industry.

Job Title of the Prospect. Let them know that you understand the
issues of their job and that you've worked with other buyers with their
same job title and in their industry.

Pain or Pains. Use high-probability critical business issues that are
typical in the buyer's particular industry. Match pains to jobs.

An Invitation to Talk. Invite the buyer to learn more. Ask, "Would
you be interested in knowing how?" The buyer response you want is,
"Yes, I'm interested. Tell me more." That's the purpose of the Business
Development Prompter.

Notice it's a problem-solution scenario, a hurt-and-rescue message.
In ending, we don't say, "Would you like to hear more?" or "Can we
set up a meeting to discuss this?" You've accomplished your objective—
introduced yourself, noted your expertise in working with other people in the same job, and you've told the person how you've helped solve

a critical business issue. Now it's up to the prospect to answer the question, "Would you like to know *how*?"

You'll get different responses. You might get a "yes." Then you have the option of booking an appointment or continuing on the phone. You could get "Yes, but now is not a good time." You could be directed to someone else who is affected by the problem in the organization, or you might even have to ask for that information. You could also hear, "No, I'm not interested."

If the VP Sales has a problem resembling the one described in your Business Development Prompter, there's a good chance the VP will be interested in learning more. Expert situational knowledge helps when it comes time to build or develop your prompters. As you gain experience in each market, you'll increase the accuracy of your Business Development Prompters.

New Opportunity with a Menu Approach

With the Business Development Prompter, a salesperson lists multiple high-probability problems rather than just one. I call this a menu of pains approach. Figure 5.2 is an example of what you can say using this approach.

The menu of pains Business Development Prompter also demonstrates situational fluency, and it gives the person receiving the information a broader range of responses. Even if none of the pains is a direct hit, the Business Development Prompter can establish enough credibility that the prospect decides to discuss it further.

Customer Referral Approach

Sometimes the prospect has connections with an existing customer. Figure 5.3 is an example of a Business Development Prompter that is particularly useful for creating new opportunities using referrals.

Name	My name is Bill Hart
Company	with _____(*selling organization*)
First-call notice	You and I haven't spoken before, but . . .
Industry expertise	I have been working with toy manufacturers for the past eighteen years.
Job title expertise	The top three issues we're hearing from other sales executives are . . .
Pain	(1) missing revenue targets, (2) inability to accurately predict sales revenues, and (3) declining customer satisfaction
You can help	We have helped companies such as Alpha Toys, Universal Computers, and HandyMan Tools address some of these issues.
Are you curious?	Would you be interested in knowing how?

Figure 5.2 Business Development Prompter, Menu Approach

Name	My name is Bill Hart
Company	with _____(*selling organization*)
First-call notice	You and I haven't spoken before, but . . .
Referral	Doug Handy, VP Sales at Universal Computers, suggested that I give you a call.
Job title expertise	We were able to help him address his frustration with . . .
Pain	missed revenue targets due to poor business development practices.
We helped	We've been able to help him address this issue.
Are you curious?	Would you be interested in knowing how?

Figure 5.3 Business Development Prompter, Customer Referral

These prompters have helped salespeople realize many successes. Our clients tell us their "interest generation rate" for first contact ranges between 30 and 70 percent compared to 2 to 10 percent before using the Solution Selling Business Development Prompters. Salespeople are far more willing to spend time prospecting and creating new opportunities with these types of success rates.

When the potential buyer says, "Tell me more," or something similar, that indicates interest. Again, the objective of the initial call is to arouse the prospect's curiosity and interest, not to close the sale. An initial positive response is an open door to advance the sales process.

BUSINESS DEVELOPMENT LETTERS AND EMAIL

Business Development Letters contain the same key components as the Business Development Prompter. Look at the examples in Figures 5.4 and 5.5 addressed to the VP Sales at Titan Games, Inc., our fictitious toy manufacturing company. The salesperson is presenting the prospect with a menu of pains.

In the Business Development Letter example, the salesperson has established expertise in manufacturing, included references of other customers, listed three critical business issues, and asked the prospect if he or she is interested in knowing more. This is a brief letter that gets to the point quickly and aims to arouse the curiosity of the reader.

The Business Development Email aims to do the same thing—arouse curiosity and interest in your product or service. Note that we provide only a brief company positioning. This is because the real focus is much like the Business Development Prompter menu approach. Share the top three issues you are hearing and then refer to three suitable companies with which you've worked. Be economical. The point is to get recipients to respond and make them curious.

Mr. Steve Jones   January 9, 20XX

VP Sales

Titan Games, Inc.

Dear Mr. Jones:

Our company is presently in the business of helping our customers increase their revenues through the implementation of e-commerce applications.

We have been working with manufacturing companies since 1996. Our clients include Alpha Toys, Universal Computers, and HandyMan Tools. Some of the chief concerns we hear lately include

- Inability to accurately predict sales revenue

- Missing revenue targets and/or new account sales targets

- Declining customer satisfaction

We have been able to help our customers successfully deal with these and other issues. I would like an opportunity to share some examples with you. If you are interested in learning how we have helped other salespeople and sales executives solve some very challenging issues, please call me at 555-215-1111.

Sincerely,

Bill Hart

Figure 5.4 Business Development Letter–Example

BILL HART January 14, 20XX 10:06 a.m.

To: sjones@tgi.com

cc:

Subject: Follow-up

Dear Mr. Jones:

In my previous letter dated January 9, I indicated that my organization has helped other senior sales executives solve some very difficult business issues.

Our focus is on e-commerce applications that help manufacturing companies achieve high value results. Are you facing any of the following issues:

- Inability to accurately predict sales revenue

- Missing revenue targets and/or new account sales targets

- Declining customer satisfaction

If the answer is yes to any of the above items, then our company may be able to help your organization. If you would like to understand how, please call me at 555-215-1111.

Sincerely,

Bill Hart

bhart@ourcompany.com

Figure 5.5 Business Development Email—Example

These letters are also used for follow-up. They allow you to contact the customer more than once. There is always the chance that reminders may stimulate prospects to take action. They may have been busy during your first contact and couldn't respond even though they were truly interested.

Let's make an assumption that you've successfully aroused the curiosity of a prospect in your Not Looking territory and now your prospect wants to talk. Now what? What do you do next? Solution Selling has a sales process aligned with how buyers buy. So let's go to the next chapter and find out what's recommended.

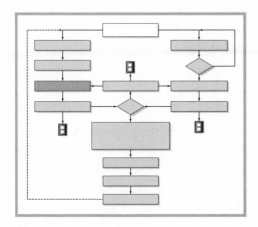

CHAPTER SIX

Defining Pain or Critical Business Issue

You are engaged in the initial sales call with a new prospect (it could be face-to-face, on the phone, or electronic). What should you say, and when should you say it? What is your goal for this first meeting, and what is the best strategy for reaching this goal?

In this chapter we go through the initial steps of a sales call. The goal is to establish the prospect's pain, or critical business issue. This is essential before the sale can proceed. The prospect's pain is central to everything that follows, because, without a compelling reason to change, the prospect will continue to do things the same way. Remember the foundational principle of Solution Selling: No pain, no change. To help you reach this goal, you will need to establish rapport, introduce the call, and tell a third-party Reference Story designed to get pain admitted.

It's interesting to see salespeople's reactions to a structured sales call model. When we first start working with salespeople, they usually think they don't need a structured sales call. Many of them go so far as to say, "I don't want information on how to make a sales call. I'm good enough already. It's like being put into a straitjacket." However, after they've seen the Solution Selling sales call model, most of them have a change of heart. They realize that they can make improvements in their own approach, even though they've been selling for a long time.

I've learned that many salespeople are unprepared for what I call normal buyer responses in a sales situation. If you've failed to anticipate the buyer's reactions, then you're out of alignment with the buyer. For every action on your part, you should anticipate all possible reactions from the buyer. It's possible to lose a sale in the early stages of a sales call. If the buyer concludes that you're insincere, incompetent, or just another salesperson trying to sell something he or she doesn't need, things are not going to go well. Since the buyer's first decision is whether or not to listen to you, building personal credibility and establishing rapport at this early stage is essential.

What would compel a buyer to be willing to reveal sensitive information about his or her company to a stranger? Solution Selling's research indicates the buyer is willing when the salesperson has accomplished the following:

- Established credibility
- Built rapport
- Established trust, sincerity, and competency
- Demonstrated situational knowledge

Prospects are willing to discuss their problems when they conclude that the salesperson is trustworthy and has the knowledge and capability to help them. Each step in the initial sales call is designed to establish your credibility.

In Solution Selling, we do not believe in or teach any type of sales trickery or strong-arm techniques. We don't believe salespeople should pretend to be something they're not. Salespeople should work on being themselves. In an initial sales call, the safest course of action is to start talking about the business purpose of your call. That's the reason you want to speak with them in the first place. The business discussion will establish rapport. By showing buyers that you understand their business, you will earn their respect. Establishing rapport takes time; don't rush it.

We've developed two job aids to help salespeople maintain alignment with the prospective buyer: the Strategic Alignment Framework and the Strategic Alignment Prompter. The Framework shows an overview of the steps involved in a first meeting, laying out each selling step. The Prompter tells salespeople what to say that leads them through these steps. We've adjusted these words over the years, and they have proven to be successful, but you should modify them to meet your style and situation.

STRATEGIC ALIGNMENT FRAMEWORK

There are seven steps in the Strategic Alignment Framework. In this chapter, I describe Steps 1 through 3; Steps 4 through 7 are covered in subsequent chapters. Not all sales situations require all seven steps. However, Solution Selling built the model knowing that you can always omit steps, depending on your industry or sales situation. For example, if you have short sales cycles or you sell over the phone, you probably won't need to use all seven steps.

Alignment with buyers is a key skill in Solution Selling. Without it, sales usually collapse. We developed the Framework to assist salespeople in maintaining proper alignment with the buyer. The Framework shown in Figure 6.1 reveals the salesperson's seven steps of the first call aligned with the buyer's perspective and decision process. As we proceed through the book, I discuss dialogue that our salesperson, Bill Hart, could have with the key players at Titan Games.

SELLER ACTIVITY		BUYER PERSPECTIVE/DECISION
Step 1: Establish Rapport	**B**	■ Do I even want to listen to this salesperson?
Step 2: Introduce Call	**U**	■ Is this person different from other salespeople?
■ State call objective	**Y**	■ Is he sincere?
■ Share positioning statement	**E**	■ Is he competent?
■ Provide company introduction	**R**	■ Do I want to share information?
■ Share relevant Reference Story/Progress to date		
■ Transition to "getting pain admitted"		
Step 3: Get Pain Admitted	**&**	■ Do I want to admit my critical business issue?
■ Ask Situation Questions (if necessary)		
■ Ask Pain Questions/Menu of Pains (if necessary)		
■ Prioritize admitted pain		
Step 4: Develop Needs: Customer Buying Vision	**S**	■ Does this person really understand the reasons for my critical business issue?
■ Diagnose/create a vision of a company-biased solution, or	**E**	■ Do I agree with his diagnosis?
■ Re-engineer a vision with company differentiators	**L**	■ Should I discuss the pain's impact on others?
■ Participate in existing vision	**L**	■ Do I agree with the capabilities articulated, the value established?
■ Introduce differentiators	**E**	■ Do I want to take responsibility for solving this?
■ Determine underlying pain (if not admitted)		
Step 5: Gain Agreement to Move Forward	**R**	■ Am I serious about moving forward?
■ Gauge desire to move to next step		■ Am I prepared to promote this to Power?
■ Move to Step 6 if buyer has not volunteered access to power		
Step 6: Determine Ability to Buy	**A**	■ Should I reveal the identity of Power?
■ "Let's say you become convinced it really is possible to (repeat buying vision) and you want to move forward, what will you do then?"	**L**	
■ Go to Step 7a (if a Sponsor) or Step 7b (if a Power Sponsor)	**I**	
Step 7a: Bargain Proof (still undefined) for Access to Power	**G**	■ Do I want to sponsor this person if he proves his capabilities to me?
■ "If we prove to you . . . will you introduce me to (Power Person?)"	**N**	
■ If buyer bargained, end call and write Sponsor Letter	**M**	
■ If buyer will not bargain, find another potential Sponsor		
Step 7b: Qualify Buying Process with Power Person	**E**	■ Am I serious enough about this to disclose my buying process?
■ "How would you like to evaluate . . . ?"	**N**	■ Do I agree with the proposal definition?
■ Legal/technical/administrative approvals?	**T**	
■ Proposal?		
■ No new information!		
■ Pre-proposal review		

Figure 6.1 Strategic Alignment Framework

The Buyer's Perspective

The Strategic Alignment Framework aligns the salesperson's activities to the buyer's perspective and decisions. In other words, the salesperson's actions are designed to match the way buyers buy.

How important is the buyer's perspective? You know the answer to this question—very important. Why don't salespeople consider the buyer's perspective more than they do? Buyers have decisions to make and therefore options to consider. While you're talking, they're thinking: Do I want to listen to this salesperson? Is this person different from other salespeople? Is this person sincere? Is this person competent? Can I trust this person? Do I want to share information with this person?

So that you can easily understand the Strategic Alignment Framework and use the Strategic Alignment Prompter, I'll break down each step and describe both the salesperson's action and the buyer's perspective.

STRATEGIC ALIGNMENT PROMPTER

We're not trying to create robotic salespeople. What I'm about to walk you through is a dialogue prompter for a suggested conversation. Note that this assumes a North American business environment, the buyer has shown curiosity and wants to talk, and this is a first-call scenario. Other business cultures may require modifications to this Prompter.

Step 1: Establish Rapport

The goal of the first step is to establish rapport with the buyer. To accomplish this, the buyer must first be willing to spend time with the salesperson and listen to what he or she has to say. This is illustrated in Figure 6.2.

STEP 1:	**Let the prospect set the tone of the meeting.**
Establish rapport	I appreciate the opportunity to meet with you.
	(Read the need for small talk or business talk.)

Figure 6.2 Step 1, Establish Rapport

In Step 1, you want the buyer to set the tone of the meeting or the exchange if it's taking place over the phone. The short pause or silence after introducing yourself gives the buyer the opportunity to say something. What comes out of the buyer's mouth will usually tell you something about the buyer and what the proper tone of the meeting should be. If you don't understand the local culture and its business practices, you could get into trouble and kill your sales opportunity early. I find the safest approach is to state the business purpose of your meeting or call. In most cases, this approach won't offend buyers anywhere in the world you're doing business.

Step 2: Introduce Call

Step 2 builds your credibility and sets the stage for encouraging the buyer to share information with you. The logic behind this step is *give to get*. Ultimately, if you want buyers to open up and share information about themselves or their situation, you have to offer them something first. Let's explore each element in Step 2.

State the Call Objective. Too many salespeople skip the step of stating the objective of the meeting. Over and over I hear salespeople begin a first-time sales call with selling—pitching their products and services. Buyers instantly push back, disengage, and put some space between themselves and the salesperson. It's too early to start selling. Instead,

STEP 2:	State the call objective
Introduce call	What I would like to do today [or during the next _____ minutes] is to

- introduce you to _____ [our company] and
- tell you about another _____ [title and industry] we have worked with.
- I would then like to learn about you and your situation.
- At that point, the two of us will be able to make a mutual decision about whether or not we should proceed any further.

Figure 6.3 Step 2, Introduce Call: Call Objective

calmly let your buyer know the objective of your call and get his or her approval.

See Figure 6.3 for a suggested way to introduce yourself and your objective. This introduction lets the buyer know that you want to cover several topics: introduce your own company, share your experiences with other buyers and companies similar to his own, and learn more about the buyer and his company. After this exchange of information, the two of you can then make a mutual decision about whether it's useful to go further; no deception, no trickery, just good business. I believe that every meeting (even with a customer you've done business with for years) should have a stated objective.

Position Your Company. Figure 6.4 addresses the positioning of your company, which is important because we want buyers to open up and share information.

I suggest that you use the "we help" theme if it's applicable and appropriate. Remember, the customer is the focal point, and it's much easier if the customer perceives you and your company as being sincere

---

STEP 2: Position your company (use "we help" theme)

Introduce call   _____ [company] is in the business of helping organizations/companies in the _____ industry. [Brief statement of how organizations use your product and services] _____

_____.

Provide company facts

- _____

- _____

- _____

- _____

(Provide three or four facts that will help the buyer reach the desired conclusions about your company. Optionally, add a personal note. Appropriate names of clients/customers can be provided.)

Figure 6.4 Step 2, Introduce Call: Positioning Statement and Company Introduction

and competent. The words you use may be similar to those in Figure 6.4, or you may want to use the words from your company's mission statement.

For example, if I were positioning my own company, it would sound something like this: "Sales Performance International is in the business of helping clients exceed their revenue and profit goals by helping them maximize both individual and team selling effectiveness."

Provide Facts About Your Company. Immediately following the positioning statement, you should offer proof of the positioning statement without sounding defensive. Proof is simply three or four facts about your company that support the positioning statement. It's important to provide facts that allow your prospective client to conclude that you are what you say you are.

Let's stop here for a moment. Try to put yourself in the place of the buyer. When I ask salespeople how they react to other salespeople making statements about (or worse, giving opinions about) their companies, I get one predictable answer—not well. If you're like most buyers, it's difficult to trust salespeople. Unscrupulous salespeople have burned too many buyers.

When stating facts about your company, a good rule of thumb to follow is to use third-party validation; for example, "According to *Fortune* magazine, we're one of the top three companies in our field." Avoid anything that may sound like an exaggerated claim (even if true). It will hurt your credibility at this early stage. You may also add a personal item that establishes your expertise in the field. And if it's appropriate, mention the names of other clients. Remember, you're trying to establish a common ground on which the buyer will develop confidence in discussing his or her critical business issues with you.

Share a Relevant Reference Story. The next part of Step 2 is to share a success story about how you and your company have helped someone in a similar job and industry solve a problem and get positive results. Solution Selling calls this story a Reference Story (described in more detail in Chapter Four). The format for developing the story and sharing it is shown in Figure 6.5.

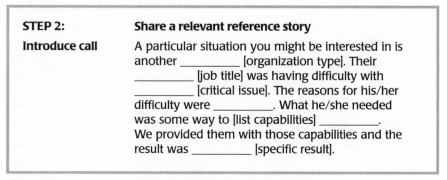

STEP 2:	**Share a relevant reference story**
Introduce call	A particular situation you might be interested in is another _____ [organization type]. Their _____ [job title] was having difficulty with _____ [critical issue]. The reasons for his/her difficulty were _____. What he/she needed was some way to [list capabilities] _____. We provided them with those capabilities and the result was _____ [specific result].

Figure 6.5 Introduce Call: Share a Relevant Reference Story

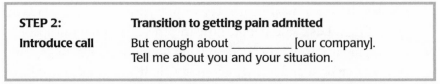

STEP 2:	**Transition to getting pain admitted**
Introduce call	But enough about _____ [our company].
	Tell me about you and your situation.

Figure 6.6 Step 2, Introduce Call: Transition to Getting Pain Admitted

Transition to Getting Pain Admitted. This is a critical element and a transition point in your sales call. Ultimately, the key is to get your buyer to admit pain (see Figure 6.6).

If the exact words from Figure 6.5 don't quite fit you, use something similar. The story's format is the important thing. It helps the buyer relate to someone similar to them with a similar problem, and then provides the punch line to end the story with quantifiable results. All this makes it possible for your buyer to open up and admit pain.

For a summary of Step 2, see Figure 6.7. It shows how you can build rapport, introduce your call, position your company, and tell a Reference Story.

Step 3: Get Pain Admitted

By the end of Step 2, the buyer must decide whether to share information with the salesperson—specifically, whether to admit his or her pain. Be prepared for a number of potential responses when you say, "Tell me what's happening with you and your company." Depending on the answer, you must decide whether to stay or disengage.

Listen carefully to the buyer's response. This is often difficult for salespeople to do. (I'm reminded of what my father said to me as a child: "God gave you two ears and one mouth; you should be listening twice as much as you are talking.") Salespeople have a tendency to have their "happy ears" on: They want to hear good news. They want to make a sale, so they hear what they want to hear.

State the call objective	What I would like to do today [or during the next 45 minutes] is to • introduce you to Our Selling Company [Bill Hart's company] and • tell you about another VP Sales in the manufacturing industry we have worked with. • I would then like to learn about you and your situation. • At that point, the two of us will be able to make a mutual decision about whether or not we should proceed any further.
Position your company (use the "we help" theme)	Our Selling Company is in the business of helping organizations in the manufacturing industry achieve or surpass their revenue targets and control operational costs by greatly reducing the amount of time spent on redundant and manual sales-related activities.
Provide company and personal introduction	Our Selling Company has worked with fifty of the *Fortune* 500 companies [conclude: our company has worked with other large organizations]. • We have offices in 49 U.S. and 100 international locations (conclude: our company can support worldwide effort]. • I have been with Our Selling Company for the last ten years [conclude: Bill Hart is experienced and knows his own company].
Share a relevant reference story	A particular situation you might be interested in is about another manufacturing firm. Its VP Sales was having difficulty with achieving his new account revenue targets. The reason for his difficulty was that his customers had to place all orders via their salesperson. In turn, the salespeople were spending all their time servicing existing customers and not developing new ones. He said he needed a way for existing customers, when wanting to order, to place their orders directly on the Internet, thus allowing his salespeople to have time to develop new customers. *continued*

Figure 6.7 Step 2, Introduce Call: Summary Example

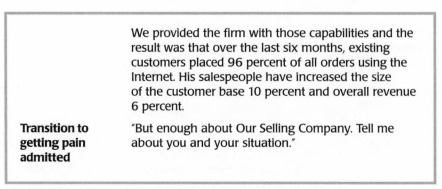

	We provided the firm with those capabilities and the result was that over the last six months, existing customers placed 96 percent of all orders using the Internet. His salespeople have increased the size of the customer base 10 percent and overall revenue 6 percent.
Transition to getting pain admitted	"But enough about Our Selling Company. Tell me about you and your situation."

Figure 6.7 Step 2, Introduce Call: Summary Example, *continued*

Five Possible Responses We've identified five responses you'll probably hear from prospective buyers after you've told your Reference Story and said, "Enough about me, tell me what's going on with you and your company." Figure 6.8 is an example of how buyers can respond.

In the first response, the prospective buyer says, "I'm having that same problem." Bull's-eye, a direct hit, a salesperson's nirvana. Pain, the pain you hoped to hear, the one that you helped bring to the surface, is on the table, and a potential sales opportunity has begun. You should now proceed to diagnose the pain—something we call *need development*—and eventually create a vision of a solution.

In the second response, the prospective buyer says, "I'm having a different problem." It's not exactly what you want to hear, but it may be something you can help them with. The prospective buyer feels comfortable admitting his or her problems in this situation, and that's a very good thing. Move on to need development and creating a vision of a solution.

In the third response, no pain or problem is admitted; still the buyer is friendly and talkative. This situation can lead to lots of discussions and maybe lots of follow-up meetings. Be careful not to fall into the trap of engaging in a situation where the pain is not compelling enough for them to change. The approach here is to get the conversation

Potential Buyer Responses	Seller Action
1. "I'm having that same problem."	Diagnose problem and create vision (Step 4).
2. "I'm having a different problem."	Diagnose problem and create vision (Step 4).
3. The buyer talks freely and is nice, but admits no pain/problem.	Ask situation questions to help direct the conversation toward the pain.
4. The buyer does not admit pain and is not friendly, maybe is even hostile.	Ask the menu of pain questions.
5. "I have the same problem, and we're already working on it."	Re-engineer the vision (Step 4).

Figure 6.8 Potential Buyer Responses

focused around a potential problem that you can address. Sometimes situation questions can help steer the buyer in this direction, for example, "Today, how do your customers get notified of new products or promotions?" or, "When a prospect calls a salesperson to ask a question, how is that call handled?" These types of questions can direct the conversation to capabilities you have that you know can help.

In the fourth and most dreaded response, no problems are admitted and the buyer is unfriendly. In this situation, you may have given it your best shot, and the prospective buyer still doesn't admit any pain or problems. On top of that, the buyer is untalkative and may even be adversarial. Have you ever encountered this kind of situation? Most of us have, and we hate it.

Still, you're a salesperson, and you have a job to do. To the extent possible, I recommend you try to engage in a conversation. Before you give up or leave, present a menu of pains that other people in that job typically have. After reciting that menu, ask, "Do you have any

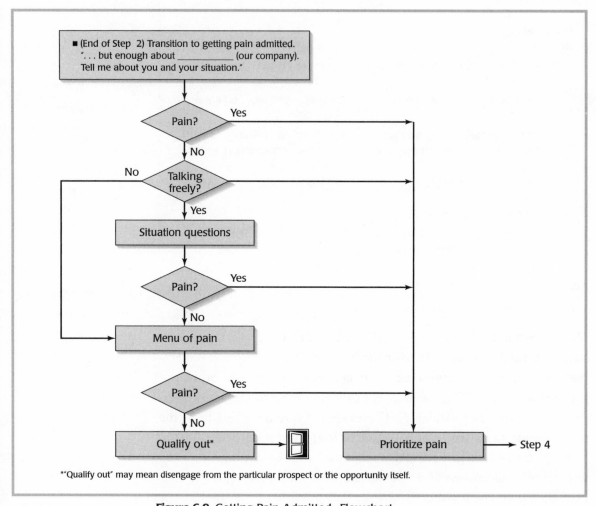

Figure 6.9 Getting Pain Admitted—Flowchart

of those problems?" We call it a menu of pains because we're almost inviting the buyer to pick one off the list. You have little to lose. Alternatively, try and discover company facts, such as who is managing what. Perhaps you can learn some useful information. You could still go back into the organization and try to get a sale going through another route.

Then there's the fifth response: "I have that same problem, and we're already working on it." A direct hit to the center of the target. Or is it? There is danger in this situation, even though it sounds exciting at first. They have the problem you want to hear, but unfortunately, they're already at vision—and you're not the person who helped them develop that vision. Someone got there before you; it may even be an in-house solution. Be careful; remember the probability or winning percentages when you're not in Column A. Here the task becomes vision re-engineering, which I discuss in Chapters Nine and Ten.

There is another way to view the five buyer responses and the possible salesperson actions (see Figure 6.9, on the opposing page).

What should we do with the pain or problems that the buyers admit to? After all, that's what we were after. We can go on to Step 4, Need Development and Vision Creation. We can diagnose the pain and create a vision of a solution. How we do this is based on Solution Selling's diagnostic model, called the *9 Block Vision Processing Model*. Let's take a look.

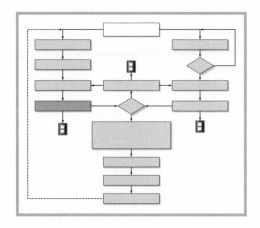

CHAPTER SEVEN

Diagnose Before
You Prescribe

Stephen Covey in his best-selling book, *The 7 Habits of Highly Effective People* (Simon & Schuster, 1990), tells a powerful story that masterfully conveys the importance of the Solution Selling principle—Diagnose Before You Prescribe. In his book, Covey describes how sick his two-month-old daughter was on the day of a really big football game in his community. Both he and his wife wanted to attend the game along with the more than 60,000 other people, but they chose not to due to their daughter's illness.

As the day progressed, their daughter's condition worsened and they sought medical assistance from their doctor. The family doctor was not available and they were directed to speak with the attending physician who was on call that day. Interestingly, the attending physician was in attendance at the big game. They chose to call the stadium and have him paged at the game to seek his advice about their daughter's condition. The page came at an important time during the game. Although the doctor did not seem to be thrilled about being interrupted during this important stage of the game, of course he spoke with Mrs.

Covey about her daughter's symptoms. As a result of the short conversation, the attending physician called in a prescription to their local pharmacy.

After hanging up the phone with the doctor on call, Mrs. Covey began to reflect on the brief conversation with him and she quickly became unsettled. Her feeling of having adequately described her daughter's situation changed to one of doubt. She felt that in her rush she may have left out some critical information that the doctor on call would have found useful and she began to question the conversation further. After all this was not their regular doctor.

The question that seemed to loom the largest in her mind was about whether or not the attending doctor knew that her daughter was only two months old. She could not remember if that fact had been discussed on the call. The Coveys wrestled with the decision to call a second time. The choice was made to call again and have the doctor paged a second time. It turns out that was a good thing that they decided to do. When Covey asked the doctor on call whether he realized that his daughter was only two months old, he admitted he did not and changed the prescription immediately.

His story drives home an important lesson: it's important to diagnose *before* you prescribe. Had Stephen Covey's young daughter received the wrong medicine, something terrible might have happened. Covey's story applies also to selling: it's important to diagnose customers' problems and then offer appropriate solutions.

SOLUTION SELLING PRINCIPLE: DIAGNOSE BEFORE YOU PRESCRIBE

Experience teaches us a lot of things, but sometimes experience can get in our way. I'm reminded of a study that tracked the performance of several hundred new salespeople. It found that as new salespeople become

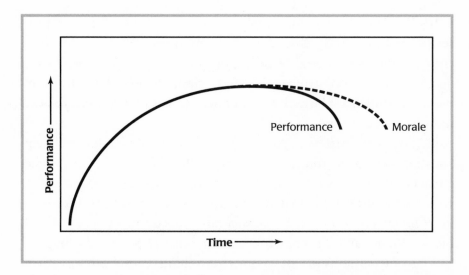

Figure 7.1 Sales
Performance over
Time

more familiar with their products and with selling itself, performance typically goes up. Morale climbs too. However, several months into most sales careers, sales performance falls off, and when that occurs, morale soon follows. Figure 7.1 illustrates this sales performance dilemma.

The big question is this: Why the drop in performance? Most people think the reason is burnout or some other motivational factor. However, research has identified the problem as behavioral, something the salespeople were doing that caused this problem—actually, it was something they were not doing. The more experience salespeople gain, the more likely they are to stop asking as many questions. Since most new salespeople don't know much about what they're selling, they're forced to ask a lot of questions. However, as they gain experience, everything changes, and not always for the good. Salespeople become experts; they think they've seen this situation before. So when the buyer admits a problem, instead of taking time to diagnose the problem, they jump straight to prescribing a solution (telling their buyers what they should do). The salesperson's enthusiasm and expertise become his or her own worst enemy.

It's like the physician in Stephen Covey's story who gave a prescription before fully diagnosing the situation. The key is to do a good job diagnosing your buyer's problem. If buyers don't trust your diagnosis, they won't trust your prescription. It's probably fair to say that the confidence a buyer has in a prescription is proportional to how thorough your diagnosis is.

This chapter introduces you to a conversation model that will help you diagnose buyer pains, uncover reasons for those pains, explore the impact of the problem throughout the buyer's organization, and create visions of solutions that match your company's capabilities. It's called the *9 Block Vision Processing Model* (also called the 9 Boxes or the 9 Block Model), and it is one of the cornerstones of Solution Selling.

Tens of thousands of salespeople, consultants, and businesspeople use this model in many different cultures and industries (technology, financial services, telecommunications, utilities, and health care, to name a few). Many people use it in their everyday lives, not just in their business lives, because it's so practical, useful, and user-friendly.

THE 9 BLOCK VISION PROCESSING MODEL

Situational experts and some Eagle salespeople have an innate talent for diagnosing problems and creating visions of solutions in the minds of their buyers. They instinctively ask questions that build rapport, help them understand the problem and the reasons, and lead buyers to solutions that use their products and services. Most of us who aren't particularly intuitive, or lack situational expertise, need a job aid, one that helps us emulate experts. The 9 Block Vision Processing Model helps salespeople do this.

It's a straightforward model, one that can be used in a variety of ways, and it's easily learned. Before you learn to use it for either Vision Creation (Chapter Eight) or Vision Reengineering (Chapter Ten), I want

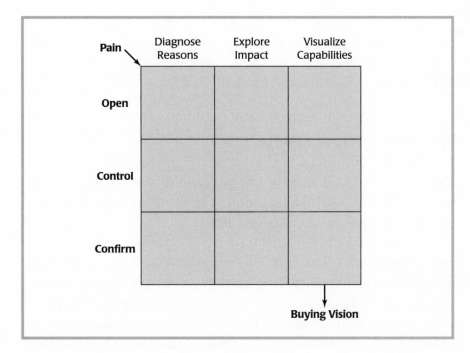

Figure 7.2 The 9 Block Vision Processing Model

you to understand the conversation strategies in the model. Let's take baby steps before running the race (see Figure 7.2).

First, three different kinds of questions are used in the model:

1. Open questions
2. Control (closed) questions
3. Confirming questions

Second, there are three main areas to investigate:

1. Diagnose reasons for the pain (problems)
2. Explore impact (throughout the organization) of the problems
3. Visualize the capabilities needed to solve the problems

As you can see in Figure 7.2, once you integrate the three rows and the three columns that form the 9 Boxes, it creates a matrix that makes remembering and using the model much easier.

Let's go through the model in detail.

THREE QUESTION TYPES

The 9 Block Model uses three different types of questions: open, control (closed), and confirming questions. I often refer to these three question types as Questioning Etiquette 101.

Open Questions Open or open-ended questions do several things. They invite buyers to talk freely (hopefully about the pain they just admitted) and respond from their experience, knowledge, and points of concern, and they earn salespeople the right to ask control questions.

Empathetic, sincere, open-ended questions are comfortable for buyers. They can answer these questions any way they want. Buyers can demonstrate their expertise and express their feelings. Buyers usually respond well to open-ended questions because they're nonthreatening, especially if the buyer has already admitted pain.

Open-ended questions do have one disadvantage. The salesperson gives up control and buyers can go anywhere they want, and many times they do. That's not good if the direction they take has nothing to do with your strengths or capabilities. But early in the buying process, it's important for buyers to feel comfortable, so salespeople are best advised to start with open questions such as, "Why do you think you're having this difficulty?"

Control Questions Control questions are basically the same as closed or closed-ended questions. We prefer to use the term *control question* because it better describes the approach we're asking you to use. Closed questions tend to be answered with a yes or no, whereas control questions tend to elicit more complete responses. Control questions might be, "Is it because . . . ? If it is, how much or how often?" Control questions guide the buyer in the direction you want your diagnostic conversation to go. Control questions seek specific pieces of information in specific areas. They help diagnose, lead, and develop the buyer's vision.

You have to be careful with control questions because buyers may start to feel uncomfortable. You must be alert and watch for this and adjust your approach according to the verbal and nonverbal feedback you receive from the buyer. If your buyer shows signs of discomfort, you may be controlling too much. Relax the situation and revert to some open-ended questions. Then, once you feel rapport is back, return to your control questions.

Research has revealed an interesting statistic. The ratio of control questions to open questions for high-achieving salespeople is three to one; it's one to three for average and below-average salespeople. What does that tell us? The very best salespeople learn to use control questions to diagnose problems and lead buyers to a vision that helps both the buyer and the salesperson.

Confirming Questions Confirming questions ensure that both the buyer and the salesperson are in sync. An example of a confirming question is, "So from what I've just heard, you said . . . Did I understand that correctly?" Confirming questions summarize the salesperson's understanding of the buyer's responses. The salesperson demonstrates an ability to listen and show empathy and exhibits his or her expertise. Good confirming questions help cast a halo around the salesperson. They show the buyer you understand his or her situation. Buyers want to do business with people who understand them. Confirming questions can also help rectify any misunderstanding that may have occurred during the dialogue. It's better to find that out sooner rather than later.

THREE KEY AREAS TO INVESTIGATE

After pain is admitted, there are three key areas we want salespeople to investigate: Diagnose Reasons, Explore Impact, and Visualize Capabilities. First, you need to find the reasons for the pain. Second, it's imperative to explore how the pain affects or impacts the organization. You need to find out not only who is impacted, but how and by how much. The idea is to connect as many people to the problem as possible. Third, now that you know the reasons for the pain and its impacts, it's time to create a vision of a solution—help the buyer to visualize (in simple terms) the capabilities he or she needs to solve the problem.

Diagnose Reasons

After the buyer has admitted having a pain, the salesperson's job is to diagnose the reasons for the pain before exploring impacts or trying to create a vision of a solution. Figure 7.3 shows how salespeople diagnose the reasons for the pain by asking the appropriate open, control, and confirming questions. The graphic depicts this concept by highlighting the area on which to focus.

Box 1: Open Question, Reasons for Pain In Box 1 of the model, the salesperson's job is to use an open-ended question and ask about the reasons for the pain; for example, "Tell me, what are the reasons you're not able to . . . ?"

This type of question encourages buyers to talk about the reasons for their problems. Some buyers respond with a detailed summary. But most buyers only provide general information at this point, forcing the salesperson to explore the situation further using control questions.

Box 2: Control Question, Reasons for Pain In Box 2, the salesperson has to diagnose the reasons for the pain and to measure the pain as much

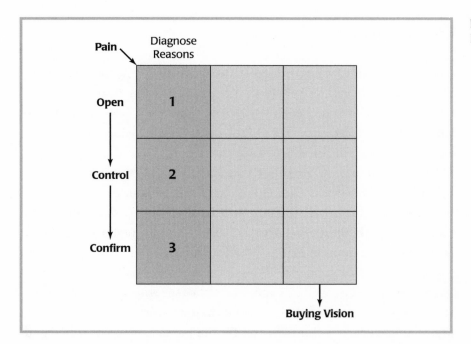

Figure 7.3 Diagnose Reasons

as possible. You establish your personal credibility and the value of your products and services in this box. If rapport and sufficient trust have been established, buyers usually answer the salesperson's control questions. Most of the salesperson's time in the diagnosing reasons area is spent in this box. Without a doubt, this is the most important box in the model. Examples of diagnostic questions are: "This [pain], is it because . . . ?" Or is it because . . . ?" "How much is [this pain] costing you?"

Box 3: Confirming Question, Reasons for Pain In Box 3, the salesperson's job is to make sure he or she is aligned with the buyer by confirming the buyer's previous responses. You want buyers to see you as patient and willing to attend to details. It's important for buyers to believe that you really do understand their issues. A way to confirm might be to say, "So, as I understand it, the reasons for your [pain] are . . . . Is that correct?"

Explore Impact

After pain is admitted and the reasons are discovered, then exploring the impact of the pain throughout the organization is essential. Impact questions are powerful because their answers reveal how far the problem extends into different parts of the organization, which then reveals how interdependent these parts are (see Figure 7.4).

Questions that explore impact frequently reveal the raw emotions behind the pain. Salespeople can broaden a critical issue to include many more people in the buyer's organization. Furthermore, such questions can give you clues about where the real power exists in the organization. Look at the middle column in Figure 7.4. Now imagine the buyer's organization chart. That's a good way to visualize this column.

Inexperienced as well as experienced salespeople sometimes forget to diagnose this area of vital information for two reasons: (1) their situational knowledge—knowing where the impacts are—is limited and (2) this area of questioning is not a regular part of their sales process.

Box 4: Open Question, Explore Impact Here your job is to use an open-ended question to explore the impacts of the pain; for example, "Tell me, besides yourself, who else in your organization is impacted by this pain and how are they impacted?" This type of open-ended question encourages the buyer to think about what other people in the organization is affected by the pain. The buyer may not always know, so you may have to explore the situation further using control questions.

Box 5: Control Question, Explore Impact Now you have to explore the impact of the pain throughout the organization. Ask, "If you're in pain, does this mean that your . . . is not able to . . . ? If that's the situation, wouldn't it also mean that . . . is probably experiencing . . . as well?" Here's your chance to discover where and how the pain spreads

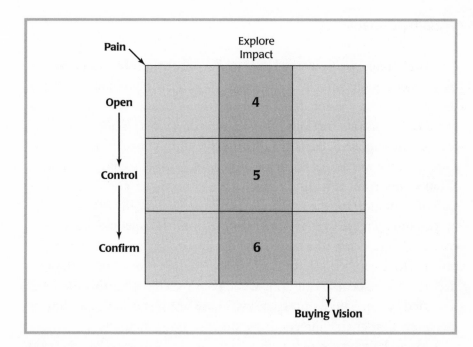

Figure 7.4 Explore Impact

throughout the organization. Who's involved? Who's connected to whom? Who's relying on whom to fix the problem? Who are the stakeholders? Is it all internal? External? What about stock price? Earnings? Profits? Sales revenue? Operating costs? HR costs? Internet costs? Regulatory compliance?

Box 6: Confirming Question, Explore Impact In Box 6, the salesperson makes sure that he or she is in alignment with the buyer by confirming all the buyer's responses. For example, ask, "So, as I understand it, [restate the pain] that we have been discussing is not only impacting you, but it is also having an impact on . . . as well as . . . . So, it's not just your problem, it's more of a companywide problem. Is that correct?"

Visualize Capabilities

Up to this point, you've worked hard to diagnose the problem and explore the impacts, but it could all be for naught if you can't participate with the buyer in creating a vision of how to solve the problem. Developing needs and creating visions are skills that you must develop to facilitate Solution Selling. An important aspect of creating a vision of a solution is ownership. In other words, it's not doing you a lot of good to have the vision. What's important is for the buyer to have the vision and take ownership of a solution for the problems that have been diagnosed.

You must create visions for buyers. Not all salespeople are able to create a good vision of a solution, but this can be learned. I know it's possible to learn, because we teach people to do it every day. With practice, most salespeople can do it well. That's really what this model is designed to do. There's no trickery. These are just good consultative questions that enable buyers to see the vision for themselves.

A key to helping create visions in the minds of buyers is having good situational knowledge, including business acumen, good capability knowledge, and the ability to ask good questions (see Figure 7.5).

Box 7: Open Question, Visualize Capabilities In Box 7, your job is to use an open-ended question to explore the buyer's vision of the capabilities needed to solve the pain. For example, ask, "What will it take for you to solve this problem?" Please note that in this example, we specifically use the word *you* in the question to achieve two things. We want to (1) know whether this person already has a vision (possibly one that competes with yours) and (2) determine if this person is willing to take ownership of the problem that's just been diagnosed. Until the buyer takes ownership of the problem, nothing good will happen.

Again, as in Boxes 1 and 4, this type of open-ended question encourages buyers to think on their own; their answers give us insight into what is on their minds. Once we have the buyers' thoughts about a solution,

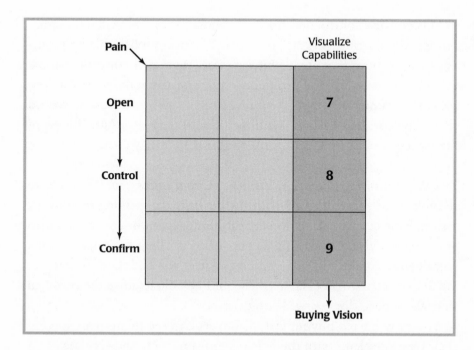

Figure 7.5 Visualize
Capabilities

it's time to support, expand, or change their vision using control questions centered on your company's capabilities. The transition from open to closed questions is achieved by simply asking, "May I try a few ideas?"

Box 8: Control Question, Visualize Capabilities Box 8 is the second most important box in the Solution Selling 9 Block Vision Processing Model. It's second only to Box 2, which uses control questions to diagnose reasons for the pain. Remember that if you didn't discover reasons for the problems, you won't be in a position to create capability visions to help the buyer solve the problems.

An analogy is the game of bowling. Bowling pins are set up one behind the other and are knocked down by the impact of the bowling ball. In Box 2, we set up the reasons—that is, the bowling pins—and in Box 8, we use capabilities—the bowling ball—to knock them over.

In Box 8, use control questions to create visions that match the capabilities of your products and services. You accomplish this by paint-
ing word pictures that enable buyers to see themselves or other people
in their company solving problems with your capabilities. For example, ask, "What if . . . when you had to . . . you could . . . . Would
that help?" or "Earlier, you mentioned one of the reasons for [the pain]
was when your . . . has to . . . . Would it help if they could . . . ?"

Box 9: Confirming Question, Visualize Capabilities Finally, you have
to make sure you're aligned with the buyer by confirming the buyer's
vision. This is particularly important because you'll want to confirm
your buyer's vision in writing as part of controlling the ongoing sale.
Here's an example: "So, as I understand it, if you had the ability to . . .
when . . . occurs, you believe you would be able to solve the problem
that we've been discussing. Is that correct?"

You now have a buying vision. Buyers can see themselves solving
their own problems with the help of your products and services.

HOW TO GAIN SITUATIONAL FLUENCY

What's difficult about this questioning model? Few people have difficulty asking open-ended questions, because they're general and nonthreatening to the buyer; for example, "What are the reasons? Who
else is affected? What is it going to take for you to solve this problem?"
And few people have trouble asking confirming questions, because anyone who has listened and taken a few notes can repeat back what he
or she has heard from the buyer.

The difficult part is *asking the control or closed-ended questions.*
They require salespeople to have situational knowledge and business
acumen. When reviewers first studied this model, they said, "You have

a great model, but our salespeople don't have the knowledge to ask the right control questions." You may be thinking the same thing. If so, relax: we've developed a job aid for sales and marketing people to use. It's called a Pain Sheet. It was designed specifically to help salespeople formulate control questions (the middle row of boxes) within Solution Selling's 9 Block Vision Processing Model. Good Pain Sheets can help salespeople develop situational fluency.

The Pain Sheet, or the Situational Fluency Prompter

The Pain Sheet, or the Situational Fluency Prompter, documents specific control questions for salespeople to use when diagnosing buyer pains and creating buying visions. Imagine, before making a sales call, having a repository of information available to you that would identify the following:

- The pains of the person you're calling on
- The reasons for those pains
- The areas of impact to his or her organization
- The capabilities that your company offers to help solve the pain

This job aid and sales tool has become a standard communication document between marketing and sales in many of the world's best companies. Companies use the Pain Sheets in several ways: to help salespeople facilitate the diagnostic conversation (via the 9 Blocks), develop their product and situational knowledge, launch new products and revamp their product training, facilitate industry and product information updates, teach nonsalespeople how to have meaningful conversations, and enable the entire company to focus on providing solutions.

Pain:	Missing new account revenue targets	
Job title and industry:	VP Sales, manufacturing company	
Our offering:	E-commerce applications	

Reasons	**Impact**	**Capabilities**
Is it because . . . ? Today?	Is this (pain) causing?	What if . . . Would it help if?
A. salespeople spend too much time handling repeat business in existing accounts (order taking versus selling)?	• missed overall revenue? • lower profits? *Is the VP Finance concerned?*	A. when: wanting to place orders who: your customers what: could view inventory levels, place an order, and have it confirmed, all over the Internet?
B. salespeople spend too much time answering frequently asked questions (FAQs) from current customers?	• impact on growth? • declining stock price? *Is the Chief Executive Officer affected?*	B. when: customers have questions who: they what: could click on a FAQ Web menu to get answers or select an "I need help" option to be connected to the appropriate person in the company?
C. prospects are unaware of your promotions?		C. when: offering promotions who: your salespeople what: could create personalized messages and broadcast them to all of the prospects via email?
D. salespeople fail to ask customers for referrals or leads?		D. when: visiting your Web site who: your customers what: could be prompted to submit referrals in exchange for discounts or promotional items?

Figure 7.6 Pain Sheet (Situational Frequency Prompter)—Example

Figure 7.6 is a completed Pain Sheet. This Pain Sheet is a fictitious one developed for our salesperson, Bill Hart, to use during his diagnostic conversation with the VP Sales at Titan Games, Inc. In this example, the pain of the buyer is "missing new account revenue goals." Bill Hart's organization sells everything from e-commerce software to the hardware and services that support it. As you study this Pain Sheet, notice that the products or services are never mentioned. On the other hand, the capabilities of the business application and supporting hardware are. The Pain Sheet leverages the knowledge base of a company.

Imagine if you could go to your computer and bring up a Pain Sheet covering the industry, the job title, and the pains of the person you're going to call. Imagine the competitive edge this would give you. Most companies have this information, but salespeople can't access it or lack a vehicle or sales process to organize it and use it effectively. A Pain Sheet is that vehicle—it collects and organizes the information that salespeople need to have meaningful conversations.

Where in the Solution Selling 9 Block Vision Process Model does a Pain Sheet fit? It fits in the middle row, the control section of the nine boxes. Figure 7.7 illustrates this.

Who should have the responsibility for building Pain Sheets and leveraging the valuable knowledge bases of companies? First, if you're a salesperson and responsible for a sales quota, take responsibility for building Pain Sheets. (Alternatively, at least take responsibility for overseeing that they're being done and maintained.) Building Pain Sheets isn't difficult. Start with your top five selling scenarios and build Pain Sheets to support those sales situations.

Many companies develop this valuable sales aid through their marketing departments or through the product marketing groups. We have clients today who insist that Pain Sheet information be made available at the same time their new products and services go on the market. Sales managers reason that if their salespeople don't have this

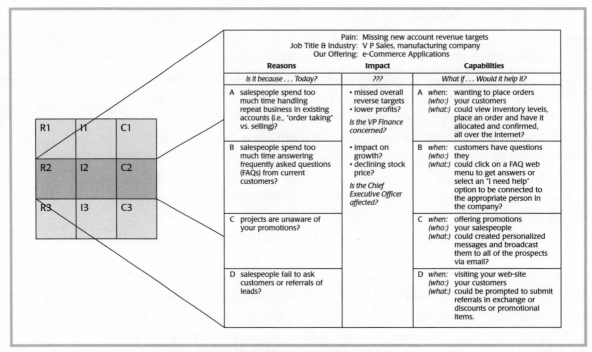

Figure 7.7 The Pain Sheet and the 9 Boxes

information, they will resort to only talking about the features and functions of the new product. And doing so will give buyers more reasons not to buy than to buy. Stop this insanity and start using Pain Sheets. Leverage your company's entire knowledge base.

In the next chapter, I take a step-by-step approach and show you how to have an actual conversation using the model.

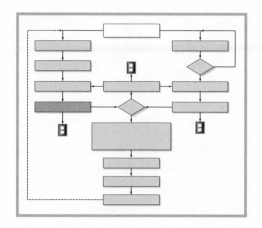

CHAPTER EIGHT

Creating Visions
Biased to Your Solution

This is a how-to chapter. It's about using the Solution Selling 9 Block Vision Processing Model. We're going to take a prospect from an admitted pain to a vision of a solution. At the conclusion of this hypothetical conversation, the salesperson and the prospect will have a shared buying vision.

The conversation you are about to read is entirely fictional. But it demonstrates the process for diagnosing the reasons for the prospect's problems, exploring their impact throughout the organization, and visualizing the capabilities ultimately leading to a customer buying vision.

Note: Your buyer is not going to follow your every lead through this approach and model. Buyers frequently go in some other direction that suits their interest at the moment. The guideline is to follow your buyer, stay in alignment, but at the appropriate time, if the buyer has taken you offtrack from executing the steps of the model, skillfully bring him or her back to the last place you were at in the 9 Boxes and continue your conversation.

VISION PROCESSING MODEL

The following script is an example of a conversation between our salesperson, Bill Hart, and the buyer, Steve Jones, the VP Sales for Titan Games, Inc.

Bill has just shared a Reference Story with Steve about another VP Sales who missed a sales goal and how Bill's company had been able to help. Bill ended the story with "Enough about that situation. Tell me about your situation and in particular about any challenges that you may be faced with."

The conversation proceeds with the prospect admitting that the firm's top-priority pain is "missing new account revenue targets." Bill then asks a few "sizing" questions to understand the scope of the problem and tries to measure by how much the new account revenue target is actually being missed. After Bill determines that the new account revenue targets are likely to be missed by $5 million, he continues the conversation starting with the first box of the 9 Block Model, Box R1.

Box R1: Open Question, Reason for Pain

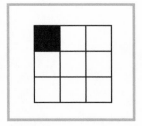

Box R1

Since the buyer has admitted a problem, the next step is to ask an open question that will empower the buyer. How much you discover at this point depends on how talkative your buyer is and his or her degree of expertise. In this example, the buyer is not particularly open, causing the salesperson to work harder.

Salesperson: Tell me about it—what is causing you to have this problem of missing your new account revenue targets?

Buyer: I've been thinking about it, but I haven't really been able to put my finger on the whole problem. I'm not sure even where to start. Let me tell you how we do it today. Our salespeople have assigned accounts. Any time an order is placed by a customer with an account, he or she must place that order through their assigned salesperson.

Salesperson: I'd like to ask a few questions. May I?

Buyer: Please, go ahead.

The open question invites the buyer to talk about the problem. In this case, the buyer doesn't know the answer, doesn't really elaborate too much, or is just reluctant to discuss it. However, having asked the open question first gives the salesperson the permission to continue on to and ask some control questions.

Note: During this conversation when the buyer admits a reason for his pain, Bill Hart then attempts to ask some additional control questions (not shown on the Pain Sheet graphic in Chapter Seven). We call these additional questions "drill-down" questions because they allow a salesperson to drill down on each reason to better understand the scope of the buyer's problem. This also allows the salesperson to establish value for his or her capabilities. These drill-down questions should be included on Pain Sheets.

Box R2: Control Question, Reasons for Pain

Having conducted precall planning and research, the salesperson has already prepared control questions. Control passes to the salesperson, which the buyer invited. The Pain Sheet example from Chapter Seven shows a list of four possible reasons for a given pain with four corresponding capabilities (visions) that address each reason. We will only demonstrate uncovering two of the four possible reasons.

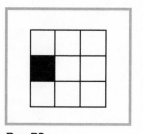

Box R2

Salesperson: Are you missing new account revenue targets because your salespeople spend too much time handling repeat business in existing accounts?

Buyer: Yes, they spend so much time doing what I call order taking and not really selling to their current assigned accounts. This takes away from the time that they could be selling to new accounts.

Salesperson: What amount of revenue is generated from this repeat business? [This is where the salesperson drills down to explore the first reason.]

Buyer: Last year we saw $80 million in revenue.

Salesperson: And what percentage of that revenue requires no selling or, to use your words, order taking?

Buyer: I would say at least 10 percent, or $8 million.

Salesperson: What percentage of a salesperson's time is spent on these order-taking activities?

Buyer: I would say 5 percent of the overall day is spent on those activities.

Salesperson: My research shows that you have approximately fifty salespeople?

Buyer: Yes.

Salesperson: What is the average quota per salesperson?

Buyer: Approximately $2 million each.

Salesperson: Back to the order-taking activities—how much of that time—5 percent—would you like salespeople focused on new account sales activities?

Buyer: Well, all of it.

Salesperson: Do you think that the same rate of revenue attainment could occur with new accounts as it does with existing ones?

Buyer: Yes, I really do.

Salesperson: Just looking at the numbers quickly, it looks like if each sales representative could spend that order-taking time focused on selling to new accounts, that could bring in $100,000 per salesperson— or $5 million a year.

Buyer: Just listening to the numbers, I don't think I would have guessed it was that high, but that does seem to be right.

In addition to establishing the first reason for the problem, the salesperson was also able to measure its value to the company. Bill continues on to uncover another reason.

Salesperson: Could another reason be that your salespeople spend too much time answering frequently asked questions (or FAQs) from their current customers in their assigned accounts?

Buyer: Oh yes, this is probably a bigger issue than the order-taking situation I described.

Salesperson: Well, again—what percentage of their time is being spent on those types of activities?

Buyer: They probably spend 15 percent of their day answering FAQs.

Salesperson: Again, how much time do you think should be devoted to that?

Buyer: Frankly, none. They're salespeople, not customer support.

Salesperson: How many new accounts did each sales rep acquire last year?

Buyer: On average, each sales rep was probably assigned ten new accounts.

Salesperson: And what was the average revenue per new account?

Buyer: I would guess conservatively that it was about $75,000 each.

Salesperson: If the salespeople were freed from answering FAQs, could they bring in one new account with the saved time?

Buyer: They probably should bring in more, but one account does sound good.

Salesperson: Is it reasonable, then, that if all fifty reps could bring in one new account each and those accounts yielded at least $75,000, you could bring in $3.75 million in revenue toward your new account revenue goals?

Buyer: Again, I never thought of the potential as that large, but I think that's a reasonable figure.

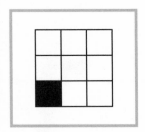

Box R3

Box R3: Confirm Question, Reasons for Pain

At some point, when the salesperson has covered the main reasons for Steve's pain, it's time to confirm the information.

Salesperson: So, it sounds like from what we've just discussed that the reasons you're not hitting your new account revenue targets are (1) that your salespeople spend too much time handling repeat business in existing accounts and (2) they're also spending too much time answering FAQs, and this is taking away from their task of prospecting into new accounts. Looking quickly at the numbers, it appears this could be costing you close to $9 million in revenue a year. Is that right?

Buyer: Yes, it is.

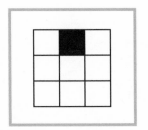

Box I1

Box I1: Open Question, Explore Impact

Having completed the diagnosis of the reasons for the VP Sale's critical business issue, it's time to move on and explore the impact of the problem on the organization.

Salesperson: Besides yourself, who else in your organization is impacted because the new account revenue targets are being missed? And how are they impacted?

Buyer: Well, I know our salespeople are frustrated because they're challenged with hitting their quotas. It tends to bring morale down.

The buyer reveals a direct impact of this problem on the salespeople, but Bill proceeds to make additional and more far-reaching connections.

Box 12: Control Question, Explore Impact

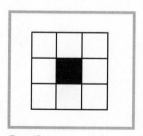

Box 12

Even though some information may have been provided by the buyer at the beginning of this part of the conversation, it's important to continue to connect the problem throughout the organization. The salesperson can either ask outright, "Is the VP Finance impacted by this problem of missing new account revenue targets?" Or the salesperson could use the Socratic method, as in the following dialogue:

Salesperson: If the new account revenue targets are being missed, is that causing your overall revenue goals to be missed?

Buyer: It really is having a huge impact on that.

Salesperson: Have you seen profits affected because of this?

Buyer: Our profits have been stagnant, but at this rate, the overall profit targets of the company will be missed.

Salesperson: Do you know what the profit margins are here at TGI?

Buyer: I think they're around 30 percent, but I'm not exactly sure.

Salesperson: Which person in your organization is going to be most impacted by missed profit targets?

Buyer: That would be Jim Smith, our VP Finance.

Salesperson: Have the declining profits had any major effect on the value of your stock?

Buyer: Well, as you can imagine, we're all shareholders here. The earnings per share have slipped, but I would say that the declining profits have affected us more in our ability to grow our business.

Salesperson: Who is looking to grow the business here at TGI?

Buyer: We all are, but this is really our CEO's initiative, Susan Brown.

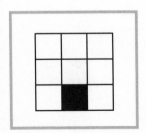

Box 13

Box 13: Confirm Question, Explore Impact

In the same way that R3 was summed up, it's time to confirm the salesperson's understanding of the impacts.

Salesperson: So, from what I just heard, it sounds like your salespeople are frustrated with the effort it requires to hit their quotas, the VP Finance is challenged with hitting his profit targets, and your CEO is finding it difficult to grow TGI's business. It sounds like this is not just your problem in sales and marketing, but a companywide problem. Is that correct?

Buyer: Bill, I can't disagree. You seem to have a real handle on our issues here at TGI.

Having diagnosed the reasons for Steve's pain and explored the impact on others at TGI, Bill can now go on to build a vision of a solution. He does this by getting the buyer to visualize the capabilities needed.

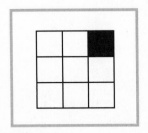

Box C1

Box C1: Open Question, Visualize the Buyer's Current Capabilities

First, the salesperson asks an open question, which empowers the buyer. The salesperson also finds out if in fact there is a competing vision or whether the buyer has come to some vision during the dialogue. Remember, asking open questions first earns a salesperson the right to explore control questions.

Salesperson: What is it going to take for you to be able to achieve your new account revenue targets for the year?

Buyer: It's apparent that we need to free our salespeople up from some of the activities that they're currently engaged in so they can focus on selling, but I'm not quite sure how we can do that. That's part of the reason I agreed to see you.

    Salesperson: I understand; can I try a few ideas on you?

The buyer doesn't have a vision and has invited the salesperson to offer whatever ideas there may be.

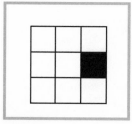

Box C2

Box C2: Control Question, Visualize Capabilities

This is where all Bill's hard work in R2 (control questions, diagnose reasons) pays off. This happens in part because he has built those questions around the capabilities of his products and services. Since there were two confirmed reasons for the buyer's pain, there are two capabilities that should be described in this conversation.

    Salesperson: Earlier, you mentioned that salespeople spend too much time order taking with their current assigned accounts. You indicated that it takes away from the time that they could be selling to new accounts. What if your customers could view inventory levels and then place an order on their own and have it allocated and confirmed on the Internet, so that the salespeople could be free from taking orders, and they could devote that time to selling to new accounts?

    Buyer: I like the sound of that a lot.

    Salesperson: If customers could do that, do you think your salespeople could bring in the $5 million in additional revenue that we figured earlier?

    Buyer: Well, Bill, since they're assigned accounts, I can't imagine that the salespeople would never have to interface with them, but I think we could realistically say that we should see a good bit of that revenue number attained.

Salesperson: Just how much?

Buyer: I would say at least 80 percent, or $4 million.

Each capability is brought up one at a time to provide the buyer with ideas on how to solve the problem.

Salesperson: Earlier, you also mentioned that salespeople spend too much time answering FAQs from their current customers in their assigned accounts. What if customers who have questions could click on a FAQ Web menu to get answers or could select a help option to connect to the appropriate person in the company, such as customer service so that the salespeople could be free from answering redundant questions, and they could devote that time to selling to new accounts?

Buyer: I like the sound of that too.

Salesperson: If customers could do that, do you think your salespeople could bring in the $3.75 million in revenue that we figured earlier?

Buyer: Well, Bill, once again, since they're assigned accounts, I think the salespeople will still have to devote some time to them, but I think we could see a good bit of that revenue number attained too.

Salesperson: Just how much?

Buyer: I would still say at least 80 percent, or $3 million.

Box C3: Confirm Question, Visualize Capabilities

This summary of the accepted capabilities is really the buying vision. Notice how it's structured: If you had the ability to do A plus B, then could you obtain your (goal)? (The goal being the inverse of the pain.) Also, note how the salesperson has calculated the value in this particular dialogue.

Salesperson: Steve, I just want to confirm our conversation here. So, if you had the ability for (A) customers who want to place orders to view inventory levels, place an order on their own, and have it allocated and confirmed over the Internet as well as (B) allow customers to answer their own questions by clicking on an FAQ Web menu to get those answers or a help option to connect to the appropriate person in the company, then could you regain what appears to be a total of $7 million in new account revenue, actually surpassing the shortfall that you shared with me earlier?

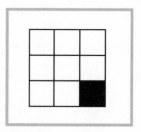

Box C3

Buyer: Bill, I really do believe that we could. How do we get started?

Our salesperson has completed the vision processing method. He has taken the buyer from an admitted pain through a diagnosis of the pain, explored the impact of the pain on the organization, and arrived at a shared vision of a solution—while establishing value for his offering.

How long does this take? Some salespeople and sales situations may only require a few minutes; others may take an extended period of time. If it's overkill—that is, the situation doesn't warrant spending this kind of time—fine; use what is applicable to the situation. On the other hand, if it's a complex situation with multiple people involved, vision processing may take place over several meetings or conference calls. You might only accomplish getting through the reasons column on the first call and the impact column on the second call, and then need a third call to describe capabilities.

Diagnosing problems and creating visions of solutions that are biased to what you sell are critical to sales success. Never underestimate the importance of this activity to you and to your prospective customers.

PART THREE

Engaging in Active Opportunities

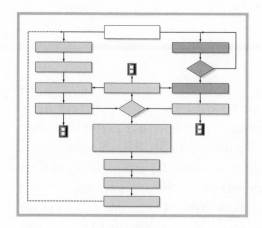

CHAPTER NINE

Selling When You're Not First

It was 3:15 A.M. when the hotel phone rang. It was Ulrich Hanson calling me from Dallas, Texas. I was in the United Kingdom and his early-morning call startled me.

"Keith, I'm sorry for calling you in the middle of the night," Ulrich said. "I have an emergency, and I was afraid I would miss you if I waited until tomorrow."

"That's okay," I said, struggling to wake from a deep sleep. "What can I do for you?"

"We've just received word that we've lost a very important strategic deal in Argentina," he said, his voice tense and filled with stress. "Time is of the essence, and I want you to help us with a competitive strategy and a tactical plan to salvage this account.

"Keith, I know this is asking a great deal of you, but can you come to Dallas right away? Can you get here tomorrow? I don't care how you do it or how much it costs. I need your help on this."

His offer made my decision easy. It was my first opportunity to fly on the Concorde, the fastest commercial airplane in the world. Because of the time difference, I effectively arrived in New York before I had taken off. I was back in Dallas later that same day and in plenty of time to participate in the first strategy session on the opportunity.

While flying from London to New York, I had time to reflect on his phone call. Ulrich Hanson, country manager for EDS in Latin and South America, was committed to implementing a sales process to help his team better manage the complex selling environment it faced in the outsourcing business. (Ulrich, along with his direct reports and his salespeople, had spent a week in Dallas learning how to implement Solution Selling—I had even taught the workshops.)

Within three weeks of the training, a large manufacturer in Argentina asked to visit the EDS facilities in the United States. The manufacturer wanted a thorough briefing on EDS's outsourcing capabilities and said it was evaluating two or three outsourcing companies. Company executives would make a fast decision. They agreed to send a packet of information ahead of time so EDS could better prepare for their visit.

Of course, EDS happily encouraged their visit. This is every salesperson's dream. Or is it? The Argentinean manufacturer was already at vision and it did not include EDS. The manufacturer only wanted EDS for comparison and price negotiations, and Ulrich and his team played right into their hands.

Ulrich realized what he and his team had done. He was angry and disappointed in himself for not seeing this one and for not doing things differently. They had played by someone else's rules in an active situation. Ulrich realized he should have deployed the End-Around competitive strategy and vision re-engineering, which he had learned from Solution Selling. Instead, his team focused on supplying the prospect with an outsourcing proposal to replace the company's existing and outdated technology.

Ironically, this was the right thing to do. However, automating the manufacturer's current chaotic processes would just result in better-automated chaos. The missing link was the need for business process re-engineering before putting the new automation into place.

Using Solution Selling's process steps, I helped the EDS team determine what the real business problems were. The manufacturer was losing more than half a billion dollars a year, and it was close to going out of business. Survival was the paramount goal. The company's current manufacturing procedures were old and outdated, and the costs of its information system were prohibitive.

Ulrich and his team got back into the opportunity by admitting to the prospect that EDS hadn't properly analyzed the manufacturer's current technology and manufacturing processes. EDS won the manufacturer's attention by disclosing a way to reduce the cost of its information system and, more important, reduce the overall costs of manufacturing by $10 million annually. EDS previously had not wanted to go down this path, because this analysis and proposal would add costs on the front end, and the customer was extremely cost conscious. Furthermore, EDS felt such an approach would delay the decision and it wanted to avoid that too.

Once the prospect agreed to listen, EDS was able to deploy an End-Around strategy and re-engineer the existing vision. EDS successfully rearranged the playing field. The approach changed the buying requirements from a technology capability focus to an industry expertise focus, where competitors of EDS could not compete or win.

EDS was very fortunate to get a second chance with this opportunity and win the business. Here is Ulrich Hansen's note to me:

Shortly after the last of three classes were conducted by our group in our SBU, we discovered an opportunity in Argentina. A major competitor of ours was about to sign the first *outsourcing contract in that country. Since we arrived late on the scene (mainly due to not having a presence in Argentina), we were not in "Column A." By using all the wisdom in your process and your strategies and techniques, we got the playing field rearranged from "technology" to our strength, "industry capability." When our competitor mistakenly accepted the new playing field, it was outplayed! In summary, we signed the first outsourcing multiyear contract in Argentina worth over $40 million.*

WHEN TO COMPETE

Ulrich Hansen's story raises several questions: When should you engage or disengage from an opportunity? And if you engage, which strategy should you employ? The right answers can lead to improved win odds, realized sales forecasts, and increased sales revenue; the wrong answers can lead to increased selling costs, missed sales forecasts, and low morale. You must decide whether to stay and compete, or disengage and move on. The cost of doing business today is too high and selling resources are too limited to pursue every opportunity that comes along.

In the past, Solution Selling focused on strategies dealing with latent, or Not Looking opportunities. Today, that's not the case. Solution Selling has been enhanced to better assist salespeople in the competitive world of active or Looking opportunities. I am a firm believer that you should evaluate every active opportunity that's out there. I also firmly believe that you will not win them unless you deploy the right competitive strategy and tactical plan, which brings me to the famous Chinese general and philosopher Sun-Tzu.

Sun-Tzu's book *The Art of War* (Sun-Tzu Ping-Fa) is the oldest account of formalized military strategies and tactics of warfare. Though he lived long ago (ca. 400–320 B.C.E.), his strategies and tactics still apply and are studied in modern business management, and his book is required reading in many business schools. Sun-Tzu regarded war as a road either to safety or to ruin, a matter of life and death, and a subject that cannot be neglected. He talked about when to fight and when not to do so and which strategy to use.

Selling is like that too. I regard sales as a road either to safety or ruin, a matter of success or failure, and a subject that cannot be neglected. We must be aware of the consequences of poor planning, wasteful selling actions, and careless personnel. Deciding when to compete and selecting the right selling strategy are crucial to success in the marketplace.

PREEMPT THE COMPETITION, GET THERE FIRST

Get there first; set the buying requirements; become Column A. Preempt the competition. That's the best strategy and the best advice I can give salespeople when it comes to winning in competitive environments. I realize that deploying this strategy may not always be possible, but there is one thing I know for sure: it cannot work unless you try.

Often we find ourselves in situations where the competition has established itself in Column A. When we do, we have to take action to replace the competition. Can you still win if you didn't define the problems and create the vision? Can you win if you're Column B or C? What does it really take to overcome someone in Column A? This chapter answers those questions.

When a buyer phones or sends you an RFP announcing that he or she is in the market for what you have to sell, it's very enticing to compete, to respond, to immediately begin selling. We fail to recognize that the buyer has a vision, and it's not one we helped create. Don't be too anxious to walk into this minefield. Step back and assess the situation.

It's difficult to compete against a competitor who is already in Column A. Remember, the research indicates that those companies and salespeople who are in Column A win more than 90 percent of the time. One of my largest clients, IBM's Software Group, tracked its results worldwide and verified the findings. IBM's results showed that 93 percent of the time some other company won the business if IBM did not define the problems and set the requirements.

The lesson is clear: if another competitor is first choice, your chances of winning are slim—about 10 percent. Put another way, you stand a 90 percent chance of losing. The staggering fact is that salespeople spend most of their time and efforts on situations they didn't create and where they have less than a 10 percent chance of winning. If you find yourself engaging in this practice, stop the insanity.

FIVE RULES FOR DECIDING WHETHER TO COMPETE OR NOT

The first step is to measure the odds of winning. Sun-Tzu said, "In respect of military method, we have, firstly, Measurement; secondly, Estimation of Quantity; thirdly, Calculation; fourthly, Balancing of Chances; fifthly, Victory."

In Solution Selling, we use five rules. Each will help you decide whether or not to engage. In the bustle and chaos of selling, there is usually little time to assess an opportunity. But when it comes to competing against competitors who are already in Column A, we have to pause and consider our actual chances of winning.

Rule 1: Don't Fool Yourself, Your Team, or Your Manager

Start by asking yourself a very basic question: Is this opportunity active (Looking) or latent (Not Looking)? If it's active, then don't fool yourself into thinking you have a good a chance of winning. The worst thing salespeople can do in competitive situations is fool themselves. The consequences of making the wrong decision can be severe, and not just in lost time, money, and resources. It can be personally and politically devastating to get involved in opportunities that you have no chance of winning.

By being honest with yourself, you can assess your real chances, select the right strategy, and build a tactical plan that gives you a realistic chance of winning. Remember, the win rate on active opportunities (when you're not first) is not encouraging. This doesn't mean give up; it means it's time to be realistic. You have limited time, money, and resources; use them wisely. Always remember, not all sales opportunities are created equal.

Rule 2: Qualify the Opportunity, Perform an Opportunity Assessment

I find that most salespeople need a job aid to assist them when they're deciding whether to pursue an opportunity. It's never too early or too late to disengage from an opportunity that does not meet a set of defined standards. The sooner you disengage from opportunities that you have no chance of winning, the sooner you can work on opportunities where you do.

I think of opportunity assessment like a game of poker. Who wins the most money? It usually isn't the person who stays in each hand the longest. He or she tends to commit more time and money and then doesn't win. Players who fold early when they realize their chances of winning are low tend to win the most money.

Why do salespeople need a job aid or a third party to assist them with making the decision whether to engage or disengage? Is it because they don't trust themselves? It seems that salespeople get too caught up in their desire to win and thereby lose their objectivity

Opportunity Assessment Worksheet					Assessment Date		
Account _____ Assessment status: Latent ☐ Active ☐ Opportunity description: _____ Potential revenue (estimated) _____		Yes	No	*Influenced by			
				Us	Competitor		
Is the customer going to buy?	Is there a key driving force causing the customer to take action?						
	Can the customer get money for the project?						
How far along was the opportunity when we found it?	Have needs been established?						
	Has a budget been set?						
	Has a time frame been established?						
	Does the customer have a vision of a solution?						
Will the customer buy our offering?	Do offerings match the customer's needs?						
	Does our offering include unique differentiators?						
	Can unique business value be demonstrated?						
Can we win this opportunity?	Does the power sponsor have a high-priority pain?						
	Is there access to the power sponsor?						
	Has a differentiated vision been created/re-engineered?						
	Can the value of the offering be proved?						
	Can the buying process be controlled?						
What is the value of winning?	Is there any risk in this opportunity?						
	Does a relationship provide an advantage?						
	Tactical (strong short-term) value in winning?						
	Strategic (long-term) value in winning?						

Should we engage?   Yes ☐   No ☐

Figure 9.1 Opportunity Assessment Worksheet

The Opportunity Assessment Worksheet illustrated in Figure 9.1 helps the salesperson answer two very basic questions: Should we compete? and, Can we win? This is especially important in active opportunities that you didn't initiate or create.

Notice in this example that we have created columns and a grading legend to help salespeople assess for themselves how they compare with their competition. Once you have decided to compete, it's important to determine what it's going to take to win.

When you use the Opportunity Assessment Worksheet, some of the key questions to ask include: Do you have access to power? Can you identify the power person's business (and personal) pains? Does the power person's vision of a solution match the capabilities of your products and services? What is the value associated with solving the problem? Can you exert control over the buying process?

Earlier, I introduced the formula for a successful sale: Pain × Power × Vision × Value × Control = Sale. This is a component of the Opportunity Assessment job aid that can be used to quickly qualify opportunities. Remember, because this is a formula, if you have a zero in any element on the left, you get a zero on the right.

Once you've assessed your chances, you should have a better idea of your competitive advantage or lack of one. If the odds look good, it's time to select a competitive strategy and determine the tactical steps that need to be implemented in order to win.

Rule 3: Select a Competitive Strategy

The key word in Rule 3 is select. To select a strategy, you first need to know what it is and how it is used. I make a big deal out of selecting, because many people unconsciously select a strategy (not knowing they have done so) that won't allow them to win. The four competitive strategies for active opportunities are:

1. Head-to-Head
2. End-Around
3. Divide and Conquer
4. Stall

Each strategy has its own strengths and weaknesses. It's important to understand each one (see Figure 9.2).

Head-to-Head Strategy Sun-Tzu said, "In the practical art of war, the best thing of all is to take the enemy's country whole and intact." He insisted that your forces must have overwhelming strength: "It is the rule in war, if our forces are ten to the enemy's one, to surround him; if five to one, to attack him; if twice as numerous, to divide our army into two." Superiority gives us a competitive advantage.

The Head-to-Head strategy is the number one strategy deployed in competitive selling situations. It's also the number one strategy selected in the majority of lost opportunities. Most salespeople unconsciously resort to it, even though it may not be the correct strategy for the situation. They are unaware of other ways to compete, and they fail to anticipate their competitors' maneuvers. Salespeople using a Head-to-Head competitive strategy simply match feature and function, competing directly with the competition, giving it their best shot—and end up losing.

In competitive situations, if a stronger competitor enjoys an entrenched position and you want to defeat the competition, don't choose a Head-to-Head strategy. It will almost certainly lead to a lost opportunity. The principles of competition dictate that to win using a Head-to-Head strategy—taking heed of Sun-Tzu's advice—you must have a greater advantage, depending on the competitor's position and level of entrenchment. Hopefully, you enjoy a 2 to 1 advantage in competitive commercial situations (preferably, a 10 to 1 or at least a 5 to 1 advantage would be better). Keep in mind, this advantage

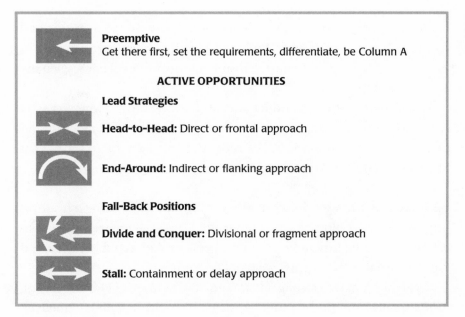

Figure 9.2 Competitive Strategies

should be considered from the customer's perspective, not your own: Does the customer think you're twice as good as the competition? Don't be unrealistic; take stock of your strengths and carefully assess your opportunity.

An example of the dangers of using a Head-to-Head strategy involved one of my clients, Texas Instruments. Several years ago, the company's software division released a software development tool that was far superior to anything else in the market. The company's salespeople could simply walk into almost any opportunity and do a product demonstration, and they would win because their product was so superior. It didn't matter if the customer was actively looking and about to buy from a competitor. Texas Instruments's product was so far superior and so much better; it clearly had a 2 to 1 or greater advantage over its competition.

Within a year, competitors caught up with Texas Instruments's product by adding additional features and functionality to their products.

However, Texas Instruments's people were slow to react to this and continued to compete using their old Head-to-Head strategy. Texas Instruments's salespeople started losing opportunities. That's when my telephone rang.

Texas Instruments's product was still good (but no longer vastly superior), and the company had to figure out a way to compete under these different circumstances. Texas Instruments went on to learn what to do—use an End-Around strategy.

End-Around Strategy Sun-Tzu was not shy about avoiding a head-to-head battle he could not win. He wrote, "If equally matched, we can offer battle; if slightly inferior in numbers, we can avoid the enemy; if quite unequal in every way, we can flee from him."

If you don't have a strong advantage, don't compete Head-to-Head; instead, select the End-Around strategy, or indirect selling maneuver. (In Solution Selling, the tactic used to support the End-Around strategy is called vision re-engineering, which is discussed in the next chapter.) The End-Around strategy is a powerful default strategy and should be used in selling situations where you are not in Column A.

How many companies and salespeople are willing to walk away from active opportunities that find them? Not very many, and I include myself in that category. Why are we like this? Is it because we're so competitive and believe our competition's rightful market share is zero? Is it because these people are buying what we're selling, and we really don't have that much going on right now? Or maybe it's because our company has labeled this account as a "strategic account" and we have "no choice"—we have to respond to every opportunity coming from this company. Always remember the concept that I introduced earlier concerning column fodder. If you're not in Column A, then you must be in Column B, C, or D, and the odds of winning are not very good.

Your product may be superior, but is it superior enough to beat the Column A vendor head-on in a feature-function competition?

Deploying the End-Around strategy means that you're not going to compete on the existing and established buying requirements. It's necessary to change the rules of the game, and you can do this by changing the evaluation matrix, changing the buying requirements, or even expanding the requirements. If you can do this and you bring value to the situation, you stand a good chance of moving into Column A. The End-Around strategy is the preferred competitive strategy when you're not first. The next two strategies—Divide and Conquer and Stall—should be used as fall-back strategies; don't lead with them. However, as the sale proceeds and you see that your chances are not encouraging, you may want to shift to one of these other two strategies.

Divide and Conquer Strategy Although you would like to win the whole opportunity and make the big sale, sometimes—despite your best efforts—you can't. Instead of competing for all the business, go after a part of the business, a part you know you can win.

Deploying the Divide and Conquer strategy keeps your competition from winning the whole thing. With a piece of the opportunity, you can, in the future, work to increase the amount of business you do with the customer—from the inside. If the competition wins the whole opportunity, chances are you'll have difficulty getting business from the customer in the future. This isn't a desirable position, particularly if you value the account.

Stall Strategy This is a delay strategy, and it's used when the features and capabilities of your company, its products and services, cannot compete effectively. Sun-Tzu assured us that "He will win who, prepared himself, waits to take the enemy unprepared." If you find yourself losing, it may be useful to stall or slow down the buyer's buying process until you can figure out a winning approach.

Companies that own market share are in a much better position to use the Stall strategy than those that do not. Market leaders often use this strategy globally in their marketing efforts. One example of this strategy involves Lotus Development Corporation and Microsoft. Lotus had established itself as the leader in work group and collaboration software with its product, Lotus Notes. Microsoft decided to deploy a Stall strategy until its work group product, Exchange, was fully ready. Microsoft preannounced Exchange and asked prospective customers who were evaluating work group software to delay making a purchasing decision. This strategy was very effective. Many customers decided to wait until the Microsoft product was on the market before making their final purchasing decision. Today, Microsoft's position in work group and collaboration software is very strong.

Rule 4: Communicate Your Strategy to the Team

Setting expectations and communicating strategy are critically important in selling, especially in team selling. In business today, it's rare to have salespeople working totally on their own without any help or assistance.

It's not fair for salespeople to use sales support people without adequately preparing them. Problems occur when salespeople know the situation but don't properly communicate and orchestrate the correct competitive strategy and tactical plan. I frequently hear sales support people complain that salespeople talk about how great an opportunity is but never share the real nature of the situation. I'd rather have a salesperson tell his or her team, "This is a competitive situation, and we didn't bring this from latent to active, so we're behind. In order to win, we'll have to deploy the End-Around strategy, which means we need to decide our most effective differentiators, meet with the prospective customer, and re-engineerr the customer's vision around our differentiation." Better this realistic assessment than pumping up team members about how great the opportunity is and mismanaging their expectations. People can deal with the truth and they will do a better job when they know the real nature of the competitive landscape. Having a process and consciously knowing what competitive strategy to follow makes the entire team better.

Rule 5: Play to Win, Invest Resources Wisely

Before you can execute a tactical plan, you must first know what it is. You should also be prepared to adjust the plan during the execution phase based on the buyer's and the competition's actions. Since our default strategy is the End-Around strategy, I will focus on how to build and execute a tactical plan to support this strategy.

When you're not first and not Column A, the strategy you want to deploy is the End-Around strategy. That's what to do. But the next question is, How do you do it? It starts with knowing what your company's strengths and weaknesses are. It's fine to say, "Change or re-engineerr the buyers vision"; it's another to know what to change.

I often recommend that salespeople use the Sales Formula—Pain × Power × Vision × Value × Control = Sale—as a basis to build their tactical plan. Start by breaking down what you know about each of these elements and honestly assess where you stand. That's what the opportunity assessment job aid helps you do. After assessment, decide how to attack each element. Get the team involved as early as possible in this exercise. The more involvement members have early on, the better. They become part of the solution, rather than part of the problem later.

DIFFERENTIATORS

Sun-Tzu identified and compared his differentiators (the enemy's strengths and weaknesses), writing, "Carefully compare the opposing army with your own, so that you may know where strength is super-abundant and where it is deficient."

I suggest using three elements in defining effective differentiators:

1. Define and list the aspects of your company and its products and services that are different from the competition.
2. Estimate the uniqueness of the differentiation compared to your competition. Use a scale of 0 to 10.
3. Estimate the value of each differentiator to your customers. Use a scale of 0 to 10.

Start with a blank piece of paper and write at the top, "Our Differentiators," and then start listing them. List anything and everything you can think of that may be a differentiator. If you're not sure, ask someone. Don't be afraid to ask—this is very important. After all, it's hard to create and re-engineerr visions if you don't know your differentiators. If you think there is something that makes any aspect of your company different, list it.

For example, if your company has been in business for fifty years and that makes you different, then write that down. It could be financial stability, international coverage, or you may have distribution capabilities that add value. Put them on the list. Do the same exercise for all your products and services.

The second step is to estimate how unique each differentiator is using a scale of 0 to 10. Zero has little or no uniqueness and ten is unique. I use the term *estimate* because it's difficult to have everyone agree. It's okay to estimate based on opinion, as you will see.

The third step is to estimate the value of the differentiator to a customer. Try and put yourself in the mind of the customer and think of value from his or her perspective as much as possible. Use a scale of 0 to 10. Zero has little if any value and ten has great value. Again, this scale is based on the judgment or opinion of the salesperson. Be careful not to overestimate the value of the differentiator unless you've spoken with the customer and he or she has specifically verified the value of the differentiator to you.

Once the list is complete with estimated weighting for uniqueness and value, it's time to plot the findings. See Figure 9.3.

On the vertical axis, rate the uniqueness of each differentiator, plotted against the horizontal axis for value to the customer. Each differentiator is rated from 0 to 10 for both parameters. You will end up with dots all around the chart.

The differentiators that made it to the upper-right quadrant are both unique and valuable. They are your strengths and they really make a difference to the customer. These are the differentiators that salespeople must make into must-have capabilities on the part of the customer.

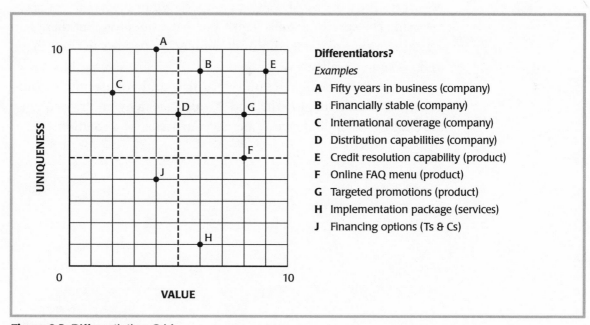

Figure 9.3 Differentiation Grid

The ones in the lower-left quadrant have little value and are not unique. The others are somewhere in between and can be used in certain circumstances, but only after you have attempted to make the upper-right quadrant differentiators real and important issues with the customer. Keep in mind that the differentiators will move from quadrant to quadrant over time. That's why it's important to keep company, product, and service knowledge along with marketing messages and materials updated as markets mature.

The importance of this exercise is to take an honest look at your differentiators and their competitive strengths. You want to get input from marketing, customer support, and other departments to help evaluate the factors of uniqueness and value. This is an eye-opening experience for many of our clients.

When you're not first, do things differently. The win rate is low, often not worth the expense of competing, unless you can change the playing field. The specific actions depend on each situation, but there is a logical sequence to competing and winning. Sometimes the best thing to do is simply walk away.

Most of the time, when you're not first and you decide to compete, you need to deploy the End-Around strategy and re-engineer the existing vision of the customer to your vision of a solution.

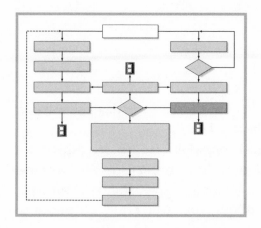

CHAPTER TEN

Vision Re-engineering

Lotus Development Corporation successfully deployed Solution Selling throughout the company. Lotus gave us lots of credit for helping it achieve significant sales results, and for that I will always be grateful. Lotus originally set a goal of selling 30 million sets of Lotus Notes, and it achieved that goal almost two years earlier than the original plan called for. The keys to this early success were an outstanding product and Solution Selling. Solution Selling enabled them to sell Notes as an enterprise-wide solution to business executives, which had been a challenge for Lotus salespeople before they used Solution Selling.

During the time that Lotus Notes was doing so well, Lotus Corporation attracted the attention of IBM. In an inspired moment, IBM acquired Lotus, and this is where my story of working with IBM and vision re-engineering really begins.

Since IBM was not a customer of ours when it acquired Lotus, we were very apprehensive about our future relationship with Lotus. Would IBM allow Lotus to continue to work with us? Would IBM come in and make wholesale changes and require Lotus to follow IBM's methods and procedures? We talked to everyone we knew at Lotus trying to find answers. Early on, no one knew, but the consensus was that Lotus would be left alone and we would be kept onboard.

Two or three months postacquisition, while on a business trip to California, I received a phone call in my hotel room early one morning from a gentleman at IBM whom I did not know. He introduced himself and told me he was aware of our work with Lotus. He said that a Lotus executive—Mark Tapling—had given him my name.

Of course, I was very excited to get a call from IBM inquiring about doing business together. Who wouldn't be? I've always admired IBM, and Mark was a person whom I had grown to respect and admire as well. My caller asked if we would be interested in preparing a proposal for IBM to do skills-based sales training for a large number of IBM salespeople.

I wanted to say, "Yes, of course, who wouldn't?" But I didn't. Instead, I said, "Tell me what you are specifically looking to accomplish with this training. What business problems are you trying to solve? What skills are you looking to improve, and why? Are you looking to incorporate these skills into a companywide sales process or roll them out as training events?"

It didn't take him long to respond to my questions, because he knew exactly what he was looking for. In fact, he was so precise that it was clear I wasn't the first person he had spoken to about this. Later, I discovered the project had been going on for almost a year, and IBM was in the final stages of making a decision. He was calling me out of courtesy to Mark Tapling, because Mark had been internally promoting our approach to IBM since the acquisition.

I realized we were being asked to participate in an active opportunity. I knew we would be just another column—and I knew we would be column fodder as well. It would be a major mistake for us to engage because of the time and effort it would take to prepare a quality proposal and because we had a low probability of winning. I thanked him for the opportunity to participate in the evaluation and respectfully declined.

You could have heard a pin drop over the telephone. After a few seconds of silence, he said, "Let me get this straight. You're doing business with Lotus, you've been training its salespeople, and you're refusing to propose to the parent company, IBM?"

I quickly said, "I hope you'll understand what I'm doing and why I'm doing this, but please let me explain. I'm practicing the methodology we teach salespeople. For me to engage at this time in your buying process would be a grave mistake. You see, we missed the first phase of your buying process. That's where you or someone else helped you define your business problems and determine what you need to solve them. You're now in the second phase of your buying process, where you already have a vision of what you need and a good idea of the company you want to do business with."

I went on to explain to him, "The only way we can make a proposal is if you're willing to take some time and help us understand the business problems you're trying to solve and then give us the opportunity to reengineer your current vision to match our capabilities. If this isn't possible, then again, I must respectfully decline."

"I don't understand," he said, "and I don't agree with your approach. We can't slow down our process just for you. However, I do respect your decision not to participate." We ended the conversation with a few polite comments that I don't remember.

After hanging up the phone, I kept hoping I had done the right thing. After all, that was IBM on the phone, one of the world's largest and most respected companies. But I wouldn't be telling you this story if it didn't have a happy ending. The happy ending began forty-eight hours later when my phone rang.

"I can't believe what you did," the same IBM executive said.

"What do you mean?" I replied.

"I've never had anybody in my life do what you did," he said. "Yet, at the same time, that's exactly what we want our salespeople to be able to do."

"Please explain," I said.

"IBM can't afford to work on deals or opportunities that don't close, or worse yet, that we lose to the competition. Many people think that because we're IBM, we have deep pockets with unlimited funds and unlimited resources, but that's not true. We have to be able to qualify out of opportunities that we can't win. I want our salespeople to do what you did with me. Can you teach us to do that?"

That was the beginning of a long and lasting relationship with IBM that continues today. Since the implementation of Solution Selling began at IBM in 1996, we have worked with and trained more than 50,000 IBM employees and business partners around the world. Solution Selling is the core sales execution component of IBM's sales process.

This story is an example of vision re-engineering. When the IBM executive first called, he was trying to get us to complete a column in his evaluation matrix. He was buying skills-based sales training, and his mind was made up about what he wanted and with whom he wanted to do business—and it was not my firm, not at first.

Fortunately, I was able to differentiate myself with my approach, which was very important in this situation. Later on, I was able to reengineer his vision and help him see that deploying a total sales process throughout IBM was the real key to improved sales results versus engaging in skills-based sales training events.

I must give the IBM executive who called back a lot of credit. That return phone call has made all the difference in the world to IBM and to my company as well.

VISION PROCESSING MODEL, VISION RE-ENGINEERING

When it comes to active opportunities and vision re-engineering, I strongly recommend following the 9 Block Vision Processing Model. You've already seen the 9 Block Model. However, this time we're going

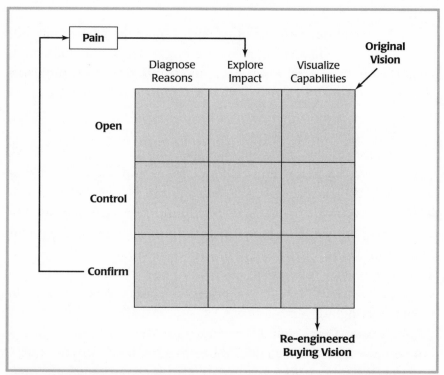

Figure 10.1 The 9 Block Vision Processing Model—Vision Re-engineering

to use the 9 Block Vision Processing Model differently. In vision re-engineering, we start in Box C1, because the buyer is already at vision. See Figure 10.1 and note the nine steps and the new sequence by which we navigate the model.

Let's revisit our sales scenario with Bill Hart and Steve Jones, but let's reverse the situation. This is not a latent opportunity. Steve Jones, VP Sales for the manufacturing company, Titan Games, Inc., calls Bill Hart. Steve briefly explains why he is calling, and then asks for Bill's product specifications, pricing, and a demonstration. Bill is told that Titan is in the market for e-commerce capabilities. Steve is inviting Bill to bid or, as we now know, to fill a column—but not Column A.

The conversation starts with the buyer calling the salesperson. Bill engages the buyer in a vision re-engineering conversation. Note how Bill navigates through the resequenced model—what he says and when he says it.

Buyer: Mr. Bill Hart, please.

Salesperson: Hello, this is Bill Hart speaking.

Buyer: Mr. Hart, my name is Steve Jones and I work for Titan Games, Inc. We're a manufacturing organization that specializes in production of toys and games . . . [the description continues in detail]. We haven't met, but we're looking for some specific e-commerce type of capabilities. We've heard great things about your company and would like to know what you have to offer. You know, the usual stuff: specifications, terms and conditions, prices—including a demonstration of your offering.

Salesperson: Thank you. I'll be happy to give you all the information you want, but before I do, I'd like to ask you a few questions. I need to know more before I'm able to talk about our offerings.

Buyer: Like what?

Here's an important Solution Selling principle: first make yourself equal before you make yourself different. In other words, first understand everything you can about the competing vision. Think about it: How will you know how to compete and what differentiators to use until you thoroughly learn about the current vision?

As you read this hypothetical conversation, note that each step has a small graphic illustrating where that step occurs in the 9 Block Vision Processing Model. It will help you follow along in the dialogue.

We enter the conversation starting with the first box (C1) of the 9 Block Vision Processing Model.

Box C1: Open Question,
Visualize the Buyer's Current Capabilities

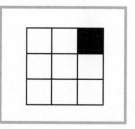

Box C1

Salesperson: What specific capabilities are you looking for, and how do you see yourself using these capabilities?

Buyer: Our salespeople have assigned accounts. Any time customers want to place an order, they must place that order through their assigned salesperson. I feel our salespeople spend way too much time doing what I call order taking with their assigned accounts instead of being out there selling into new accounts. Given all that, we've decided to implement an e-commerce application that will allow those existing customers to place their own orders. First, they'd be able to view inventory levels, then place the order on their own and have it allocated and confirmed on the Internet. We really think this will allow the salespeople to devote their time to selling into new accounts.

Salesperson: [Clarifies initial vision.] So, it sounds like when existing customers want to place an order on standard items, you want them to easily and at any time be able to do that via the Internet without involving the salesperson, is that right?

Buyer: Yes, that's what we're attempting to do.

You will find all types of active buyers. The buyer may be active but has not selected a vendor. The buyer is truly shopping for the best alternative. In this case, the salesperson may have some latitude to further explore Box C1 and ask some probing questions to better participate in the existing vision. It's possible that the buyer will even share the pain early on that is driving the requirements.

Unfortunately, this is not usually the case. We will proceed with the dialogue assuming a worst-case scenario. The buyer is not very talkative and has not admitted a pain, and the salesperson doesn't feel he has earned the right to explore the current vision too much. The salesperson must attempt to establish valuable differentiators to earn the right to continue. After Bill has gained a good understanding of Steve's existing vision, the next step is to differentiate himself—that is, change the buying requirements so they include his strengths. The goal is to move into Column A and become the company and salesperson of choice. Let's assume that Bill has a good idea of the buyer's existing vision. It's now time to make himself different.

Box C2: Control Question, Visualize Capabilities

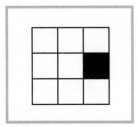

Box C2

Note: This is a sensitive area, because Bill is exploring areas outside Steve's original vision. The Pain Sheet example from Chapter Seven showed a list of four possible reasons for a given pain with four corresponding capabilities (visions) that address each reason. In this re-engineering scenario, the buyer has offered one of the four capabilities listed on the Pain Sheet as his existing vision. This allows the salesperson to attempt to provide a differentiating capability among the ones left.

First Differentiating Capability (Capability B)

Salesperson: Steve, as part of your e-commerce initiative, are you also looking for a way for customers who are at your Web site and have questions to click on a FAQ to get those answers, or, alternatively, select a help option to connect to the appropriate person in the company?

Buyer: That's not currently part of our initiative, but it does sound interesting.

Note: Bill has two options here: (1) he can continue positioning all his differentiators and then explore the possible value of them (reason column), or (2) he can bounce back and forth through the boxes. That is, once interest is shown in a new capability, Bill might go straight to the reason columns to establish value for the new capability before introducing a second new capability. The chosen style will vary by salesperson and opportunity.

For the sake of this illustration and to learn the sequence, we will have Bill continue positioning his differentiating capabilities in Box C2 before exploring their value.

Second Differentiating Capability (Capability C)

Salesperson: Steve, we will certainly explore that further, but let me ask you this: Are you also looking for a way, when offering promotions, for your salespeople to create personalized messages and broadcast them to all the prospects via email?

Buyer: Not really. Our sales force doesn't get involved with creating promotions. It's something we've looked into, but I really don't want to explore that today.

Although Steve wasn't interested in the second differentiating capability, Bill is not discouraged. He explores another differentiator.

Third Differentiating Capability (Capability D)

Salesperson: Well, I respect that. [Moves on to additional capability.] Do you think it would help if, when visiting your Web site, your customers could be prompted to submit referrals in exchange for discounts or promotional items?

Buyer: Again, this is not part of our current initiative, but that does intrigue me.

Now that Bill understands Steve's current vision and has piqued his interest in exploring some additional capabilities, it's time to find out what it currently costs the buyer to do business without the desired capabilities and why the buyer is seeking those capabilities. Again, you find all types of active buyers. Some may allow you to back up in their buying process to establish the "cost of doing business today." In this case, the salesperson may be able to ask some probing questions to better establish value for the existing vision. Once again, this is not usually the case. Often, buyers who have already gone through the due diligence process don't want to repeat it. In that case, the salesperson should respect their decision and focus on establishing value for his or her differentiating capabilities only. We'll proceed with the dialogue assuming the latter, worst-case scenario.

Note: When Bill explores Boxes R1 and R2, the boxes seem to merge together. The dialogue fluctuates between the two.

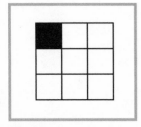

Box R1

Box R1: Open Questions, Diagnose Reasons

Salesperson: Tell me about it—how do you manage your accounts today without these capabilities?

Buyer: Specifically in regard to handling FAQs, I was intrigued by your description, because today when customers have a question, they go straight to their assigned sales reps. They usually call on a direct line. If they don't get their reps that way, they usually can reach them on their cell phones.

Salesperson: I'd like to explore that a little further, if I may.

Buyer: By all means, go ahead.

Box R2: How They Do Business Today Without Capability B

The dialogue below is very similar to the drill-down conversation that I explained in Chapter Eight showing the establishment of value during Vision Creation.

Salesperson: Today, how much time do salespeople actually spend answering these types of questions?

Buyer: They probably spend 15 percent of their day answering FAQs.

Salesperson: Well, how much time do you think should be devoted to that?

Buyer: Frankly, none. They are salespeople, not customer support. This really takes away from the time that they should be selling into new accounts.

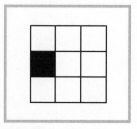

Box R2

Salesperson: How many new accounts did each sales rep acquire last year?

Buyer: On average, each sales rep was probably assigned ten new accounts.

Salesperson: And what was the average revenue per new account?

Buyer: I would guess conservatively that it was about $75,000 each.

Salesperson: If the salespeople were freed from answering FAQs, could they bring in one new account with the saved time?

Buyer: They probably should bring in more accounts, but one account sounds good.

Salesperson: Is it reasonable then that if all the reps—all fifty—could bring in one new account each and those accounts yielded at least $75,000, that you could bring in $3.75 million in revenue from new accounts?

Buyer: I never thought of the potential as that large, but I think that's a reasonable figure.

Once Bill had established the cost of doing business today without the first differentiating capability, he would then explore the second differentiating capability by asking the open question of R1. He would have then explored the cost of doing business today in R2 without the second differentiating capability. The dialogue is similar to the drill-down conversation that took place for the first differentiating capability. In the next dialogue, Bill confirms how the firm does business today.

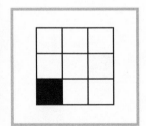

Box R3

Box R3: Confirm Questions, Diagnose Reasons (Cost of Business Today)

Salesperson: So, it sounds like from what we just discussed, the way you're doing business today is that (A) your salespeople spend too much time handling repeat business in existing accounts, (B) they're also spending too much time answering FAQs, and this is taking away from their task of prospecting into new accounts, and (C) they also fail to ask customers for referrals and leads. Looking quickly at the numbers, it appears that not having these additional capabilities could be costing you close to $4.75 million in revenue a year. Is that right?

Buyer: Yes, the figures I gave you are accurate.

Admission of Pain Between Boxes R3 and I1 When conducting Solution Selling Workshops, I (jokingly) call this moment in the Vision Re-engineering Model the "out-of-box experience." Here we're assuming the worst-case scenario, where the buyer has not admitted his or her pain to us. It may become obvious to the salesperson (via the exploration of how the firm does business today) that the pain is driving the opportunity, but it's important that the buyer be the one to admit it. Here we would ask a leading question:

Salesperson: What is the effect on you and your business of doing it this way?
Buyer: Well, quite frankly it's having a real bearing on my ability to hit our new account revenue targets.
Salesperson: What is your target? And how short of it do you think you will be?
Buyer: Our goal is $5 million. At this rate we won't even come close.

Note: Bill would explore the impact column in the same method as he did for Vision Creation. Feel free to skip the dialogue and proceed to Box C3.

Box I1, Open Question, Explore Impact

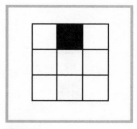

Box I1

Salesperson: Besides yourself, who else in your organization is impacted because the new account revenue targets are being missed? And how are they impacted?

Buyer: Well, I know our salespeople are frustrated because they're challenged with hitting their quotas. It tends to bring morale down.

Box I2: Control Question, Explore Impact

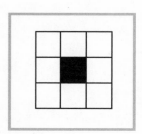

Box I2

Salesperson: If the new account revenue targets are being missed, is that causing your overall revenue goals to be missed?

Buyer: It really is having a huge impact.

Salesperson: Have you seen profits affected because of this?

Buyer: Our profits have been stagnant, but at this rate the overall profit targets of the company will be missed.

Salesperson: Do you know what the profit margins are here at TGI?

Buyer: Approximately 20 percent.

Salesperson: Which person in your organization is going to be most impacted by missed profit targets?

Buyer: That would be Jim Smith, our VP Finance.

Salesperson: Have the declining profits had any major effect on the value of your stock?

Buyer: Well, as you can imagine, we're all shareholders here. The earnings per share have slipped, but I'd say that the declining profits have affected us more in our ability to grow our business.

Salesperson: Who is looking to grow the business here at TGI?

Buyer: We all are, but this is really the initiative of our CEO, Susan Brown.

Box I3: Confirm Question, Explore Impact

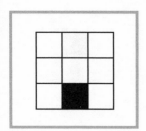

Box I3

Salesperson: So, from what I just heard, it sounds like your salespeople are frustrated with the effort it requires to hit their quotas, the VP Finance is challenged with hitting his profit targets, and your CEO is finding it difficult to grow TGI's business. It sounds like this is not just your problem in sales but a companywide problem. Is that correct?

Buyer: Bill, I can't disagree. You seem to have a real handle on our issues here at TGI.

Having established the cost of doing business today, positioned differentiating capabilities, and explored Steve's pain and the impact on others at TGI, Bill can now confirm his understanding of the total situation at TGI.

Box C3: Confirm Question, Visualize Capabilities

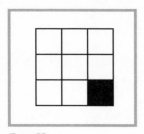

Box C3

This summary here attempts to establish a new reengineered buying vision. Notice how it's structured: "When you called, you said you needed [A = original vision]. But you also said you needed [B and C = additional capabilities]. If you had all these capabilities, could you [address your goal]?" Also, note how the salesperson ties back in the value established.

Salesperson: Steve, I just want to confirm our conversation here. So, when you called, you were looking at e-commerce to give (A) your customers who want to place orders the ability to view inventory levels, place an order on their own, and have it allocated and confirmed over the Internet. You also said you needed a way to (B) allow customers to answer their own questions by clicking on a FAQ Web menu or a Help option that would connect them to the appropriate person in the company. (C) You also wanted your customers to be prompted to submit referrals in exchange for discounts or promotional items when visiting your Web site. If you had all three of these capabilities, could you regain what appears to be a total of $7 million in new account revenue [including value of Capability A]—actually surpassing the shortfall that you shared with me earlier of $5 million?

Buyer: Bill, I really do believe that we could.

There you have it. You've taken a competing vision and learned all you can about it, and then you reengineered it with your most competitive differentiators.

However, before leaving the subject of vision re-engineering, there is one more important topic: Requests for Proposal (RFP) and Request for Information (RFI).

THE RFP (REQUEST FOR PROPOSAL)

RFPs, RFIs, tenders—all these purchasing vehicles are different from culture to culture, industry to industry, and company to company, but the general philosophy and approach for handling them is the same.

The question is—what should you do in active opportunities that come to you as an RFP? The simple answer—don't waste your time on them unless you wrote them. If you did not define or contribute to all or part of an RFP's buying requirements, your chances of winning are much less than 10 percent—most customers tell me less than 2 percent. It also costs a great deal of time and money to answer them, and it takes you away from activities that are more productive.

Salespeople often respond to RFPs wired for their competition because they have nothing better to do. The sad reality is that the RFP is their best prospect.

Chapter Nine addresses the rules for competing in active opportunities—an RFP is definitely an active opportunity, so those rules apply. If you understand those rules and you decide to use them, then your responsibilities are clear. If for some reason they're not clear, go back and read Chapter Nine, paying particular attention to the Five Rules for Deciding Whether to Compete or Not and the Opportunity Assessment Worksheet (Figure 9.1, page 140).

Rule One says don't fool yourself into thinking you've got just as good a chance of winning as anybody else. You don't. You have to assume the RFP was written for and by someone else. I have salespeople argue with me over this issue all the time. They don't want to be told not to waste their time. They ask, "How can you say it was written by somebody else?" They also ask, "What if the RFP was written by a third party?"

My response is that most organizations don't have the time or the expertise to put together RFPs totally on their own. Even if the RFP was developed internally, it was probably influenced by outside consultants or a vendor. So stop kidding yourself. Almost every RFP is biased in some shape, form, or fashion. If you will just accept that fact, you will be able to adopt the proper competitive strategy and deploy the right tactical approach that will improve your chances of winning.

Deploying the Right RFP strategy

What competitive strategy should you use? The End-Around strategy should be the default strategy with RFPs that you didn't develop. Tactically, you want to re-engineer the vision in the RFP and bias the requirements in favor of your differentiated capabilities.

When attempting to re-engineer an RFP, I recommend using the following eight specific tactical steps.

Tactical Step 1 Call the sender and offer to respond to the RFP in exchange for three one-hour interviews (that's your *quid pro quo*). Whether you're looking for three interviews or two, the point is that you need a chance to meet with the key players impacted by the scope of the project or you will have no chance at influencing the requirements of the RFP in your favor. If granted, go to Tactic 4.

Tactical Step 2 If your request for a meeting is denied, send a letter to the sender stating that it will be impossible to respond to the RFP without the three one-hour interviews. Include with the letter marketing and sales collateral equal in volume to the RFP. Figure 10.2 is an example of the kind of letter you might send.

Note that the people in the job titles I asked to meet with were determined from reading and analyzing the scope of the RFP. The reason for the marketing-related materials is an attempt to send the message, "My company has a lot to offer, and it's difficult to respond without knowing more about the situation than I do now." This letter can be adapted slightly in the event a third party is involved, such as a consultant. The same message and tactical approach still apply.

Tactical Step 3 When the prospect calls again, offer to respond to the RFP in exchange for three one-hour interviews. If they seriously want you to respond or if they simply need you to fill a column, they will find a way for you to talk to the right people. Maintain the *quid pro quo* of only responding to the RFP once the interviews are granted.

Tactical Step 4 When an interview is granted to you, ask each line executive, What are the two primary issues behind the project? You're trying to determine each one's pains so you can re-engineer their buying visions.

Dear Mr. Doe:

Thank you for the opportunity to propose to your organization. We appreciate your confidence in us. As I mentioned on
the phone, our practice is not to respond to Requests for
Proposals until we have personally interviewed the department heads impacted by the scope of the project. We have
found that this practice enables us to do more complete work
on behalf of our potential clients, resulting in a more satisfac-
tory implementation of the project. The client is the major
beneficiary of this practice.

If you would arrange for us to meet with the VP Opera-
tions, VP Finance, and the CIO for one hour each, we will then
invest the time and resources to respond to the RFP to your
satisfaction.

In the meantime, I have enclosed some detailed information on our products and services. If you have any further
questions, don't hesitate to call.

Sincerely,

Bill Hart

Figure 10.2 RFP Initial Response Letter—Example

Tactical Step 5 Prepare your response to the RFP as agreed.

Tactical Step 6 Send a cover letter with the proposal to the person controlling the RFP. Specifically point to the executive summary and how it
documents the buying vision of each line executive with whom you spoke.

Tactical Step 7 Highlight the key capabilities you can provide in the
executive summary. The executive summary attempts to highlight the
differentiating capabilities that you established during the interviews

and vision-processing sessions. It specifically points out how important the differentiating capabilities that you discovered are in helping the firm solve its business problems. You can make your case stronger and give it a compelling reason to do business with you if you can quantify the negative impact of not having these unique capabilities.

Tactical Step 8 Copy the cover letter and the RFP and send them to the line executive with whom you had the best rapport.

THE RFI (REQUEST FOR INFORMATION)

An RFI is distinct from an RFP in one important way: the buyer probably doesn't have a fully formed buying vision. Therefore, respondents have a chance to form part, if not all, of the buying vision. This situation provides a much easier opportunity for the salesperson to influence the buying criteria and requirements than at the RFP stage. The RFI is generally used as a precursor to the RFP step in an organization's procurement process. RFIs are commonly used in government and highly regulated sectors.

Companies and organizations use RFIs for several reasons, including finding out if capabilities exist to help solve a problem, establishing buying criteria and budgets, and looking for a team of vendors or suppliers who can work together. I recommend you deploy the eight tactics previously discussed at the RFI stage in regulated and government sectors.

The goal in responding to RFIs and RFPs is to obtain the interviews so that you can create or alter the buying requirements. The buying requirements must include your unique capabilities—your differentiators—to give you a reasonable chance of winning.

If the RFP is part of a highly regulated industry or company, always request a Bidder's Conference if one is not already scheduled. Also, in highly regulated situations you may find that you can use this tactic at the Request for Information (RFI) stage of the process if access is denied once RFPs are published.

The Bidder's Conference

The Bidder's Conference represents an opportunity, and maybe the only opportunity you have, to affect the requirements. Whether it's regulated or nonregulated, public or private sector, you really have no other choice—that is, if you want to compete.

Participate as though you were in a regular face-to-face sales call or meeting, except that you want to be the salesperson asking all the questions. In other words, make yourself equal and learn everything you can about the company's pains, reasons, impacts, current vision, and so on.

Next, make yourself different. Try to alter the buying requirements. You must re-engineer the RFP in front of the other competitors who are also attending the Bidder's Conference.

Don't worry about what your competitors may be thinking or doing. What difference does it make what they think? After all, in this situation, if you can't deploy the End-Around competitive strategy and tactically re-engineer the requirements of the RFP, you've learned you have almost no chance of winning.

PART FOUR

Qualify, Control, Close

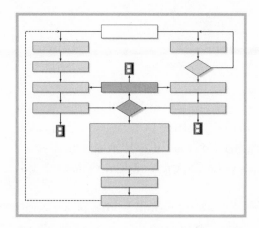

CHAPTER ELEVEN

Gaining Access to People with Power

A few years ago, while I was teaching a Solution Selling workshop in Stanford, Connecticut, a young lady, Christine Matson, came up to me at the end of the third day and said, "I wish I had been given the Solution Selling process in my previous company. I know I would still be there if I had. Would you mind if I passed your name along to my former boss? I still stay in touch with him." "Of course not," I said.

That was on a Thursday. The following Monday, I received a phone call from—guess who? Her former boss, a sales manager, who asked, "What exactly do you do and what is Solution Selling all about?" This was an open invitation for me, a salesperson, to reach in my pocket, pull out my product or service, and begin to sell.

If you take nothing else away from this book, remember this: Don't lead with your product. Learn to keep your products and services in your pocket until you have fully diagnosed the situation. Remember the Solution Selling principle: *diagnose before you prescribe*. The products or services you represent may give buyers more reasons not to buy than to buy.

Back to the sales manager on the phone—I said, "I'll be glad to tell you about Solution Selling. However, before I do, would you take just a minute and tell me what Christine told you that sparked your interest? I'd also like to hear about your situation and any sales-related problems you may be having."

I let him know that with this information I would be in a better position to describe specifically how Solution Selling capabilities apply to his business. He agreed, and with just a little prompting, he told me all about his business and his challenges. This allowed me to begin diagnosing his situation before I introduced Solution Selling's capabilities. In fact, as I continued to ask questions about his situation, he started to form his own opinion about Solution Selling and me.

After a few minutes of conversation, mostly me asking questions, he asked, "When can you come to Dallas and show me your Solution Selling process?" My temptation at this point was to ask, "When would you like me to come?" and volunteer to show up whenever he wanted me to, but I didn't.

The good news was that he was interested and wanted me to fly to Dallas for a demonstration of our capabilities. This provided me with the opportunity to ask for something from him that I wanted—the perfect *quid pro quo* scenario. You are never in a better position to ask for something than when a prospective customer wants something from you. So, what did he want? A demonstration or proof of Solution Selling's capabilities. What did I want? If you're thinking money, you're wrong. I wanted access to power. I then suggested a bargain, a *quid pro quo*.

"I'll be glad to come to Dallas in exchange for the following: you arrange to have both your division president and the VP Sales in the meeting, and you agree to pay for my expenses to come to Dallas." You can imagine his reaction. He had a problem with—you guessed it— paying for my expenses.

"You've got to be kidding me!" he said. "I can't believe you want me to pay for your expenses; we don't do that in Texas." At least those are the words I'm willing to use here in this book.

To put him at ease, I quickly explained my reason for making the request to have the executives in the meeting and for my expenses to be covered. I said, "If you cover my expenses, then we're both committed. You will have invested your time and money, and I will have invested my time and shared my expertise, for which I usually get paid."

I also knew that if he didn't make a financial commitment, or have "skin in the game," as we sometimes say, there was a good possibility that I would show up, but his executives would not. With his financial commitment, I was much more confident of getting access to the right people and having the executives involved.

As we were ending the conversation, he sheepishly asked, "Is this the kind of stuff you teach in your class?" With a slight chuckle, I proudly said, "As a matter of fact, it is." It took him some time, but he agreed to set up the meeting with the executives and to pay for my expenses. In the meantime, I sent a letter confirming our conversation. The letter documented his sales challenges, the reasons for the challenges, and the ideas we had discussed on ways to improve the situation. The letter spoke directly to his and his company's business issues.

In Dallas, I was greeted by the sales manager. As we were exchanging pleasantries, the president of the division walked into the meeting room, looked directly at me with an expressionless face, slid a sheet of paper across the boardroom table, and asked, "Are you the person who put this letter together?" By this time, the letter had traveled across the conference room table and was resting squarely in front of me.

I looked at it, knowing I had written it, and thinking to myself, "Yes, that is indeed my letter. I sure hope you liked it," but not knowing what she thought of it. I answered her, "I certainly did write that letter."

At that point her demeanor warmed. She smiled and said, "It's apparent to me that you really understand our business."

My outward reaction was calm, but on the inside, I was yelling "yes, yes, yes!" Why? Because I knew I had just differentiated myself from everyone else, and people want to do business with someone who really understands their business.

That was the start of a very long relationship with the largest out-sourcing company in the world—EDS.

GAINING ACCESS TO POWER

Whether you initiate an opportunity from latent pain, as we discussed in Part Two, "Creating New Opportunities," or find an active opportunity, as discussed in Part Three, "Engaging in Active Opportunities," eventually you must qualify the opportunity by gaining access to power. In Solution Selling, we define power as someone who has the absolute authority to buy or the influence to get what he or she wants, regardless.

If you discover that the person whom you initially contacted doesn't have the authority or the influence to make the decision, then you need to get that person (a Sponsor) to provide you with access to the person or persons who do (a Power Sponsor). In some cases, he or she offers to take you there, but in many cases, you need to negotiate for this access to power. In such a negotiation, the most powerful leverage you have is the vision of a solution that you either created or re-engineered.

The best way to gain access to power is to find a prospect in pain, diagnose the pain, and create or re-engineer a vision of a solution. People get very excited when they see or hear for the first time how to solve a difficult situation that they've had for a long time. Naturally, this excited individual wants to see and be offered proof that this solution exists. This desire for proof becomes a strong bargaining chip for access to power. The salesperson that begins by demonstrating his or her products and services loses this bargaining chip.

POWER PRINCIPLE: YOU CAN'T SELL TO SOMEONE WHO CAN'T BUY

Many salespeople spend an enormous amount of time trying to sell to someone in the organization who can't make the buying decision.

This is often referred to as "selling too low." They also fall into the trap of trying to sell to a person with a title. They assume this person has absolute authority, and all they have to do is reach that person. Both these selling behaviors cause difficulties for the salesperson.

In the case of selling too low, salespeople tend to call on people they like and who are similar to themselves. It's human nature to want to spend time with smiling enthusiasts who tell you what you want to hear, rather than frowning skeptics or executive-level people with whom you don't have anything in common. We see this situation often with technical products and services and other complex selling situations. The technical people in the prospect's organization love to talk with salespeople and get a free education on all the latest products and technology. But salespeople eventually have to deal with someone who has the authority or influence to make a buying decision.

In the case of selling to a title or person they think has absolute authority, salespeople fall into a different trap—the trap of sketching out an organization chart and thinking they only need to sell to the person at or near the top. The problem with this situation is the organizational chart only maps out the formal organization of a company. Although this is helpful to know, it won't tell you which person has the most influence—the real power to get something he or she wants.

How does someone gain influence, the key ingredient of power? There are many contributing factors, such as age, experience, tenure, and politics. In some organizations, it is who you know and what your last name is. However, I have found that those who have made significant contributions to an organization tend to be very influential.

In Chapter Six, I used a structured sales call model called the Strategic Alignment Framework (Figure 6.1, page 88) to demonstrate the steps of a first meeting or sales call. I used this framework and a prompter to demonstrate how a salesperson can remain strategically aligned with his or her buyers through the first four steps of an initial call. Once again, I want to use that same framework and prompter to leverage the vision that has been created and negotiate access to power.

HOW TO MOVE THE BUYER TO COMMITMENT

You have diagnosed the prospect's pain and created a vision of a solution that is biased toward your product or service. Now you must move the buyer to commitment. In this case, we're only asking for a commitment to explore further, not a commitment to buy anything. We will go from an agreed-upon customer buying vision (Step 4) to determining the customer's ability to buy (Step 6) by first gauging how willing the customer is to move forward (Step 5). There are two approaches or options to this transition in Step 5.

Step 5: Gain Agreement to Move Forward

Option 1. I'm reasonably sure we can provide you with those capabilities. I want to check some things with my resources within the company. If they confirm what we just discussed, will you further evaluate my company and our capabilities? [Get buyer's agreement.]

Option 2. I'm confident we can provide you those capabilities, and I would like the opportunity to prove it to you. Would you give me that opportunity? [Get buyer's agreement.]

If during the process the buyer volunteers access to power, schedule the meeting and end the call. If the buyer does not volunteer access to power, go to Step 6.

Option 1 is the conservative option. You give yourself an out. When you say that you're reasonably sure, you give yourself the ability to go back and check. If your company's resources confirm what was discussed, then you're asking the buyer to seriously evaluate what you have to offer. Some salespeople like this option because it sounds more consultative, like they don't have all the answers. Others think it sounds weak to a buyer when they aren't more confident. I personally like Option 1 because you arrive at the same place as Option 2 without sounding too sure of yourself. For example, what if you discovered something in your conversation with the prospective buyer that you are unsure of and you really do need to check things out? If that occurs, you don't want to say, "I'm confident we can provide you with those capabilities."

Option 2 is more aggressive, but you still have to offer proof. Don't forget, your job title is still salesperson, and it is still early in this relationship. It likely will take time for you to establish trust with your prospect. Option 2 may be more appropriate when time is limited—such as in re-engineering scenarios—or if you are talking to a Power Sponsor and you feel this may be your only chance to meet with him or her.

In this example, you have the buyer's agreement to explore further. What's next? What should you do now? Before you proceed, you must determine if this person has power. At this point in this example, you're not trying to determine the organization's need for the product or whether there is a budget. You must determine if this person has the influence or the authority to say yes. In other words, does he or she have the power to buy? Don't make the mistake illustrated in Figure 11.1.

AT POWER? IF NOT, BARGAIN FOR ACCESS

This is a crucial question at this point in the sales call. Although there are many beneficiaries of your product in the prospect's organization, there are probably few who can approve or make the actual purchase happen. How can you politely determine this person's ability to buy? The question can be made less threatening by asking about the buying process, as shown in Step 6.

Figure 11.1 Getting to the Right Person

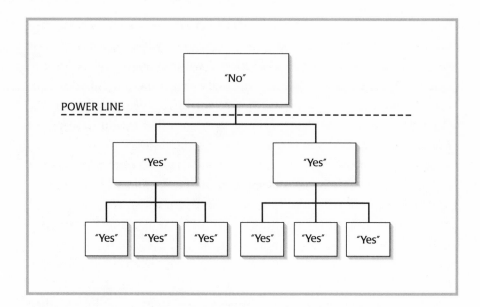

Step 6: Determine Ability to Buy

Salesperson: Let's say that you become convinced that it really is possible to [repeat buying vision] and you want to go forward. What do you do then? Who else would need to be involved?

The answers to these questions should reveal whether you have a Power Sponsor who has the ability to buy, or a Sponsor who will provide access to power, or neither. Before we go on, let's take a moment to clearly distinguish between a Sponsor and a Power Sponsor:

Power Sponsor. Power Sponsors have enough influence (regardless of their job title) or authority to make the purchase, even if it is not budgeted. They can and will take you anywhere in the organization you need to go. They can and will negotiate the steps leading to a buying decision.

Sponsor. Sponsors can promote your proposed solution inside the their organization, but they do not have the power to make a buying decision. Sponsors are important. They "sell internally" by promoting your product or service to everyone. They provide you with internal information that you need and set up meetings, but most important, they provide access to power.

If your Sponsor does not provide you with access to power, then he or she is not a good Sponsor and you need to find one who will. The real job and role of a Sponsor is to provide you with access to power. No exceptions! For now, let's assume that your Sponsor has revealed the name(s) of the power person(s), and proceed to Step 7a.

Step 7a: Bargain with Proof for Access to Power

Salesperson: Could we get on his calendar?

Buyer: That may be premature at this point.

Salesperson: I would like to make a bargain with you. I'm not yet sure of the best way for us to prove these capabilities to you. I first want to consult with my company. Whichever method we end up using to prove these capabilities, it will take some of my company's resources. I'm willing to make that commitment today. If through that effort we succeed in proving to you that you will be able to [repeat buying vision], at that point, will you then introduce me to [power person]? Is that fair? [Get buyer's agreement and end call.]

Salesperson: Thank you for your time. I'm going to consult with my company. I will then write you a letter [email] confirming my understanding of your situation. In that letter [email], I will propose a specific way for us to prove these capabilities to you. You should receive the letter [email] shortly.

There is an extremely powerful phrase in the wording of the bargain. The salesperson hasn't used it up to this point in the sales call to preserve its power. The salesperson saved it to negotiate for access to power because access to power is so important. The phrase is "Is that fair?" Notice that the actual question being asked is not "Will you introduce me to the power person?" You are actually asking the Sponsor if it is fair, and it is.

Quid Pro Quo

The Latin expression *quid pro quo* should be an integral part of every salesperson's life. It means that you will not give without getting something in return. Literally translated, it means "this for that." I'm going to give you something, and I expect something in return.

This is one of the most important business concepts that all businesspeople and especially salespeople need to learn. It is a key concept in any business relationship or negotiation. Some people have said that this is the single most important concept in Solution Selling.

Too often, salespeople cater to a prospect rather than being good stewards of themselves and their company's resources. They fall into the trap of doing anything and everything the prospect wants: the prospect says, "Jump," and the salesperson says, "How high?"

Prospective buyers want, demand, and need many things from salespeople, and salespeople should be attentive and responsive. But if you're willing to give, they must be willing to give. You make a commitment to prove your capabilities, and in return, you want access to the person with the power. I ask you, Isn't it fair that prospects provide you with access to power-level people within their organization if you have used your resources to prove to them you can help them solve a business problem?

The Sponsor Letter

I'm convinced that salespeople have to differentiate themselves by the way they sell. If they don't, then they're not bringing much value to their company or to their customers. In many cases today, it's difficult to differentiate products and services, so salespeople must become a part of that differentiation. Let me say it in a different way—salespeople must add value to the mix. If not, they'll be eliminated. Salespeople can be the most important differentiator in winning opportunities. Think of all the other salespeople who have interfaced with a buyer before you have. Is that buyer grouping you in the same category of "just another salesperson"? Or are you standing out in the buyer's mind by your approach?

I often ask salespeople, "How would you feel if after a meeting with a salesperson he or she wrote you a letter that documented the business issues that you discussed, the reasons for them, and the capabilities needed to solve the problem?" Their response is always very positive. Then I ask, "Do you do that with your prospective customers?" In most cases, the answer is no. If they do correspond, the letter or email usually sounds something like this:

"Thank you for seeing or talking with me. I enjoyed the meeting. Enclosed is product literature. I will follow up."

This type of letter or email does very little to differentiate the salesperson from every other salesperson out there. It is critically important that salespeople have business issue conversations and then document those conversations. People want to do business with people they believe understand their business. A strategically planned letter can prove that you understand their business.

Solution Selling provides salespeople with a job aid called the Sponsor Letter that helps them document conversations with prospective customers. The framework of information included in a Sponsor Letter helps differentiate salespeople in the minds of their customers.

The Sponsor Letter is written after a salesperson has negotiated access to the power person. Take a look at the sample Sponsor Letter in Figure 11.2. Notice the six key elements in the body of the letter:

1. Pain
2. Reasons for the pain

3. Vision
4. Agreement to explore
5. Bargain for access to power
6. Next step or proof step

This is very similar to the letter I sent to the EDS sales manager I spoke about in the beginning of this chapter. You read the reaction from the division president when she said, "It's apparent to me that you really understand our business."

I ask managers to check these six elements in the Sponsor Letters their salespeople write. I find it's a very good way to reinforce the Solution Selling process, particularly during the critical first few weeks after a company adopts the process. This is the time when habits are formed. Trained managers are able to evaluate the effectiveness of their salespeople based on the strength of their follow-up Sponsor Letters. After all, if salespeople can't write good follow-up letters based on their conversations with prospective customers, what does that say about the quality of those conversations? Salespeople must be good businesspeople, able to define and diagnose business problems.

It is also important for salespeople to document the agreement to explore and to gain access to power. This will help to smoke out prospects who are not serious about evaluating your products or services and will save you a lot of time that would be better spent on serious prospects.

How well does the Sponsor Letter work? One reason we write a Sponsor Letter is because our buyer didn't volunteer to take us to power. We have to bargain. The Sponsor Letter restates the vision that is the foundation of the bargain. This letter works so well that about 50 percent of the time, the Sponsor shows up at the proof session and at least one power person is also there.

Dear Steve:

Thank you for your interest in our company. The purpose of this letter is to summarize my understanding of our meeting and our action plan.

We discussed the following:

❶ Your primary critical issue is missing new account revenue targets by $10 million.

❷ Reasons you are missing your new account revenue targets:
- salespeople spend too much time handling repeat business in existing accounts instead of developing new customers
- salespeople are spending too much time answering frequently asked questions from customers
- prospects are unaware of promotions
- your salespeople are not asking existing customers to refer potential new business

❸ Capabilities you said you needed:
- whenever wanting to order, your customers could view available stock, place their order, have it allocated and confirmed using the Internet
- when customers have questions, they could click on an FAQ menu on your Web site and select a Help button to be connected to the appropriate person in your company
- when offering new promotions, your salespeople could create personalized messages and broadcast them to all their customers via email
- customers to be prompted to submit referrals for new business when they place an order on your Web site.

You said if you had these capabilities, your salespeople would have the time to develop new customers, allowing you to achieve your new account revenue targets, increasing revenue annually by $11 million.

Our next steps:

❹ You agreed to move forward with our company and

❺ said if we succeed in proving we can give you these capabilities, you will introduce me to Jim Smith, your VP Finance. You mentioned Jim is not happy with the revenue shortfall and its impact on profits.

❻ I would like to propose that we arrange a meeting with another sales executive who has implemented an e-commerce application with our help. I'm confident you will like what you see and will introduce our company to the rest of your organization. I'll call you Monday to discuss it further.

Sincerely,

Bill Hart

Figure 11.2 Sponsor Letter–Example

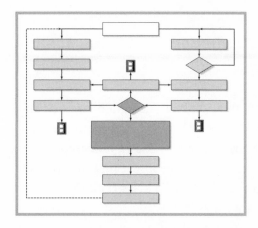

CHAPTER TWELVE

Controlling the Buying Process

There I was—the proverbial elephant hunter trying to drag home a live, adult elephant. A large organization in the financial services industry had agreed to explore doing business with us. I was excited and eager, but I knew there was a big risk—I could lose control of the elephant.

The path had been cleared; I had found a great Sponsor. Meetings with the Power Sponsor had gone extremely well. On the basis of his agreement to explore doing business with us, I suggested that I go back to my office, document our discussion, and propose a way for him to evaluate our capabilities. He had agreed, and asked if I could be ready the next day with something for him to look over. I said yes, and we agreed to meet for lunch and review the Evaluation Plan.

After lunch the next day, I gave him my letter with its attached Evaluation Plan. He began to review the letter and plan. Looking at his body language, I wasn't sure what he was thinking; he seemed a little puzzled. He then reached into his inside jacket pocket, pulled out a pen, and began to edit the plan. At that point, I smiled to myself. Why? Because he was doing exactly what I wanted him to do—take ownership of the Evaluation Plan.

After he finished editing the Evaluation Plan, he handed it back and said, "I think this sequence of events will work better for us." He had requested some schedule changes, nothing too significant.

At that moment, something came over me and I just had to ask, "Would you agree that we're in the middle of a sales cycle?"

"Yes," he responded, "I guess we are."

"Who would you say is in control of the sales cycle at this point in time?" I said.

"I am, of course," he said without hesitation. "I just took control when I changed your suggested sequence of events. The changes made it my own."

"That's exactly what I hoped you would say," I responded.

He paused for a moment and then picked up the proposed Evaluation Plan from the table and tore it into pieces. He looked over at me and said, "I don't think I'll need this."

I became very anxious and nervous. I thought my curiosity about my process had gotten me into trouble. Why couldn't I have left well enough alone? Why did I have to ask that question?

A smile returned to his face. "If you can teach our salespeople to do what you just did," he said, "which is to control the buying process and have the buyer believe he's in control of buying, that alone is worth doing business together. We don't need to evaluate any further. How soon can we get started?"

YOU WIN WHEN YOU CONTROL THE BUYING PROCESS

This control principle specifies that the salesperson controls the buying process—not the buyer. Keeping control of the buying process and letting the buyer buy without pressure appear to be mutually exclusive, but they are not. Solution Selling is about keeping control while letting your buyers direct themselves. The role of the salesperson in Solution Selling is to be a buying facilitator.

I often ask salespeople who are engaged in active opportunities what elements of control they have been able to put in place during the buyer's evaluation process. If the answer is none, I know they have a low probability of winning, so I work with them on strategies and techniques to put controls in place. If this can't be done, I encourage them to disengage. Remember the concept of column fodder? It's alive and well. Stop wasting time on opportunities that won't allow you to exert any control: those are opportunities you're unlikely to win.

The job aids I introduce in this chapter help salespeople work professionally and collaboratively with their buyers to solve their critical business issues and reach a mutual decision to do business together. Exerting control may be as simple as establishing the time frame to make a decision or as specific as defining the exact evaluation criteria on which their decision will be based.

One way to control the buying process is through project management techniques. *Project management* is not a term used very often in selling. However, when you use good project management techniques, you put standard processes in place to deal with all contingencies, which enables you to achieve predictable results. This is important in most sales campaigns because there are so many variables.

Think about it. How often does a development project, or sale for that matter, come in on time and within budget without a plan? We all know that the answer is not very often, if at all. Incorporating project management techniques into the sales process helps transform selling activities from a series of random events into a logical sequence that concludes with a successful sale.

Project Management

The aim of project management is to organize the activities to achieve a goal within a specified time frame. In Solution Selling, the fundamental documents we use are the Power Sponsor Letter and the Evaluation Plan. If a salesperson can get a buyer to agree to an Evaluation Plan, including the sequence of events and a time line for each event, he or she will win these opportunities most of the time. This is not control of the buyer or the final decision, but control of the buying process.

Why would buyers allow a salesperson to exert any level of control over their buying process? The answer is that most buyers don't buy (or go through the evaluation process) very often, so therefore they want and need help when they do buy. When salespeople demonstrate good situational knowledge by defining the buyer's pains, diagnosing the reasons for the pains, and creating or re-engineering a vision of a solution, the buyer usually welcomes the salesperson's proposed plan of action.

POWER SPONSOR LETTER

The Power Sponsor Letter used in Solution Selling is a classic example of how to incorporate project management techniques into selling. It helps Journeypeople look and act like Eagles.

Power Sponsor Letters help buyers buy and salespeople close business deals. Such letters help management predict the amount of business in the pipeline and when that business will close, and they help qualify opportunities and optimize resources by giving managers a view into the future. Without a doubt, this tool is the number one job aid used by the more than 500,000 salespeople who have been trained in Solution Selling globally.

Power Sponsor Letters have two components: (1) a letter written to the Power Sponsor and (2) a suggested Evaluation Plan with a sequence of events for the prospective customer to follow.

The Letter

The letter itself outlines the salesperson's understanding of the situation: the pain, reasons for the pain, vision of a solution, organizational impact, agreement to explore doing business with the salesperson's company, and an Evaluation Plan.

As you can see, the Power Sponsor Letter incorporates many of the same elements that are in a Sponsor Letter. The major differences are the request to commit resources to the evaluation process and the Evaluation Plan attached to the letter. I believe a good Power Sponsor Letter contains the following major elements (the numbered paragraphs correspond to the circled numbers in Figure 12.1):

1. *Pains*. The principle *no pain, no change* also applies to Power Sponsors. It's important to document and get verification of the critical business issue your Power Sponsor faces. Reconfirming your understanding of the pains in the letter also helps to establish personal credibility.

2. *Reasons for the Pain*. You discovered and confirmed the reasons for your Power Sponsor's pain in both the Diagnose Reasons and Explore Impact columns using Solution Selling's 9 Block Vision Processing Model. Reconfirm the reasons in the letter as well.

3. *Buying Vision*. This is Box C3 in the 9 Block Model and is critical to include in your letter. It should be clear and powerful and contain the capabilities that you helped the Power Sponsor see that he or she needs.

4. *Organizational Impact*. This is where you confirm what the Power Sponsor has told you about the impact of the pain throughout the organization. Much of this came from the conversation that took place during Boxes I1 and I2 of the 9 Block Model. This helps to build the business case and the compelling reason to take action.

Dear Jim [VP Finance]:

Thank you for meeting with Steve Jones and me earlier today. I believe the time was well spent for both TGI and our company. We discussed the following:

❶ Your primary critical issue is declining profits due to the revenue shortfall. You said you were about $8 million below plan.

❷ Reasons for declining profits:
- Missing new account revenue targets
- Rising operational costs
- Increasing credit write-offs

❸ Capabilities you said you needed:
- When visiting your Web site, your customers could place and confirm orders via the Internet, get questions answered through a FAQ menu, be notified of promotions, and be prompted to submit referrals, or customers would be able to click on an FAQ Web menu to get their answers and only require a CSR for extraordinary situations.
- Before accepting an order, your Web site could alert your customer to outstanding credit issues needing to be resolved and give them the ability to speak to someone in your accounting department.

❹ You said if you had these capabilities, Steve could meet his revenue targets, Donna Moore could reduce operating expenses, your controller could reduce the average age of receivables, and you would be able to increase your profits by at least $4.5 million.

Our next steps:

❺ When I told you I was confident our company could help you integrate an e-commerce application with your existing internal accounting and inventory system, you agreed to commit the resources needed to evaluate our ability to do so.

❻ Based on my knowledge to date, I'm attaching a suggested Evaluation Plan for your further exploration of our company. Look it over with Steve, and I'll call you on February 11 to get your thoughts.

Sincerely,

Bill Hart

cc: Steve Jones

Figure 12.1 Power Sponsor Letter—Example

5. Agreement to Explore. This reminds your Power Sponsor of his or her agreement to take the next step and explore ways of solving the pain. It's important to remind him or her of this in the letter because it's more difficult for people to change their minds after things have been committed to writing.

An Attached Draft Evaluation Plan

The draft Evaluation Plan (Figure 12.2) is attached to the Power Sponsor Letter. This plan details the evaluation process. It lists critical events necessary to get to the close, each event's scheduled time line for completion, and go/no go decision points. Ultimately, the plan helps a salesperson exert control over the buyer's evaluation process. A good plan should contain all the critical Milestones that will help you get to a win and the buyer to obtain your offering.

The Event column breaks down what to do into a sequence of interdependent steps. The Week Of column gives suggested dates for each event. If dates are missed, the salesperson should negotiate new time lines and send out an amended plan. The Responsibility column designates who is responsible for a given event.

The Go/No Go column is a powerful qualifier because it requires that a decision be made about whether or not to proceed further in the evaluation. Read the footnote in the figure that says going forward or not is a mutual decision. This empowers both the buyer and the salesperson to make a mutual decision to proceed or not to proceed at each step along the way. This key element assures the buyer that he or she is in control of buying.

The Billable column is optional and may not be applicable in all cases. However, this can imply to the buyer that your activities or services are valuable. Any billable item may be negotiable, but it's hard to negotiate it if it isn't first in the plan.

Event	Week of	✔	Responsibility	Go/ No Go	Billable
Phone interview John Watkins (CIO)	Feb 7		Us/TGI		
Phone interview Donna Moore (COO)	Feb 14		Us/TGI		
Summarize findings to top management team and agree to evaluation plan	Feb 21		Us/TGI	*	
Prove capabilities to top management team	Feb 28		Us	*	
Perform detailed survey of current TGI systems	Mar 4		Us	*	Yes
Present preliminary solution/design	Mar 11		Us		
Implementation plan approval by IT department	Mar 18		TGI	*	
Determine value analysis	Mar 18		Us/TGI	*	
Agree on preliminary success criteria	Mar 18		Us/TGI		
Send our license agreement to legal	Mar 18		Us		
Gain legal approval (terms and conditions)	Apr 4		TGI	*	
Visit corporate headquarters	Apr 11		Us		
Preproposal review meeting	Apr 18		Us		
Present proposal for approval	Apr 25		Us	*	
Transition kickoff and finalize success criteria	May 10		Us/TGI		
Measure success criteria	Ongoing		TGI		

*Mutual decision to proceed

Figure 12.2 Draft Evaluation Plan—Example

Why Use an Evaluation Plan?

Simply put, the Evaluation Plan is the best closing tool I've ever used. It helps keep sales campaigns on track and provides a high level of predictability. It helps the buyer stay in control of the buying process and helps the salesperson stay in control of the selling process. Evaluation plans provide continuous feedback about where buyers are within their buying cycles and where salespeople are within their sales process. It's not likely that a buyer would go through the time and effort to engage in an Evaluation Plan with someone with whom he doesn't see himself doing business.

Why Make a Draft Evaluation Plan?

Initially, an Evaluation Plan is just a draft plan or a proposed sequence of events. It's not the final Evaluation Plan—not until the buyer accepts it. So what's the best thing you could wish for after you submit the plan and call to get the prospective customer's feedback? You want them to suggest or make changes to the plan. Remember, if they change it, they own it. Just as in my story at the beginning of the chapter, buyers usually want to review it, change it, and make it fit their organization before they feel comfortable executing it. You want buyers to own the plan. It's not your plan, it's theirs. Buyers are more likely to execute their own plan than yours.

The Number of Events in an Evaluation Plan Varies

The number and sequence of events in an Evaluation Plan vary according to the scope of the opportunity. There are many variables, including the players involved, the industry being sold to, and the complexity of products and services being sold. In less complex sales, where you can close the sale quickly with one call, you construct the plan verbally and then work through each element with the prospective customer. In more complex sales, the list of events should be more extensive.

Never propose more steps than you think are necessary. You don't want the buying process to be too complicated and cumbersome. On the other hand, a good and thorough evaluation is important for everyone involved.

Possible evaluation events in longer sales cycles or complex selling situations can open a number of opportunities to you. It's also important to specify certain criteria so that you minimize surprises between yourself and your buyer (or buying committee). Evaluation events can provide opportunities for you to

- Gather all necessary information and details about the situation
- Interview all key players and beneficiaries
- Summarize and confirm findings to top management
- Specify when the costs and the associated value will be revealed
- Present a preliminary solution
- Specify when and how proof will be revealed
- Develop a value justification/value analysis
- Develop an implementation/transition plan
- Specify legal/technical/administrative steps to follow
- Specify a preproposal review
- Determine Success Criteria
- Specify ongoing measurement of Success Criteria

Remember, each sales situation is unique. Don't fall into the trap of thinking, "This is the way we always do it" or "This is the series of steps we always follow." But because many of the opportunities you'll engage in are similar, use Evaluation Plans and sequences of events that have been successful in the past. Each event in your proposed plan should have a specific purpose. For example, summarizing your initial findings to top management can help you build momentum and qualify the opportunity further. The plan also serves the customers by making sure they are fully committed and not wasting their time and resources.

ADVANCE YOUR EVALUATION PLAN WITH VALUE JUSTIFICATION

By definition, justification is a reason, fact, circumstance, or explanation that justifies or defends the action being taken. Justification answers the question, Does the end justify the means? Unless you're dealing with a single individual who has the power, money, and authority to buy without answering to anyone else, justification must be done. Too often salespeople leave this important step up to the prospect or customer to do. They don't have a model to work from, or they're afraid to get involved because they don't know how. I recommend that salespeople initiate the activity and participate with the customer in the value justification activities. If you don't know how, you must learn.

A COMPELLING REASON TO ACT

Value justification gives customers a compelling reason to take action. People will spend money if they can see that doing so will enable them to make more money or save money they're currently spending.

Salespeople have been participating in ROI (return on investment) analysis and cost justifications for years. Many times I've observed salespeople frustrated because, though their proposal was completely justified with a fantastic ROI and a short time frame for payback, the customer still didn't take action. Why? One reason is that the return and the payback are in the mind of the salesperson and not the buyer. The only way prospective buyers can get the same vision and understand the real value of the solution is if they understand and own both the problem and the solution. As long as salespeople are telling buyers, "We can solve your problems," they're not enabling prospective buyers to take ownership.

Historically, salespeople and customers have used terms such as *cost justification* and *ROI analysis* instead of *value justification* or *value analysis*. I stress the term *value justification* because I want salespeople to focus their customers and prospects on value. It's very important for salespeople to know that the higher the price, the more important it is to sell value. Remember, in Solution Selling we define value as Total Benefits minus Total Cost or Total Investment.

Why Participate in Value Justifications?

There are several reasons for participating in value justifications. They include sale cycle initiation, closing a sale, discounting, proof, and avoiding no decisions.

Initiate Sale Cycles Once you know the value you bring to situations, you can leverage this to help initiate new opportunities and create curiosity in your prospect or customer more easily and quickly.

Close Sales Value justification creates compelling reasons to take action. With a compelling value justification, buyers often ask to get started early. In other words, the cost or impact of delay is so overwhelming that they can't afford to wait any longer.

Minimize Discounting When the buyer and the salesperson know the real (measured and quantified) value, this onerous pressure can be greatly reduced. The buyer is less likely to ask for (or at least expect) a discount, and the salesperson is less likely to feel he or she has to give one.

Provide Proof Visionaries see how the implementation of your offerings will give them an advantage in the marketplace. However, these visionaries only make up 20 percent of buyers in the market. The other 80 percent are more pragmatic and conservative. They need proof and the demonstration of high value to mitigate the risk that buyers naturally feel at the close of sell cycles. Value justification and value analysis are very important to this segment of the market.

Avoid No Decision For one reason or another, some opportunities never conclude. The customer makes a no decision (we call this No Decision, Inc., or NDI). One of the main reasons buyers end up making a no decision is that they see no compelling reason to act; they don't see enough value in the solution.

I contend that we actually do lose these opportunities because buyers do make a decision—they choose an alternative project. They don't go with you or your competition, but they choose instead to invest that budgeted money with someone else. We all need to stop kidding ourselves about this situation; we lost.

Think of your buyers as people who hold the money like bankers. They don't sit on the money; they invest it to get a return. You may well be competing against an accounting system, a new fleet of trucks, furniture, and so on, not just your usual competitors. Expect your buyers to go with the projects that provide the greatest value and the greatest return.

THE VALUE JUSTIFICATION MODEL

I recommend that every company provide its salespeople with a model to assist them with value justification. Keep in mind that every prospective customer will have his or her own way of analyzing value and the return on investments. Nonetheless, you're always better off being prepared and presenting a projected ROI based on what you've learned. Unless you're asked otherwise, keep it simple, and if the customer wants to take the analysis further, you'll gladly assist him or her. (See Appendix A for a sample value justification.)

VALUE JUSTIFICATION ELEMENTS

The key to a successful value justification is making sure the customer owns it. After all, it doesn't matter what you think; it's what the customer thinks. I encourage salespeople to answer the five following questions with their value justification models:

1. What elements of the customer's business will be impacted and measured?
2. Who is responsible for the changes in the impacted areas?
3. How much impact and value is possible, and over what period of time?
4. What capabilities will be needed?
5. When will the investment pay for itself?

Element 1: What Will Be Measured?

Many elements and measurements are superfluous. You can clutter your buyer's vision if you choose measurements that detract from the real issue. Find out the few elements that if changed will make a significant difference. When two or three elements or reasons for the problem align with your products and services, make those the key points in the value justification. Examples include the following:

Profits Remember, this is the reason most organizations exist. If you don't include profits as one of your elements in the value justification, you're making a mistake.

Revenues This element is very powerful because businesses (and even nonprofit organizations) depend on it to survive. Cash flow is critical, and revenues are needed to sustain good cash flow. Organizations depend on revenues to pay staff, suppliers, and shareholders, so revenues tend to have immediate, direct consequences. Revenue measurement can focus great buying attention on your capabilities.

Cost Whether absolute or relative, I'm talking about cost reduction or cost containment. This is a very big area of opportunity because every part of every organization is a cost center. The two types of cost reduction you should focus on are displaced cost and avoided cost.

Displaced Cost If your products and services can displace or get rid of an existing cost, you want your buyer telling you how and by how much.

Avoided Cost If your products and services can help a customer avoid future spending, again, you want your buyer telling you how and by how much.

Intangible Benefits These benefits, such as employee morale, customer satisfaction, image, reduced stress, goodwill, and quality of life, are hard to put a dollar value on. However, if the customer is willing to assign a value to them based on the capabilities of your solution, I suggest you include them in your value justification model.

Element 2: Who Is Responsible?

It is critically important that the customers own the value justification. This comes into play when the customer is ready to make a decision. If the person ultimately responsible for making the decision asks about the value justification and the response is, "I don't know where those numbers came from" or "I don't know if we can achieve those results or not," the decision to move forward with your proposed solution will likely not happen. On the other hand, if the person being asked responds, "Yes, those are my numbers, and yes, we can achieve the results because of the capabilities being proposed," the decision to move forward with you will happen.

Element 3: How Much Total Value Is Possible?

How much can profits improve? How much can revenues increase? How much can cost be reduced, either displaced or avoided? The value justification must answer all these questions, and the answer needs to cover a period of time—one year, two years, and so on.

Element 4: What Capabilities Will Be Needed?

The value justification must state what capabilities will help change the business. If this question can't be answered with assurance, why would a prospective customer take the risk? For example, if a company was experiencing rising costs in the customer service department and this was negatively impacting profitability, you would want to link specific capabilities you offer to reducing or avoiding additional cost in the customer service department. For example, it might sound something like this: "What if you could allow your customers to access their own accounts online and see frequently asked questions from other callers, thus eliminating your need to hire three new customer service representatives and the additional $250,000 in expenses you're scheduled to take on this year? Would this help? Would this be of value to you?"

Element 5: When Will This Investment Pay for Itself?

Value justification must answer this question. Buyers want to know when the breakeven point is. They want to know when the numbers start to turn from red to black. The answer is when the cumulative total benefits, including the increase in revenues and the reduction in cost, exceed the cumulative investments made to acquire and implement the products and services, including services suggested in any Implementation Plan. (See Appendix A: Part 2 for an example.)

ADVANCE THE EVALUATION PLAN: PREPROPOSAL REVIEW

Go back and take a look at the Evaluation Plan in Figure 12.2. Toward the bottom of the plan, note the event, Preproposal review meeting.

One way to ensure that your final proposal wins the business is to have the customer review the proposal before it is due and take ownership of the document. You want all the work that's been completed to date to be the customer's work. It needs to be the customer's proposal, not yours.

Before the preproposal review is conducted, the salesperson should make sure all legal, technical, and administrative approvals have been cleared and all value has been established. If you don't have these items completed, then you give the committee an excuse to delay accepting the proposal.

During the preproposal review meeting, review and reconfirm all go decisions. These were the mutual decision points in the Evaluation Plan to proceed. Be sure to review organizational interdependence from the perspective of each key player by recapping the Pain Chain. Review the value justification elements and all the other work that has been done, making sure that nothing has changed.

Overall, this approach should satisfy the buying committee members that you have accomplished some powerful things: (1) you've gone through a mutual process with their organization, (2) you understand their business, (3) you've brought operational capabilities to help them resolve their critical issues, (4) you're prepared to help them (via your products and services) get from where they are today to where they want to be, and (5) you've established the value and a payback (using their numbers) that is compelling. Finally, you can make sure that nothing has changed on the customer's behalf.

When ending the preproposal review, and if everything appears in order, suggest an early close. You might do this by saying, "I know you weren't planning on approving the proposal until next week, but it seems like everything is in order. Does it make sense that we approve this today so you can start realizing the benefits of the capabilities sooner?" If the review has been compelling, the buying committee itself may even approve an early closing. Depending on the committee's reaction, you may need to schedule another preproposal review due to competition or items that need to be completed.

Sometimes, no matter how much they might like your proposal, the buying committee members feel they should wait and get final proposals from the other vendors. In that case, you should ask to come back after all the other vendors have presented. This allows you to address any new issues that may arise from competing vendor presentations.

Here's a story I like about Ross Perot. In 1957, after an honorable discharge from the U.S. Navy, Perot became a salesperson for IBM's data processing division in Dallas, Texas. While with IBM, Perot is said to have developed the "yellow pad" proposal (the forerunner to the preproposal review). Legend has it that Perot provided each member of the buying committee with detailed notes (on yellow legal pads) concerning all the activities and events of the buying process up to that point. His goal was to review the content in a draft format and get his customers' input before presenting them with a final proposal.

If he felt everything was in order, he would suggest an early close, even leaving the room to allow the committee to talk in private. Upon his return, if the committee was not ready to move forward, he would pick up his yellow pads and explain that he must have missed something if they weren't ready to move forward. He would leave, saying that he would "fix it" and return.

As the story goes, Ross never left a draft proposal behind. One of his claims to fame is that he never delivered a final proposal to a customer that he didn't win.

ADVANCE THE EVALUATION PLAN: SUCCESS CRITERIA

One item on the suggested Evaluation Plan that deserves special attention is Measure Success Criteria. The objective of putting together a list of Success Criteria is to determine if and when a project is successful. The approach is straightforward: It establishes a baseline and measures how business is done before your solution is implemented, monitors the postsale results, calculates the delta (the improvement), and then reports the findings.

Success Criteria identifies specific elements that the buyer and salesperson agree will be impacted and that should be measured once the capabilities have been implemented. It could be one or two items or it could be a long list, but it's essential that they be measurable. The actual criteria are mostly derived from information uncovered during the vision processing conversations and the elements defined in the value justification.

Establishing Success Criteria helps salespeople in multiple ways. Initially, it helps to establish credibility and trust—key ingredients in any relationship. It's important for the salesperson to let the customer know that he or she isn't going away, that the salesperson is interested in the customer's overall success, not just in making the initial sale. Success Criteria allow the salesperson to put a stake in the ground to measure against postsell. It's often hard to go back and get baseline metrics after the sale is closed.

I recommend that you measure performance quarterly, though this may vary depending on your customers' business. Look at the example of a Success Criteria chart in Appendix A.

YOUR SUCCESS DEPENDS ON YOUR CUSTOMER'S SUCCESS

There are important benefits to establishing Success Criteria during the evaluation process and then measuring to determine the amount of success later on. When your customers achieve a measurable change in their business, it's a success for them and it's also a success for you. Their success becomes a Reference Story that you can leverage.

Reference Stories tell of other customers who reduced costs or increased profits by a specific amount because they used your capabilities. The best way to obtain these compelling results is to determine the elements to measure during the evaluation process and, postsale, follow up and measure them on an ongoing basis. Today's success becomes tomorrow's Reference Story.

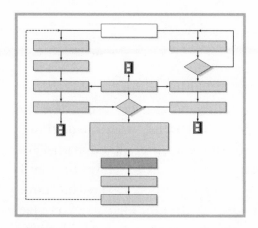

CHAPTER THIRTEEN

Closing: Reaching Final Agreement

I was asked to speak at a company's national sales meeting held near Tampa, Florida. I was warned that the president was very strong willed and that I should solicit his input for my speech. I called the company in advance to discuss my participation so that I could better support the theme of the meeting and the president's message.

Because of the president's schedule, we had a difficult time meeting before the event, but he agreed to pick me up at the airport on the day of the event so we could have thirty to forty-five minutes to talk during the drive from the airport to the meeting.

After we exchanged pleasantries, I asked him, "What message is important for me to deliver to your salespeople?"

He turned and looked at me, taking his eyes completely off the road, scaring me half to death. He said, "Keith, the one thing they really need help with is closing. They need to learn how to ask for the order and close more sales. I want your message to be close early, close often, and do not take 'no' for an answer."

He concluded his minitirade by hitting his clenched fist against the steering wheel, emphasizing the point, and asked, "Can you do this?"

What should I say to this man? I thought. After all, I don't believe in the approach he was describing, and that was certainly not what I planned on speaking about. I pondered the question, Do I tell him now, or do I wait? After all, it was very close to the time I had to go onstage and speak. However, being true to myself and true to what I believe in, I looked at him and said, "That's not my philosophy on closing and that's not what I had planned on speaking about."

"What do you mean, that's not your philosophy on closing?" he said.

I confidently said, "I don't believe in nor do I teach people to close the way you're describing."

"Let me get this straight. You're a sales consultant and a sales trainer and you don't teach people how to close?"

Before I could respond, he said, "Why did we fly you down here, agree to pay you a lot of money, and ask you to be our keynote speaker if you're not going to talk about closing?"

I could tell he was more than a little agitated. I figured I had better start to explain the logic behind my statement before he pulled the car over to the side of the road. I said to him, "I do have every intention of talking to your people about how to successfully close opportunities; however, my focus won't be on this big event at the end of a sell cycle that everyone refers to as 'the close.'" He began to calm down. Looking at me with a puzzled grin, he said, "Please continue."

So I did. I said, "I believe that closing should be the natural evolution of the sales process. If everything is done well throughout the sales process, then the close becomes almost a nonevent. When salespeople have problems closing, it's usually because of something they did or didn't do earlier in the sales process."

He didn't say anything, but his nodding head provided me the approval I was looking for. Knowing that I had his attention, I continued, "Don't get me wrong—I've been in plenty of negotiations near the end of a sale where closing the deal was a challenge. I think of those situations as hurdles associated with reaching a final agreement. No matter what your sales process looks like or the steps you've taken prior to the end of the sale, having to deal with obstacles and hurdles near the end are inevitable. I do plan on sharing thoughts around those types of circumstances with your people today." A relieved look appeared on his face.

I further explained to him that sales research has verified that there is a direct correlation between the effectiveness of closing techniques and the size of the price of the item being purchased. In other words, the pressure associated with closing techniques works better when the price of the item is low and the impact of the decision on the buyer is not so great. On the other hand, closing techniques appear to be less effective and in fact harmful with expensive and major-impact purchases.

My comments on the research got his attention, because his company developed and sold higher-priced strategic application systems. I then asked, "How do you feel when you know that someone is using a closing technique on you?" He sheepishly said, "I don't like it."

The keynote address was a hit. The president hired us to help him implement Solution Selling.

CLOSING MISCONCEPTIONS

There is not a sales book on the market that doesn't have something to say about closing. There is more written about closing than any other topic related to selling. Yet, with all that has been written and all that has been said about closing, it still comes up as the number one problem facing salespeople.

When I ask sales managers, "What's the number one skill deficiency of your salespeople?" the most common answer is closing. When I follow up and ask, "What do you mean they have a problem closing?"

The typical response is, "You know, asking for the order, getting the business, doing the deal, making their numbers."

Most organizations equate salespeople's results with the skill of closing. The theory goes, if salespeople aren't making their numbers; they must have a problem with closing. I've spent the majority of my professional life working with individuals and companies to improve their sales performance, and I can say without any hesitation that closing, the so-called skill of asking for the order, is not the big problem. Often my clients discover that the real problem with closing is not adequately defining or diagnosing the prospect's problems in the first place.

CLOSING IS THE NATURAL EVOLUTION OF THE SALES PROCESS

The Solution Selling philosophy on closing is that closing is the natural evolution of the sales process. The best close is to not have to close *per se*. In other words, when buyers can see themselves solving their problems with the capabilities of your products and services and they realize the negative financial impact of delay, closing comes naturally. If salespeople are having a hard time closing business, it probably means that either they're not following a proper selling process or they've skipped a critical step in the process.

The closing doesn't start at the end, when you're asking for the order; it starts at the beginning and continues throughout the sales process. The best way to pinpoint the source of selling difficulties is to implement a clearly defined sales process—a sales process with identified Milestones that salespeople and managers can measure, evaluate, and refine. Emphasis and measurement points within the process include defining the problem, diagnosing the problem, creating the vision of the solution, gaining access to power, exerting control within the buying process, and quantifying value.

Though our goal is to create situations where the buyer wants to buy, this doesn't mean that you should wait for your sale to close by itself. Using the natural evolution of the process inherent in Solution Selling's Evaluation Plan means that you provide your buyer with a written plan to follow, and part of that plan includes getting written commitments.

One of my best closing stories comes from an IBM software sales specialist who never wanted to be in sales in the first place. This person was hired to be a systems engineer, and he moved into a sales role due to a business downturn in the early 1990s. I'm sure there are a lot of people reading this book who can relate to not wanting to be in sales.

By following the Solution Selling sales process, this IBM sales specialist was able to secure an agreement with one of his customers worth more than $50 million. In addition, the solution IBM provided the customer helped it gain additional market share valued at more than $2 billion.

So how did he do this? He used an Evaluation Plan similar to the one described in Chapter Twelve. Each step of the plan helped the customer discover the value of the proposed solution. At the end of the evaluation process, the close was simple because the customer wanted to get started. The close was the natural evolution of the process.

CLOSE WITH VALUE

Back in Chapter Four, I introduced the concept of a Value Proposition. Previously, Value Propositions were used as a job aid to help stimulate interest. If you recall, I called it an initial, or preliminary, Value Proposition. By the time of closing, the initial Value Proposition has evolved. It has been researched, possibly refined, validated, and confirmed during the evaluation process. It can now be used to help close the sale, because the numbers in it have been verified—they are the buyer's numbers. A closing Value Proposition might look like this:

> ABC Motors will be able to reduce inventory carrying costs by
> 20 percent (an annual savings of over $108 million) through the
> ability to identify car buyer preferences. This will be made possible
> by employing [your company's name] Internet-based business intelli-
> gence solution. The investment of $2.5 million will provide a ROI
> of 125 percent in the first year.

Notice the first words, "ABC Motors will be." In the preliminary
Value Proposition, the first words are "We believe ABC Motors." In the
confirmed, final Value Proposition, ownership of the preliminary Value
Proposition has been transferred from the salesperson to the buyer. The
initial Value Proposition has been researched and validated with the
prospective buyer, and it now belongs to it. After all, it's not important what the salesperson or his company believes is possible. Ultimately,
what is important is what the prospective buyer believes.

The closing Value Proposition can only be crafted after the buyer has
shared detailed information during the sales process. For example, ABC
Motors's current state of marketing and inventory analysis has been
diagnosed. Things like inventory days carried and its costs are known.
The projected savings from using the new business intelligence has been
researched and confirmed. Since the investment cost is known—$2.5
million—a first-year ROI has even been calculated to be 125 percent.
This provides the buyer and her company a compelling reason to act
and provides the salesperson with a natural way to close the business.

CLOSING CHALLENGES:
BUYING AND PROCUREMENT TACTICS

Over the years, I've learned many different buying and procurement
tactics. Professional buyers and purchasing agents are being taught how
to buy, just as professional salespeople are being taught how to sell and

increase their productivity. I want to make you aware of some of the more popular ideas out there and provide you with some strategies and techniques to deal with them. After all, no matter how much someone wants to do business with you, it doesn't mean the buyer is not going to negotiate and make sure he or she gets the best deal possible. A key ingredient in closing is the salesperson's ability to negotiate and withstand the buyer's pressure for a lower price and better terms and conditions at the end of the sales cycle.

Smart Buyers

Smart buyers are people who have been trained in procurement procedures and in negotiating. Here are some of the most popular tactics that smart buyers and negotiators are trained to use. Smart buyers

- Never sole source
- Know their positions in advance
- Assign sponsors to each alternative
- Never let you know you're winning
- Never let you know you're losing
- Negotiate price in reverse preference order
- Take it away from you at least once
- Are aware of your deadlines

Never Sole Source. This straightforward concept simply means that buyers are taught to never have a single source. They're told that they will not get the best deal if there's only one supplier. The goal is to keep as many competitors in the game as long as they can, because the more competitors they have at the end, the better the deal for the buyer. Smart buyers, particularly if an evaluation is complex, will put at least three suppliers through their paces.

Know Their Positions in Advance Smart buyers keep themselves and each member on the buying committee informed. They determine ahead of time what they want to accomplish in any final negotiation. Salespeople tend to have a high opinion of themselves and their negotiation skills, when in fact their skills are often not very good and many times untested. Professional buyers and in particular procurement specialists are trained in negotiations, and they buy things for a living every day. This means they're more experienced in negotiations than the average salesperson. It's vitally important to never underestimate the negotiation prowess of smart buyers.

Assign Sponsors to Each Alternative Smart buyers assign a Sponsor to each competitor in the evaluation, keep the assigned Sponsor actively engaged in the evaluation process, and make sure the Sponsor is there at the end of the process. In this way, each competitor is more likely to draw false conclusions, such as he or she is the favored vendor, he or she is the one occupying Column A, the buyer is using the salesperson's list of buying criteria to solve whatever the problem may be, and his or her assigned sponsor is the Power Sponsor.

Never Let You Know You're Winning Why would a buyer not let a salesperson know he or she is winning? The answer is so the salesperson will feel pressure to discount and give better terms and conditions. Simple fact: when you're losing, you tend to try harder. As I previously mentioned, buyers are taught to avoid sole sourcing whenever possible. They need multiple competitors so they can arrange optimal contracts and agreements for themselves.

Never Let You Know You're Losing Why would a buyer not let a salesperson know he or she is losing? Because the buyer doesn't want the salesperson to walk. Remember, buyers need competitors in the game as long as possible to ensure the best deal at the end. Most smart salespeople would leave if they knew they were losing. After all, why waste selling resources on hopeless opportunities?

Negotiate Price in Reverse Preference Order This tactic is particularly enlightening for many salespeople. It can also be discouraging if it has ever happened to you and you weren't aware that it was happening until it was too late.

Buyers are taught first to negotiate with the supplier in last place. They get their best and final offer and use it (assuming it's a lower price or better terms and conditions) to negotiate with the more favored suppliers.

Buyers are taught to then work up to their favored supplier. They use the lower price and the improved terms and conditions obtained from the column fodder suppliers to negotiate with Column A, the most favored supplier. Using this tactic, the buyer is armed with concessions he or she can use to wrestle the Column A supplier down in price.

This tactic alone is an important enough reason to know the value of what you offer the customer so you can withstand this pressure. Using Power Sponsor Letters and knowing what column you're in are also important. Don't waste a lot of time and money chasing rainbows with no pot of gold at the end.

Take It Away from You at Least Once The buyer tells the favored supplier he or she has made the decision to do business with someone else. The buyer may say, "I know you've done good work for us, and I'm embarrassed to admit this, but we've had budget cuts across the board, and I no longer can spend the amount we agreed on. We're going to do business with someone else, even though we really don't want to." The buyer uses this tactic to make sure he or she is getting the best deal with the preferred supplier.

This tactic is particularly painful and difficult to endure. If the salesperson isn't aware of what's going on, it can cause him or her to panic and make unnecessary concessions. Salespeople have to learn to anticipate this tactic. Of course, it's a lot easier to deal with if you know the competitive landscape, you've been able to exert control of the buying process, and you've done a good job identifying and proving the value in your offering.

Are Aware of Your Deadlines Smart buyers are well aware of salespeople's critical deadlines. Month-end, quarter-end, and year-end quotas make them salivate because they know how important those dates are for salespeople. They know if they hold out on one of these critical measurement points, they're likely to get a better deal.

Although this is difficult to overcome, if you're above quota, you'll have the power to walk away. Another simple tactic is not to tell your buyers how badly you need deals to make your quota or special incentive deadlines. Don't give them negotiating leverage; make them obtain that information on their own.

NEGOTIATING

At negotiation time, in the mind of the buyer, the salesperson is like a washcloth. What do most people do with a washcloth full of water? They wring it out until the water stops dripping. Just to make sure, most people give it that one extra squeeze and then shake it out just to be sure.

In any negotiation, buyers squeeze salespeople until they believe they're getting the best possible deal. This includes both price and terms and conditions. The sooner the salesperson is willing to draw the line and walk away, the sooner the squeezing stops.

Even though you'll be negotiating with buyers, I strongly recommend that you remove the word *negotiate* from your vocabulary. Buyers frequently ask salespeople if an item being discussed is included in the price. If a salesperson responded, "That's negotiable," it implies that other buyers have avoided paying extra for it. Again, it's important that buyers believe they're getting the best deal possible. If they think something is negotiable and they don't get it in the deal, it's very upsetting to them.

SOLUTION SELLING NEGOTIATING PRINCIPLES

If You're Not Ready to Walk, You're Not Ready to Sell This means that you have to be able to withstand the pressure and walk away from business you want when your buyer is demanding too much. You may think that's easier said than done, particularly when you're below quota. The best advice I can give salespeople is to keep a full pipeline. Having enough other opportunities to work on is the best position a salesperson and his or her company can be in. A full pipeline gives salespeople the strongest position from which to negotiate—the ability to say no.

Don't Close Before It's Closeable Don't get caught pushing a string uphill. Unless your buyer (and your buyer's negotiator) has the power to buy, the payback (ROI) is agreed to, legal and technical and administrative approvals are in place, the Evaluation Plan is completed, and the costs are known, it is not closeable. Any one of those items can stop a deal from closing. If you can think of a reason why the opportunity is not closeable, you can bet the buyer can too. Reaching the final agreement is hard work for both sides. Buyers want to achieve their objectives, and salespeople want to do the same thing. Each side has an emotional hurdle to clear: the buyer must believe he or she is getting the best deal possible, and the salesperson must be willing to walk away. It's important for salespeople to know this and plan around both issues.

Plan Before You Begin Negotiations

Ask yourself at least three questions: (1) Is it closeable? This means checking that all technical, legal, and administrative requirements are known and in place. (2) What will you accept? It's useful to review what you will minimally accept. (3) What are you willing to give? Prepare a Give/Get List, one that analyzes your and the buyer's positions. The list outlines each party's interests and priorities. It aids the negotiation process, helps achieve successful outcomes, and helps you look professional. Figure 13.1 is our template for a Give/Get List to help you prepare for negotiating.

There are four things you want to plan for before you negotiate: (1) what you want to get, (2) what you're willing to give, (3) what you definitely will not give during the negotiation, and (4) the values behind your gets and gives. You should attempt to associate value with each get and give, as well as determine the ranking of importance for each give to the buyer and each get for you. I think it's important here to be flexible and try to understand the interests behind the issues to be negotiated. Naturally, each party will try to maximize its own self-interest.

For several years, I dealt with a software buyer who oversaw the implementation of new software applications. His tolerance for risk was very low because he had lived through several failed implementations with other suppliers. Minimizing risk was more important to this buyer than getting the lowest price. I knew that he had a good relationship with one of our implementation specialists, Roger Owens.

Because of the software buyer's concerns over implementation, I planned ahead before each negotiation with this buyer. I checked into Roger Owens's schedule to make sure that he would be available when the implementation was scheduled to occur. This is one of the gives that I was preparing to possibly use. I figured that it would be one of the buyer's interests. I also calculated how many hours of Roger Owens's time would be required, so that I would be prepared to share the value

Our priority	Get	Potential value ($) ◄──►		Give	Projected customer priority
1	Larger (volume deal)	$100K	$15K	Payment terms/special financing	2
2	To become a reference account	$?	$20K	Training discounts	1
3	Lower cost of sales via avoidance of demo/proof	$5K	$10K	Short-term rental licenses	4
4	Introduction to business partner with similar needs	$?K	$10K	Refund on proof of concept already conducted	3
5	Pay software cost for Phase II at the same time as Phase I	$2K	$1K	Reduce software cost	5
6					
7					
8					

No way	1. Maintenance discounts 2. Free consulting 3. _____

Figure 13.1 Give/Get List—Example

of his time with the buyer. I developed other gives too, but I ranked implementation risk as the highest priority.

Remember the principle *don't give without getting*. Don't give up something without getting something in return when making concessions. For instance, you might want an earlier close date or to combine multiple phases of the project, or you might want to add to the project and increase the amount of the sale.

Give Reluctantly and Slowly (If Necessary)

This is easier said than done. However, it's easier if you know the real value your solution brings to the customer. That knowledge is very powerful.

Be Prepared to Resist Buyer Squeezes Anticipate at least four squeezes by the negotiator. In turn, be prepared to make four stands. I suggest that your stands center around four of the five variables in the formula that helps win sales: pain, vision, value, and control (P × V × V × C).

Don't Give Without Getting I've already discussed this, but just as a reminder: get something of equivalent value for what you're being asked to give up and learn to say, "The only way I can do something for you is if you can do something for me first." Buyers almost automatically reply, "Like what?" The psychology has changed. Now the salesperson gets to put forth the gets before anything is conceded.

Be Willing to Walk Away In the same way buyers are trained to take away a potential sale from salespeople, salespeople too must learn sometimes to walk away. The better your Value Proposition, the easier it is for you to do this.

For salespeople who are below quota, this isn't so easy. In such cases, I suggest that sales managers go along and help out. Desperate salespeople can't negotiate from a position of strength.

Risk Assessment

Risk is a bigger factor in buying decisions and negotiations than most salespeople realize. I know a retired bank CEO whose bank grew past its computer systems capabilities. He was in the market for a main-frame-based system. The bank asked four suppliers to pitch their wares, one of which was IBM. After all was said and done, the bank's buying committee, chaired by the CEO, ranked the four suppliers and IBM ranked third.

However, the CEO started having nightmares, and it was always the same bad dream: he dreamed of banknotes (what else?), except that the banknotes had legs, and every time he reached for the banknotes, they ran away out of his reach. Then he would wake up. Eventually, he began to wonder what bad thing would happen to him if the winning supplier went bankrupt or important technical personnel changed jobs. To make a long story short, IBM won the contract—not with the best price or the best technology, but with risk management. For the CEO in my story, value was for him personal job risk management.

Find out what is the highest priority in your power buyer's mind. If you were to flip back to Figure 2.4 (page 24) you'd see Shifting Buyer Concerns. Keep in mind that in Phase III, price is not the most important concern, risk is. So what is the message? As salespeople, we should first recognize that risk is normal, and second, that mitigating it can be one of our strongest negotiating tactics versus focusing on price concessions. Sometimes dropping price can even scare a buyer and throw him or her into further risk.

The Negotiation Worksheet

In Solution Selling, we've developed a Negotiation Worksheet to help salespeople anticipate buyer demands and to help them withstand their buyers' demands for concessions. When I first saw this worksheet being developed, I asked, "Will experienced salespeople use this job aid? Why do they need it?"

The answer to the first question has been a resounding yes. And the answer to the second question is that the deals are too big and too important to wing it. As salespeople, we have good intentions to stand our ground, but in the heat of negotiations, we often lose our intention to battle for our positions. A prepared, written document is harder to dismiss when the going gets tough (see Figure 13.2).

For example, the dialogue during negotiation could sound something like the following:

Salesperson: Are you ready to sign the contract and get started with this implementation?

Buyer: I am, but I do think you need to come down on price. You don't expect us to pay full price for software and hardware.

Salesperson: [Using Stand 1: Plan Stand] I don't understand. Our published plan shows an implementation starting next Monday. Is this issue worth the delay?

Buyer: Look, I don't want to delay the project, but I don't pay full price to anyone.

Salesperson: [Using Stand 2: Value Stand] When we calculated the payback, you told me that even with all the costs included, the return was higher than you expected and the project would pay for itself in ten months.

Buyer: We're now looking at next year's budgets, and I need to save a little more this year to carry over.

Salesperson: [Using Stand 3: Pain Stand] We've spent the last four months together because you're not meeting your new account revenue targets. That issue will not go away until you gain these new capabilities. Don't you think solving that problem is well worth the investment?

Buyer: I need you to do something here so I can go back to my committee and tell them I got something out of this negotiation.

Taking stands, or drawing lines in the sand, are psychological messages to the buyer that you're not giving easily—at least not without

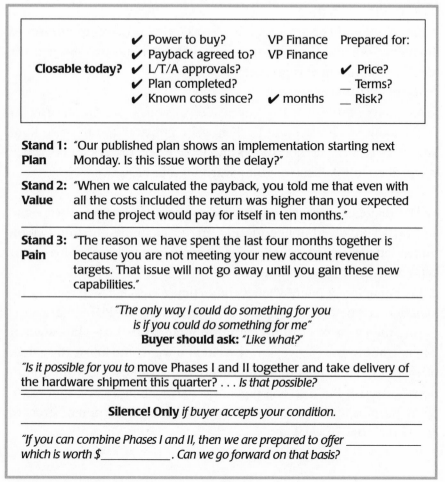

Closable today?
- ✔ Power to buy?   VP Finance   Prepared for:
- ✔ Payback agreed to?   VP Finance
- ✔ L/T/A approvals?   ✔ Price?
- ✔ Plan completed?   _ Terms?
- ✔ Known costs since?   ✔ months   _ Risk?

Stand 1:
Plan "Our published plan shows an implementation starting next Monday. Is this issue worth the delay?"

Stand 2:
Value "When we calculated the payback, you told me that even with all the costs included the return was higher than you expected and the project would pay for itself in ten months."

Stand 3:
Pain "The reason we have spent the last four months together is because you are not meeting your new account revenue targets. That issue will not go away until you gain these new capabilities."

"The only way I could do something for you
is if you could do something for me"
Buyer should ask: *"Like what?"*

"Is it possible for you to <u>move Phases I and II together and take delivery of the hardware shipment this quarter?</u> *. . . Is that possible?*

Silence! Only *if buyer accepts your condition.*

"If you can combine Phases I and II, then we are prepared to offer _____ *which is worth $_____ . Can we go forward on that basis?*

Figure 13.2 Negotiation Worksheet—Example

getting something of equivalent value in return. It's important to follow up your stands with a conditional offer.

Salesperson: [Realizing a conditional offer will need to be made] The only way I could do something for you is if you could do something for me.

Buyer: Like what?

Salesperson: [The salesperson's first Get] Is it possible for you to move Phases I and II of this project together and take delivery of the hardware shipment this quarter?

Buyer: Yes, that's possible.

Salesperson: [Only if the buyer accepts your conditional offer] If you'll combine Phases I and II, then we're prepared to offer two hundred extra implementation support hours of Roger Owens's time, which is worth $27,000. Can we go forward on that basis?

This dialogue is meant only to give you an introduction to strategies and tactics involved in negotiating. In our example, the salesperson traded services (which usually have lower markups in technology markets) for bottom-line advantages.

In closing (not a pun), when it comes time to reach a final agreement, I encourage you to: (1) Prepare and use Evaluation Plans that incorporate the event of closing. (2) Build a Give/Get List—know what you're empowered to give, know what you want, and know the values of each. (3) Think through your negotiating stands and your conditional offer. (4) Build strong pipelines—have enough sales opportunities in the pipeline to allow you to negotiate from a position of strength rather than one of weakness.

PART FIVE

Managing the Process

CHAPTER FOURTEEN

Getting Started with the Process

I received a phone call from one of my clients, a VP Sales. He was troubled by a phone call he'd received from a prospective customer. The prospective customer had called him and asked that a particular salesperson not be allowed to call on the firm again—he was too pushy and unprofessional. The VP wanted me to spend some one-on-one time with this sales rep. He asked me to assess the salesperson's skills and help him to determine if he had made a hiring error.

When I met the salesperson, it didn't take long to find out that he wasn't pleased with his boss's decision to send him to me for help. He felt that spending time with me was a waste of good selling time and that he would be better served making more sales calls. After just a few minutes with him, it was apparent that selling a solution was the last thing on his mind. His idea of selling was to push features on anyone who would listen and then "overcome" all objections before he closed. "No" was not in this guy's lexicon.

Nothing I had to say or suggest seemed to resonate with this man. Finally, after much discussion and my best attempt to create a vision for him, the salesperson agreed to give it a try. We started with the account that didn't want to see him. A letter of apology was written asking for a second chance. He enclosed a Reference Story in the Solution Selling format and suggested that if given a second chance to work with company employees, his entire focus would be on their critical business issues and coming up with capabilities that would bring measurable change to their business. He also enclosed a sample of the output he would provide them if they would give him the opportunity to come back and diagnose their situation.

Fortunately, this worked and he got a second chance. While there, he used the 9 Block Vision Processing Model to diagnose their situation, and the Power Sponsor Letter (including a proposed Evaluation Plan) as a follow-up. The prospective customer couldn't believe the change.

Less than six months from the date of my first meeting with the salesperson, the VP Sales called me and read a letter he had received from that same prospective customer who had asked for the salesperson not to return.

> We are a happy customer today. We have implemented your new automation system and it is exceeding our expectations. I wanted to tell you we would not be a customer if it had not been for your salesperson. Our initial impression was not favorable, but he quickly overcame our concerns and truly differentiated himself from the the rest. He is the only salesperson who focused on our business and what it would take to solve our problems. Everyone else was simply trying to sell us their products. Your salesperson is a real asset for your company.

Solution Selling has enabled both businesses and individuals to become more effective. However, the primary beneficiary of Solution Selling is the customer. When salespeople use the Solution Selling concepts of defining the pain, diagnosing the pain, and creating visions, customers have realistic expectations of the products and services they buy. They are more likely to succeed with the products and services they buy from Solution Selling salespeople.

Getting started with Solution Selling is not difficult. There are many job aids that you can apply in the short term that will have a significant impact. Whether it's learning or applying something new or transforming from selling products to selling solutions, change may be required. In this chapter, I focus on activities that will enable the transformation from a product sale to a solution sale and how to implement the Solution Selling process. I follow up with sales and executive management implementation activities in Chapters Fifteen and Sixteen.

GETTING STARTED ACTIVITIES

Getting Started activities for salespeople include the following:

- Build your pipeline by scheduling "sacred prospecting time" in your planner or diary.
- Build your situational knowledge by developing Pain Sheets for your top five selling situations.
- Determine the Milestone status of your existing opportunities by completing the Pipeline Milestone Worksheet.
- Convert your top three opportunities to C status (part of the Pipeline Milestone Worksheet).
- Make three vision processing sales calls followed by a debriefing from your manager or other designated person within one week of starting your implementation.
- Get all Power Sponsor sales calls debriefed by your manager or other designated person for at least thirty days after start of implementation.

- Take back outstanding proposals over thirty days old.
- Write Pain Sheets, Pain Chains, and Value Justification for all C status opportunities.
- Personally interview an existing customer (end users and beneficiaries) and develop a new Reference Story each month after starting your implementation.
- Use the Pipeline Analysis Worksheet to project revenue attainment.

To better assist salespeople to implement Solution Selling, I will break down each bulleted activity and provide examples and Solution Selling job aids where possible. Keep in mind that Solution Selling is a sales process that requires salespeople to define problems and create visions, as well as a sales methodology with sales techniques designed to increase overall sales productivity.

Schedule Sacred Prospecting Time on Your Planner

I first mentioned scheduling sacred prospecting time in Chapter Five, but it bears repeating: schedule 10 percent of your time, approximately four to six hours per week, to prospect for opportunities in the latent, or Not Looking area. Recommended job aids and tools for prospecting are covered in Chapter Five.

Prospecting into the latent, or Not Looking, area gives you the opportunity to develop your skills in Vision Creation. You will benefit if you take it seriously and make sacred prospecting time an integral part of your work. Sacred time means that nothing else is more important. Make sure that the appointment you've made with yourself can't be changed or manipulated. If you do this, you'll build bigger and better pipelines, making you even more successful.

Develop Pain Sheets for Your Top Five Selling Situations

Buyers want to do business with salespeople who are knowledgeable about their situations and about capabilities that will help them, so this recommendation is very high on my list. Start by developing at least five Pain Sheets and then add one per month until you've covered the majority of the selling situations you encounter. Think about how important it is for salespeople to understand the problems or pains of the people they call on, the reasons for the problems or pains, the impacts of those problems on others in the organizations, and, last but not least, the capabilities needed by the buyer to help solve the problem. Pain Sheets help develop your situational knowledge and your conversations with your buyers.

The Solution Selling Pipeline Milestone Chart

If I had to pick one Solution Selling job aid to talk about, I'd pick the Solution Selling Milestones. Milestones guide salespeople through the sales process. Each Milestone (Territory, Qualified Suspect, Qualified Sponsor, and so on) provides a series of steps or activities that need to be accomplished before proceeding to the next Milestone (see Figure 14.1). The Milestones help you identify, measure, and analyze where you are and what actions you should take with each opportunity in your pipeline. The Solution Selling Pipeline Milestone Chart has four major components, indicated by the four columns in the chart:

1. The letters T through W in the first column are Milestone grades that correspond with each Milestone description: T = Territory, S = Qualified Suspect, D = Qualified Sponsor, C = Qualified Power Sponsor, B = Decision Due, A = Pending Sale, W = Win.

Milestone	Yield	Milestone Description	
T		Territory	☐ Opportunity identified in territory
S	10%	Qualified suspect	☐ Meets marketing criteria ☐ Potential sponsor identified ☐ Initial contact established (verifiable)
D	25%	Qualified sponsor	☐ Pain admitted by sponsor ☐ Sponsor has a valued buying vision ☐ Sponsor agreed to explore ☐ Sponsor granted access to power ☐ Agreed to above in sponsor letter
C	50%	Qualified power sponsor	☐ Access to power sponsor ☐ Pain admitted by power sponsor ☐ Power sponsor has a valued buying vision ☐ Power sponsor agreed to explore ☐ Evaluation plan proposed ☐ Evaluation plan agreed upon
B	75%	Decision due	☐ Evaluation plan underway ☐ Preproposal review conducted ☐ Asked for the business ☐ Proposal issued, decision due* ☐ Verbal approval received
A	90%	Pending sale	☐ Contract negotiation in progress
W	100%	Win	☐ Signed documents
			☐ Update prospect database

*Premature delivery of a proposal is *not* a sign of progress

Figure 14.1 Solution Selling Pipeline Milestone Chart

2. Yield percentage indicates the amount of good business that is likely to come from the total revenues associated with this collection of opportunities.

3. Milestone descriptions identify general categories and qualifications and provide a common language for everyone to work from.

4. Milestone process or activity steps list selling activities that need to be accomplished. They provide a road map for salespeople: telling them where they are, where they are going, and how to get there. For instance, if you're at Milestone D, your Sponsor has admitted pain, you have a mutually shared vision with your Sponsor, the Sponsor has agreed to explore doing business with your firm, access to power has been agreed to, and confirmation of all this has taken place in writing in the form of a Sponsor Letter.

The Milestone Chart has one underlying rule: All process or activity step boxes in a particular Milestone must be completed before you can achieve that Milestone grade. Failure to do so means that the opportunity stays at the previous Milestone category.

Each step leads to completion of a major Milestone, which is the process. Milestones allow you to measure where you are in your sale. This is particularly important when you are selling large-ticket items and only close a few transactions a year. In that situation, you may not experience success often enough to sustain you. Using Pipeline Milestones helps you emotionally sustain yourself, and you can grade where you are in your sales cycles.

The Pipeline Milestone Worksheet

Now that you have an understanding of the Solution Selling Pipeline Milestones, it's time to grade a sample opportunity (see Figure 14.2).

You should immediately recognize the Milestones. Milestone action steps are listed vertically, and individual sales opportunities are entered across the top. Simply fill in the date you complete each step in the Solution Selling process. This may be trying at first because you haven't been using the process. That's all right; do the best you can. Part of the value is identifying what you don't know. The worksheet allows you to grade the status of the opportunity as well as see what you have or have

Opportunity	1	2	3	4	5	6	7	8	9	10	
											Latent or active
											Potential sale amount $K
T											Opportunity identified in territory
											Meets marketing criteria
											Potential sponsor identified
S											Initial contact established (verifiable)
											Pain admitted by sponsor
											Sponsor has a valued buying vision
											Sponsor agreed to explore
											Sponsor granted access to power
D											Agreed to above in sponsor letter
											Access to power sponsor
											Pain admitted by power sponsor
											Power sponsor has a valued buying vision
											Power sponsor agreed to explore
											Evaluation plan proposed
C											Evaluation plan agreed upon
											Evaluation plan underway
											Preproposal review conducted
											Asked for the business
											Proposal issued, decision due*
B											Verbal approval received
A											Contract negotiation in progress
W											Signed documents
											Update prospect database

*Premature delivery of a proposal is *not* a sign of progress

Figure 14.2 Pipeline Milestone Worksheet

not accomplished at each process step or activity. In many cases, it also helps you see execution patterns. Gaps in execution allow you to see what action steps need to be taken.

Convert Your Top Three Opportunities to a C Milestone Status

Once you've graded your existing opportunities using the Solution Selling Pipeline Milestone Worksheet, it's time to take your top three opportunities through the process. If those three opportunities are not yet at a C grade, I suggest you start by promoting them to C status. Here are three things you can do to start this activity:

1. Schedule refocus meetings with your buyers.
2. Create/clarify buying vision(s).
3. Send Power Sponsor Letters with Evaluation Plans (or Sponsor Letters, if more appropriate).

A refocus meeting clarifies all the issues and makes sure you're in sync or aligned with the buyers in the opportunity. You might encounter some resistance when you ask for this meeting. Be prepared to tell buyers that if they'll spend the time with you, you will document the discussion for them, and it should help everyone involved.

Keep in mind that your buyers probably need you—if only to fill out a column in their buying matrix. You should at least be able to discuss the status of your deal. If you can't get them to speak with you, then it's a definite negative signal. You might as well find out now before you waste any more of your valuable time and resources.

The goal depends on what level you're at in your sale and what steps you've completed. Remember, a C grade means you're at power and that the power person has admitted pain, is at vision, and has agreed to an evaluation plan. If that's the case, you're on sound ground.

Make Three Vision Processing Sales Calls

Do this within one week of starting your Solution Selling program. Your goal is to have at least three discussions with customers or prospective customers in which you try to define the buyers' pains and use the 9 Block Vision Processing Model to diagnose the situation and create a vision of a solution.

Use your manager or a third party to debrief your activities. Do this to reinforce the model and turn your new selling behavior into a habit. It's simple to do. You've just read the book or been to a workshop, so use it or lose it. Skills require repetition and practice to remain sharp.

Have All Power Sponsor Sales Calls Debriefed by a Manager

For at least the first thirty days after you begin your Solution Selling implementation, have your manager debrief your Power Sponsor calls and meetings. Because Power Sponsor meetings and discussions are so critical, getting a second opinion only makes sense. Having meaningful business discussions with a power person is one of the most challenging sales tasks for a lot of people. Debriefing with your manager or with some other mentor will help you build depth in your situational knowledge.

Again, it reinforces the Solution Selling process.

Take Back Proposals over Thirty Days Old

Taking back month-old proposals will free up selling time. In my experience, if you have outstanding proposals and prospective buyers who have not committed to do business with you within thirty days, you're probably not going to win the business. So stop wasting your time.

Salespeople often resist this recommendation. They say, "Oh, wait,

I just know they're going to buy something. Trust me." But taking back your proposal will test whether the prospect really is interested. The buyer may be stimulated to talk with you again. If so, then stay engaged. If not, cut the prospect loose. This frees you up mentally and physically to focus on other opportunities.

Write Pain Sheets, Pain Chains, and Value Justification for all C Milestone Opportunities

The purpose of this recommendation is to make sure you know and understand the issues. Remember, people generally need a compelling reason to act. Knowing the pain, the impact of the pain on others, and the value associated with resolving the pain can provide compelling reasons for you to sell your solutions to your prospects. By documenting these issues, you see for yourself how valuable the solution is. Once you're convinced, helping the prospective customer see it becomes much easier. It's much easier and much more effective to tell a story if you were personally involved or have firsthand knowledge.

Develop a New Reference Story Each Month

Meet with existing customers. Where there are success stories, collect and maintain them. The Reference Story format used in Solution Selling enables salespeople to leverage their customers' past successes to generate additional business. After all, who would not be interested in knowing how someone else, in a similar position, has solved a problem with which they're currently dealing?

You develop Reference Stories by talking with your Power Sponsors, Sponsors, beneficiaries, and users. Keep in touch with your customers and go after the valuable information.

Use the Pipeline Analysis Worksheet to Project Revenue Attainment

Determining if you are going to make your numbers is an important part of a salesperson's job. However, I find that salespeople too often estimate and make guesses. In Solution Selling we've developed a Pipeline Analysis Worksheet to help salespeople determine if they're going to make their numbers at an individual level. This same tool can be used by sales mangers at the unit or company level.

This analysis is based on the pipeline. Three key elements of the pipeline are used to determine revenue attainment: (1) year-to-date attainment or business you've already closed, (2) current business in the pipeline that you expect to close, and (3) any future business that is not yet in the pipeline and is likely to close in the current year or reporting period. Figure 14.3 illustrates the different pipeline components. Depending on where you are in your accounting period, you have different options available to you at different times.

The key to understanding the pipeline and the Pipeline Analysis Worksheet (Figure 14.4) is that the process is the pipeline and the pipeline is the process. As you analyze your pipelines, you move opportunities through the process; you are actually managing the sales funnel. Look at Adams's pipeline report (Figure 14.5) as of March 1.

As you can see from the pipeline report, Adams has a quota of $2 million for the year and collectively his current pipeline is valued at over $4 million. Is he going to make quota? Most people look at this example and say yes—after all, it's early in the year and he has more than two times his quota in his pipeline.

The Pipeline Analysis Worksheet helps determine this by translating our history, with the estimated "good business" in our current pipeline and an estimate of the future, or the likely business we will gain after the current pipeline for the year.

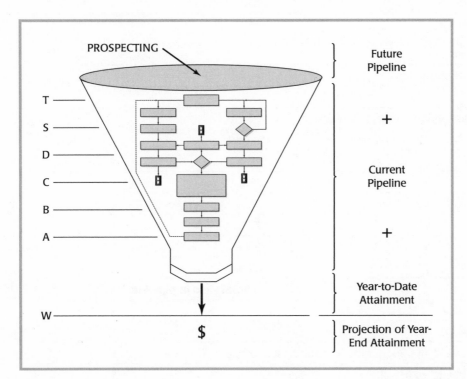

Figure 14.3
The Pipeline

Let's first explore what we know of the facts in Figure 14.6. The quota of $2 million and the current month, March, was shown on the pipeline report earlier. The average opportunity size was calculated from the pipeline chart by dividing the total dollar volume or opportunities in the pipeline by 39, the number of total opportunities. The year-to-date attainment in this example is $200,000. The average sell time for an opportunity must be estimated, and in this example it is six months.

Using the Pipeline Analysis Worksheet, the yield that is expected from the current pipeline is $1,054,500. This yield is calculated by multiplying the revenues associated with each status code by the win odds to attain the yield. When added to the YTD attainment of

A	Quota:					
B	Average sell time:					
C	Average size of opportunity:					
D	Current month:					
E	Year-to-date attainment not reflected in Ws:					
F	**Sell cycle code**	**Revenue**	×	**Win odds**	=	**Yield**
	S	$	×	10%	=	$
	D	$	×	25%	=	$
	C	$	×	50%	=	$
	B	$	×	75%	=	$
	A	$	×	90%	=	$
	W	$	×	100%	=	$
				Total yield in pipeline:		$
G	Revenue under way (E + F):					$
H	Shortfall to go (A − G):					$
I	Likely additional yield (F ÷ B × number of months left to sell):					$
J	Remaining shortfall to go (H − I):					$
K	New Ss required (J ÷ C × 10):					

Figure 14.4 Pipeline Analysis Worksheet

		S		D		C		B		A		W		Total units	
Sales rep	**$ Quota**	**$K 10%**	**#**	**$K 25%**	**#**	**$K 50%**	**#**	**$K 75%**	**#**	**$K 90%**	**#**	**$K 100%**	**#**	**$K**	**#**
Adams	2M	1,725	17	1,490	10	526	5	75	2	75	2	119	3	4,010	39

Figure 14.5 Pipeline Report—Example

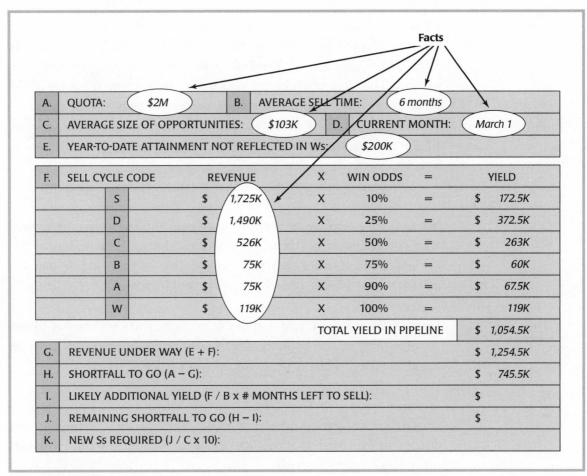

Facts

A.	QUOTA:	$2M	B.	AVERAGE SELL TIME: 6 months
C.	AVERAGE SIZE OF OPPORTUNITIES: $103K		D.	CURRENT MONTH: March 1
E.	YEAR-TO-DATE ATTAINMENT NOT REFLECTED IN Ws: $200K			

F.	SELL CYCLE CODE	REVENUE	X	WIN ODDS	=	YIELD
	S	$ 1,725K	X	10%	=	$ 172.5K
	D	$ 1,490K	X	25%	=	$ 372.5K
	C	$ 526K	X	50%	=	$ 263K
	B	$ 75K	X	75%	=	$ 60K
	A	$ 75K	X	90%	=	$ 67.5K
	W	$ 119K	X	100%	=	119K
				TOTAL YIELD IN PIPELINE		$ 1,054.5K

G.	REVENUE UNDER WAY (E + F):	$ 1,254.5K
H.	SHORTFALL TO GO (A − G):	$ 745.5K
I.	LIKELY ADDITIONAL YIELD (F / B x # MONTHS LEFT TO SELL):	$
J.	REMAINING SHORTFALL TO GO (H − I):	$
K.	NEW Ss REQUIRED (J / C x 10):	

Figure 14.6 Pipeline Analysis Worksheet with Facts

$200,000, you have current revenue underway of $1,254,500. Based on the calculation thus far, what looked like a pretty sure thing now indicates a shortfall in current yield of $745,500.

We need to calculate the likely additional yield for the rest of the year by extrapolating our yield. This is the period that goes beyond the current six-month period. Six months of yield produces $1,054,500 in our current pipeline. Assuming a similar run rate for the rest of the year, we have to cover the four months remaining in the current year. Four months divided by six months multiplied by $1,054,500 equals $703,000, the business that will likely be done for these uncovered four months. This does not take any seasonality into account, but we could make the necessary adjustments if they were known.

Adding the likely yield to the current revenue underway of $1,254,500 gives us $1,957,500 and a remaining shortfall gap of $42,500 from the needed $2 million quota.

In the case of a shortfall, you have recourse to several actions:

Increase Your Win Odds Follow the process and engage yourself more with Power Sponsors, the people who have the authority to buy or the influence to get what they want regardless of title. A sale usually advances much faster once you have access to power.

Shorten Your Sales Cycle Using the process, you can attempt to get opportunities into an evaluation plan. You can also attempt to get your buyer to agree to buy or start the project earlier.

Increase the Size of Your Opportunities There may be opportunities where you can increase the size of a sale. Using the Pain Chain, you can document the impacts across an organization and start to cross-sell other products and services.

Find More S Opportunities In other words, particularly if it's early in the quarter and you have relatively short sales cycles, get out there and prospect. Find new opportunities.

In this chapter, I have dealt primary with getting started and with implementing the Solution Selling process from the salesperson's perspective. In Chapter Fifteen, I explore sales management's role in the implementation and introduce additional job aids that both salespeople and managers can use to manage the process.

Sales Management System: Managers Managing Pipelines and Salespeople

The purpose of this chapter is threefold: (1) to help increase the performance and productivity of sales managers by introducing you to a sales management system, (2) to introduce you to forecasting methods and aids, and (3) to assist you with specific recommendations for getting started with the Solution Selling process.

First, it's important to realize that outstanding individual sales performance doesn't happen by chance. Although most world-class athletes are born with a lot of talent, that talent must be nurtured to reach its maximum potential. The same requirement applies to salespeople. There are very few natural-born superstar salespeople. Most of them need sales process and training. The most important roles a sales manager can play are coach, mentor, and trainer. This can be especially difficult for sales managers who weren't prepared for these roles.

Research and results prove that the very best sales managers follow a sales process for selling and use a sales management system for managing. When it's time to develop or coach salespeople, they draw on their expertise in these two areas to ensure success.

If you're a sales manager, consistency is a key element of your success with your salespeople. It is also what most salespeople are looking for from you. Salespeople want to know that if they need help, you'll be there with a consistent approach that always works, and you won't be an overactive, aggressive sales manager questioning their decisions. The best thing you can do as a sales manager is to have a sales process and a management system that prompts you to consistently ask the right questions. The right questions can lead salespeople to positive and predictable outcomes. The rate of sales success rises sharply in direct relationship to a sales manager's leadership.

Leadership is essential. Sales managers must set the example by their focus and actions. They must use a common language throughout the organization and ask the right questions. They must have appropriate expectations and communicate those effectively. They must set goals and measure against them. They must motivate and coach individuals to maximize sales results.

SALES MANAGEMENT CRITERIA

Most sales managers strive to meet three success criteria: (1) make the revenue numbers, (2) forecast sales revenues accurately, and (3) coach and develop the right team of people to get the job done. Which of these three criteria is most important may shift over time, but these three always seem to make it to the top of the list.

According to a recent Sales Performance International survey of sales managers at 134 different companies, inaccurate forecasting had become a big problem for them. In the survey, sales managers cited poor forecasting more often (54 percent) than either declining revenue (49 percent) or inadequate coaching (34 percent).

Sales managers certainly don't like missing their revenue goals, but they really hate getting the forecasts wrong. It's no wonder. In today's mistrustful climate stemming from large corporate failures, they're under more pressure than ever because companies need to know exactly where they are at all times, especially publicly traded companies. Wall Street doesn't respect a management team that's not in full control of the business, and that becomes evident when the business misses a forecast, negative or positive.

Forecasts are missed for many reasons. Whether it's the economy, misunderstood sales pipelines, customer budget cuts, competition, market shifts, product inadequacies, or supply shortages, they all affect the forecast. Wall Street's expectations compound the pressures. Good forecasting facilitates good goal setting, the right inventory levels, and maintaining manufacturing and customer service levels and ultimately revenues. As a result, accurate forecasting is one of the sales manager's most critical responsibilities.

FORECASTING CHALLENGES

In the past, forecasting depended solely on a sales manager's experience and judgment, which in turn depended on input from the sales force. But sales methodologies and processes have since emerged that need specific customer feedback to track such things as chains of selling events or pipeline Milestones and thereby improve forecasting accuracy.

For technology companies and companies selling large-ticket items or strategic applications, the challenge is even greater, because they have long and highly complex selling cycles. Some sales take over a year to close, so it's not surprising that such companies are among the first trying to make forecasting a more reliable, systematic process.

The number one question CEOs ask their sales managers is, Are you going to make your numbers? Sales managers must answer this question and answer it correctly. I find that if sales managers are offended by this question (let's call it what it is, "pressure"), it's probably because the forecast is out of sync with reality. Consequently, sales managers always live with the anxiety of not being able to meet the number that the executive wants. This challenge will probably never go away, but it can be made much less risky by implementing two things: a reliable systematic sales process and a sales management system.

SOLUTION SELLING SALES MANAGEMENT SYSTEM

Our goals in developing the Solution Selling Sales Management System are to help sales managers (1) make their revenue numbers, (2) forecast revenues more accurately, and (3) coach and develop the right team of people to get the job done.

Figure 15.1 is a flow chart of our sales management system. On the basis of the Solution Selling Milestones you learned about in Chapter Fourteen, Coaching and Diagnosing (shown on the left axis) become two primary functions in this system. The flow goes like this: sales managers are able to diagnose pipeline content and quality, including individual pipeline opportunities; certain findings can be discovered and remedial action decided on; and then two kinds of coaching can take place—opportunity coaching and skill coaching. All this is followed up and reflected in corporate reporting, allowing a more accurate reality. I will discuss diagnosing and coaching separately.

Diagnosing

The sales pipeline is the cornerstone of the sales management system. In this pipeline is information about opportunities that will eventually deliver the much-needed revenues. Whether pipeline information

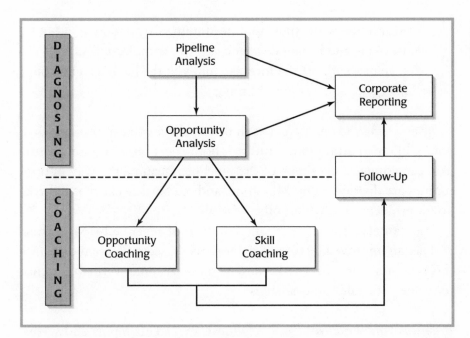

Figure 15.1 Sales Management System Flow Chart

(reporting) is automated or manual, very few sales managers have been taught how to diagnose their pipelines.

Diagnosis involves pipeline analysis (macromanagement) and opportunity analysis (micromanagement). Pipelines, pipeline reports, and pipeline analysis are the tools of the trade for sales managers, much like balance sheets and income statements are for accountants.

When you analyze a pipeline, what are you looking for? What do you want to find? Likely you are looking for the following:

- A pipeline's overall health, including the projected sales revenue attainment for the quarter, the year, and beyond
- Bottlenecks in the pipeline
- Deficient selling behavior, such as the inability to get to Power
- Sales support deficiencies, such as inadequate presale technical support

- Marketing weak spots that need immediate action
- Revenue and timing deficiencies. For example, will sales revenues support the forecast, and will the likely revenue be adequate and at the right time?

By assessing the opportunities in the pipeline, you can project what you're likely to attain in the future—both short term and long term. You can compare the shape of the pipeline, meaning the way opportunities are distributed by Milestone, and see bottlenecks that tell you about problems you would otherwise miss.

You can also compare the distribution of revenue by Milestone and get an improved picture of the forecast based on factual data. All this becomes more effective because you use customer-verifiable events to define your sales process steps.

Business Unit Pipeline Look at Figure 15.2. This report shows the pipeline for a sales unit. In Chapter Fourteen, I introduced this pipeline report, and we looked at it from an individual salesperson's perspective.

In Figure 15.2 you see a chart of eight salespeople, each with a quota, followed by their individual pipelines graded according to Milestone codes. Gross totals are calculated in the two columns to the far right. At the bottom of the chart are the sales unit's unweighted and weighted yield pipeline totals. In case you didn't see it, the total row (second from the bottom) is multiplied by the Milestone grade (yield) percentage probability (second row from the top), resulting in the unit's yield (the last row).

Although the unit's total work in its pipeline is $40,100,000, the actual likely yield given all the work-to-date is only $10,503,000. That's a different reality! That's a different bottom line.

But can this aggregate data be analyzed in such a way that you know the total yield in your pipeline relative to your quota? For example, are

Sales rep	$ Quota	S $K 10%	#	D $K 25%	#	C $K 50%	#	B $K 75%	#	A $K 90%	#	W $K 100%	#	Total units $K	#
Adams	2M	1,915	31	146	10	27	3	5	1	8	3	10	4	2,111	52
Bond	2M	3,034	49	1,988	26	631	15	268	4	70	7	89	7	6,080	108
Chang	3M	3,400	11	2,072	7	530	3	9	1	602	5	1,000	6	7,613	33
Davis	1M	376	7	818	8	240	15	389	4	11	1	15	2	1,849	37
Eades	3M	2,769	40	2,130	19	499	8	38	3	53	5	60	6	5,549	81
Fisher	3M	2,529	11	97	1	165	1	9	1	0	0	2	1	2,802	15
Gomez	4M	384	3	6,281	14	3,045	4	0	0	0	0	1	1	9,711	22
Hart	2M	2,845	14	1,373	18	121	3	30	2	6	2	10	3	4,385	42
Total	20M	17,252	166	14,905	103	5,258	52	748	16	750	23	1,187	30	40,100	390
Yield		1,725		3,726		2,629		561		675		1,187		10,503	

The table is headed **Milestone codes** spanning columns S, D, C, B, A, W.

Figure 15.2 Business Unit Pipeline Report

you over or under the quota? What's the shortfall, if any? What can you do about it?

Pipeline Analysis Worksheet Chapter Fourteen went into some detail about how an individual salesperson can use a Pipeline Analysis Worksheet. Let's advance our analysis and look at the whole sales team.

Can you reliably estimate the amount of good business in your current pipeline? Are you able to estimate future pipeline sales? Can you answer the question, Are you going to attain your goals for the year? I believe you can if you use our sales management system.

Examine the example of a Pipeline Analysis Worksheet in Figure 15.3. Take note of the following:

A	Quota: *$20 million*					
B	Average sell time: *6 months*					
C	Average size of opportunity: *$103K*					
D	Current month: *March*					
E	Year-to-date attainment not reflected in worksheet: *$2 million*					
F	**Sell cycle code**	**Revenue**	×	**Win odds**	=	**Yield**
	S	$	×	10%	=	$1,725K
	D	$	×	25%	=	$3,726K
	C	$	×	50%	=	$2,629K
	B	$	×	75%	=	$561K
	A	$	×	90%	=	$675K
	W	$	×	100%	=	$1,187K
					Total yield in pipeline:	**$10,503K**
G	Revenue under way (E + F):					$12,503K
H	Shortfall to go (A – G):			$7,497K		
I	Likely additional yield (F ÷ B × number of months left to sell):					$7,002K
J	Remaining shortfall to go (H – D):					$495K
K	New Ss required (J ÷ C × 10):					48

Figure 15.3 Pipeline Analysis Worksheet—Example

- The Average Size of Opportunity (row C) was calculated from the previous business unit pipeline report by dividing $40,100,000 by 390—the total number of opportunities. The result is an average opportunity size of $103,000.
- The Year-to-Date Attainment (row E), which is not reflected in the pipeline, tells us that in January and February, business closed at $2M.
- In this example, we know from past experience that the normal average sell time for an opportunity is six months (row B).

- The current month, March, is shown in D. This means that this worksheet covers business that will close, on average, in the months of March through August.
- The total yield in the sales unit's existing pipeline is calculated in row F.
- The unknown (the likely additional yield that will happen in the months remaining in the year but not covered by the pipeline) can be seen in row I. This covers the months of September through December.
- Row J indicates and warns that there is a shortfall of $495,000.

We can use this early warning of a shortfall to calculate what additional effort is needed to close the gap. If you are facing a shortfall, you have at least four options.

Option 1 You could ask your sales unit to generate additional opportunities. The question here is, How many? If you choose this option (row K on the Pipeline Analysis Worksheet), you must know how many new sales must be initiated. To find out in this example, simply divide $495K (row J) by $103K (row C)—you will need 4.8 additional opportunities to close the gap. But you take this one step further. Since you only close one out of ten S Milestone opportunities, multiply 4.8 times 10. Thus you need to get your sales unit to generate forty-eight new opportunities to allow you to close the gap. So, you've got to hit the prospecting trail.

Option 2 You could ask your salespeople to increase the average opportunity size. You would go back to selected pipeline opportunities and renegotiate larger transactions.

Option 3 You could work with your salespeople and get them to improve the win odds of selected opportunities. What do I mean? You could, for example, where salespeople are not yet at Power, move them to dealing with the Power people. Or you could examine your salespeople's evaluation plans and improve any weak plans. Or you could improve your buyers' perceived value.

Option 4 You could work with your salespeople to shorten the length of the sales cycles. For example, for those pipeline opportunities that have not yet reached the Evaluation Plan stage, you could coach your salespeople to shorten their sales cycles. For deals already in the Evaluation Plan stage, you could ask your salespeople to renegotiate the events and their timing.

Whichever option you choose and manage successfully, you now have the ability to look ahead to the end of the year and estimate whether you will make your revenue goals. What is comforting in the example we evaluated is that ten months remain in which to close gaps discovered as of March 1. The forecasting enables a sales manager to avoid the mad scramble of December.

In our workshops, participants learn other things about pipeline opportunity identification and analysis. For example, they learn to analyze whether opportunities are moving through the pipeline consistently. They also learn to determine whether revenue is positioned to close in a particular target quarter. Our sales management system addresses these and other questions.

Coaching

Go back and take a look at the left axis in Figure 15.1, page 247. Since you've diagnosed a pipeline—both its aggregate and individual components—you are now in a position to manage by exception. Doing so saves time and money, and management by exception helps keep salespeople focused on what to do first.

When sales managers get into opportunity analysis, they enter the world of coaching. On a short-term basis, a manager ought to be prepared to coach each sales opportunity with the idea of winning the business and, if required (it usually is), be prepared to coach selling skills for long-term performance improvement.

Consistency is the key to good coaching. The sales process gives us consistency by defining the selling activities and the standard for results. Today I find it hard to imagine how to coach effectively without a well-defined sales process. Being a sales process expert and enabling salespeople to see things for themselves are two important aspects of good coaching. In major sporting events, coaches don't play the game; players do. It should be the same in selling. Unfortunately, too many times sales managers take over the opportunities, and little, if any, coaching, mentoring, or training takes place.

Effective coaching requires sales managers to (1) coach key opportunities based on objective information, not subjective information, and (2) participate in and conduct regularly scheduled training and practice sessions that address selling skill deficiencies as well as reinforce the sales process.

Too many companies and too many sales managers hire experienced salespeople, believing they know how to sell. However, even the very best salespeople need ongoing coaching, mentoring, and training to maintain their peak performance.

Sales Management Job Aids Managers can use two job aids to objectively determine the status of an opportunity and uncover potential salesperson deficiencies: the Key Opportunity Debriefing Guide and the Strength of Sale Check.

The Key Opportunity Debriefing Guide (See Figure 15.4.) This guide can help you track where a salesperson is in his or her execution of the Solution Selling sales process for a specific opportunity. In addition, it

Competitive Strategy

Check these items to validate status
Opportunity assessment conducted supports strategy

T
- □ Opportunity identified in territory → Opportunity or territory plan
  - □ Meets marketing criteria
  - □ Potential sponsor identified → Name and title of potential sponsor
  - □ Initial contact established (verifiable) → Business development letter or date of conversation

S
- □ Pain admitted by sponsor → Pain articulated by sponsor
- □ Sponsor has a valued buying vision → Differentiated vision articulated by sponsor
- □ Sponsor agreed to explore
- □ Sponsor granted access to power → Power sponsor's name and title
- □ Agreed to above in sponsor letter → Sponsor letter sent and content agreed upon

D
- □ Access to power sponsor → Date of conversation
- □ Pain admitted by power sponsor → Pain articulated by power
- □ Power sponsor has a valued buying vision → Differentiated vision articulated by power sponsor
- □ Power sponsor agreed to explore
- □ Evaluation plan proposed → Power sponsor letter and attached draft plan sent
- □ Evaluation plan agreed upon → Evaluation plan changed and/or agreed upon

C
- □ Evaluation plan underway → First step accomplished (step completion letter)
- □ Preproposal review conducted → Audience, date, and time of preproposal review
- □ Asked for the business → Who was asked? What was their response?
- □ Proposal issued, decision due
- □ Verbal approval received → Who gave approval? What was their indication.

B
- □ Contract negotiation in progress → Who? What is agreed upon? (negotiating worksheet)

A
- □ Signed documents

W
- □ Update prospect database

Sponsor name/title _____   Power sponsor name/title _____
Pain _____   Pain _____
Reasons _____   Reasons _____
Vision _____   Vision _____
Value _____   Value _____

Figure 15.4 Key Opportunity Debriefing Guide

provides you, the sales manager, with a list of verifiable outcomes that helps you measure the actual progress of your sales rep's opportunity.

After a brief overview of the selling situation—such as what is being sold and to whom and the opportunity size—the Milestone status code is determined. If, for example, the opportunity is a D, the sales manager should ask to see the Sponsor Letter. A Sponsor Letter is an excellent point of validation. Review it for quality and for the customer's agreement to the letter.

If no letter exists, this Milestone cannot be validated. Whether verbal or written, you need Sponsor Letters in order to validate the position of the opportunity in the Milestones.

If a Sponsor Letter exists, the manager should review it for six key points—pain, reasons, vision, agreement to explore, bargain for access to power, and proof. In this way, the manager can verify that the appropriate communication has occurred. If the manager is satisfied, then the Milestone is a confirmed D. If not, it is reset to S or T. The manager then discusses how to achieve the next Milestone for that opportunity. This focuses the salesperson on actions that will improve the chances of winning the sale.

Figure 15.5 shows another way you can look at and diagnose a situation where a salesperson is having difficulty moving from one Milestone status to the next.

There are many selling difficulties—some severely disabling, others not so important. Figure 15.5 is used by a number of sales managers to identify why a salesperson is having difficulty moving from one Milestone to another. For example, if a salesperson is having trouble moving from Milestone D to C, the sales manager should look for (1) trouble validating power, (2) difficulty getting the Power Sponsor to admit true pain, (3) inability to effectively create or reengineer the power person's vision, or (4) inability to get the power people to buy into an Evaluation Plan.

Difficulty moving from	Typical reasons
T to **S**	• Ineffective prospecting
S to **D**	• Difficulty getting sponsor to admit true pain
	• Inability to effectively create or reengineer a vision
	• Difficulty determining power
	• Inability to successfully negotiate for access to power
D to **C**	• Trouble validating power
	• Difficulty getting the power sponsor to admit true pain
	• Inability to effectively create or reengineer power's vision
	• Inability to get power to buy in to evaluation plan
C to **B**	• Incapable of maintaining control after issuing proposal
	• Difficulty getting the buyer to see compelling value
	• Challenge of staying in alignment (proposal too early)
	• Failure to plan ahead
B to **A**	• Difficulty negotiating

Figure 15.5 Selling Difficulties

This opportunity debriefing approach helps determine the true status of the opportunity from a process execution perspective. It gives some insight into how much work and time are required to close the business, but it can be difficult to judge progress well enough to forecast with confidence. Another job aid that can help judge quality of the sale, and the progress through the sales process, is the Strength of Sale Check.

Strength of Sale Check In Chapter Two I introduced the formula for sales success and talked about its five critical elements: Pain, Power,

Vision, Value, and Control. Experience has shown us that if we focus our efforts on these five elements, we increase our probability of success. Our job aid, the Strength of Sale Check (Figure 15.6), does three things: measures the five elements, estimates the strength of the opportunity, and determines the remaining effort required to complete the sale.

There are different levels of customer commitment in each of these five elements. Putting metrics on each task or step within an element allows you to determine the actual strength of each element, and it also helps you to estimate how long it will take to complete the sale.

If you can attain level 20 for each of these five elements, it means that the sale is imminent and you will almost certainly win the opportunity. As a sales manager, it is frequently difficult to objectively determine the strength of any particular opportunity. This job aid can help you with this difficulty.

FORECASTING

Forecasting is a critically important part of a sales manager's job. A primary reason for implementing this sales process and sales management system is to improve the accuracy of the sales forecast.

One of the important elements of forecasting is, first, to recognize the sources of revenues that make up the forecast. Next, it's important to apply an appropriate forecasting method.

In Figure 15.7, Forecast Elements, two different revenue sources and the three forecasting methods that apply to them are identified.

Revenue Sources

Most people are familiar with the revenue that a sales organization produces from opportunities that are in its traditional pipeline. These

Sponsor	Pain scale	Power sponsor
0	Seller cannot describe need, pain, or reasons	9
2	Seller assumes customer's needs	10
3	Seller assumes pain	11
4	Customer admits needs	12
5	Customer admits reasons/symptoms	13
6	Customer admits pain	14
7	Pain/reasons documents to customer	16
8	Customer agreed to or modified	20

Power scale

0	Power sponsor not identified	
4	Potential power sponsor identified	
8	Buying and decision process understood	
9	Sponsor granted access to power	
10	Power sponsor agreed to explore	
14	Power sponsor agreed to evaluation plan	
16	Power sponsor agreed to proposal	
20	Power sponsor agreed to buy	

Vision scale

0	Vision not created (or competitive vision)	7
1	Vision created in product terms	8
3	Differentiated vision created in situational terms	10
4	Differentiated vision documented to customer	15
6	Differentiated vision agreed to or modified	20

Value scale

0	Vision not identified or competitive vision	8
1	Customer wants a solution, not quantified	9
2	Seller identifies value	10
3	Customer states the value	12
4	Customer performs value justification	14
5	Customer performs value justification with seller	16
6	Joint value justification conducted	18
7	Customer agrees joint value meets financial criteria	20

Control scale

0	No documentation	
2	Sponsor letter sent	
4	Sponsor letter agreed to	
8	Power sponsor letter and evaluation plan sent	
10	Power sponsor letter agreed to	
14	Evaluation plan modified/agreed to	
16	Preproposal review conducted	
20	Evaluation plan complete	

Figure 15.6 Strength of Sale Check

include key selected opportunities, often called "must-wins," and the balance of opportunities that we work on that are more routine. However, these are not all the revenues we need to consider when forecasting. There are also nonpipeline sources, such as through third parties or unsolicited orders.

Forecast Method

As indicated in Figure 15.7, there are three forecast methods: Run Rate, Forecast QuickCheck, and Yield Analysis.

Run Rate What does this mean? It means using the historical financial performance or revenue results of a company's or unit's nonpipeline

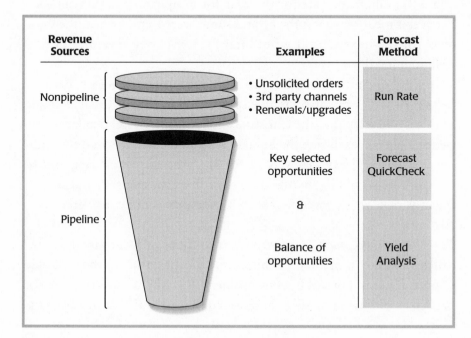

Figure 15.7 Forecast Elements

revenue (for example, annuity income) and extrapolating it into the future. For example, some software companies take their renewing software licenses for a given accounting period and extrapolate them into the future. They call it their run rate.

So, there are nonpipeline sources of revenue that never hit the pipeline. As you can see from Figure 15.7, unsolicited orders, third-party distribution channels, and product/services renewals and upgrades all make up nonpipeline revenue. Although these may not be revenue sources that the organization manages through the sales process, they still need to be forecast. So when I talk about your Run Rate, I'm asking you about your nonpipeline revenue.

In the context of extrapolating future performance, the run rate helps put the company's or business unit's latest results in perspective. For example, if in its first quarter a company had nonpipeline revenues of $10 million, the sales manager might say, "Our latest quarter puts us at a $40 million run rate for the year for nonpipeline opportunities." What this means is that if the business unit were to perform at the same level for the next year, it would have nonpipeline revenues of $40 million annually.

A word of caution: you have to be careful using a run rate, because certain variables can affect it, like seasonal industries. A great example of this is a retailer after the Christmas holiday. Almost all retailers experience higher sales during the holiday season. It's unlikely that the coming quarters will have sales as strong as in the fourth quarter, and so the run rate would likely overstate the following quarters and, subsequently, next year's revenue if such seasonality is not considered.

Forecast QuickCheck Here you want to focus on your key opportunities, which can include (1) big opportunities and (2) the strategic opportunities important to your business—usually where you have the best chance of winning. For these we combine the five elements of the formula for sales success (Pain, Power, Vision, Value, and Control) with the Forecast QuickCheck method.

This method establishes measurable guidelines that become forecast thresholds using the five elements. We use the same 20-point scale for each of the five elements discussed earlier in the Strength of Sale Check.

Figure 15.8 illustrates how you can get a Forecast QuickCheck. You are trying to forecast the likelihood of closing a specific key opportunity in any particular given time period.

If the opportunity doesn't have all the five elements at the predetermined forecast thresholds, then the opportunity is not likely to close during the forecast period. On the success side of the ledger, your forecast will include those key opportunities that meet or exceed the predetermined forecast thresholds. Those below the thresholds will not be included. This allows you to communicate quickly and easily with all interested parties about the strength and predictability of a key opportunity. Thus, the Forecast QuickCheck analyzes a simple set of variables that provide a basis for forecast discussions.

Note that the thresholds may also be different depending on when the forecast is being made. For example, a forecast done at the beginning of a quarter will have a different threshold from one done one week before the quarter ends. Each selling organization must establish the right set of thresholds for its own forecasting environment.

Yield Analysis This is business as usual—the grading of your normal pipeline opportunities. Recall that yield is the expected revenue from a collection of opportunities in the pipeline. Yield represents the total revenue by Milestone multiplied by the win odds or probability.

This method is based on the Solution Selling Milestone probabilities. (You learned about Milestones earlier in this chapter and in Chapter Fourteen.) The key to good forecasting rests on accurate Milestone grading and validation of where each opportunity is in its Milestone status.

Figure 15.8 Forecast
QuickCheck

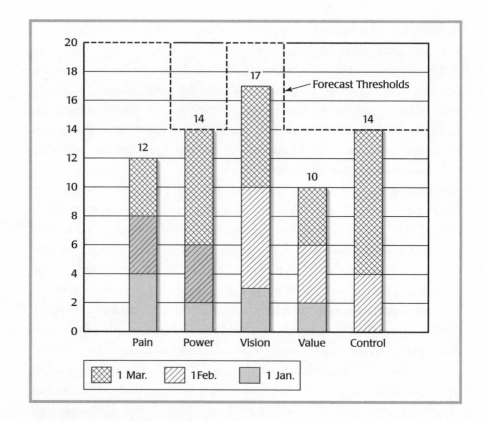

GETTING STARTED WITH THE SALES MANAGEMENT SYSTEM

I've covered a lot of ground in this chapter, and if you're like most people, you're probably asking yourself, How do I get started? We originally thought we should start with pipeline analysis. We encouraged clients to analyze their pipelines. That seemed logical. That's the way most managers would start. Once that was completed and operating, people could begin to manage pipeline opportunities. The objective was correct. Start with pipeline analysis, identify problem opportunities, and deal with the exceptions. It sounded great, but most clients discovered they were going in the wrong direction.

This approach assumes that there is good data in the pipeline—and this is usually wrong. The reality is that there usually isn't good data in the pipeline. It's badly flawed. So, it turned out to be a wrong assumption.

Here's my recommendation. Instead, start the sales management process by working with your salespeople and help them to use the pipeline Milestones, to grade their pipeline opportunities—opportunity by opportunity. You want to ensure the quality of the sales information. If you do that, then pipeline analysis will work, because it's based on fact, not opinion.

Recommendations for Getting Started

- Ask each salesperson to complete the Pipeline Milestones Worksheet
- Debrief pain, reasons, buying visions, and next step with each key opportunity
- Ask salespeople to convert current key opportunities to C status
- Participate in refocus calls (conference calls or face to face) on key opportunities
- Review and edit Sponsor and Power Sponsor Letters before they are sent
- Schedule role-play sessions with each salesperson within the next two weeks
- Using the Milestones, regrade all opportunities and determine the actual health of your pipeline
- Build the pipeline to a level that will enable you to achieve your sales goals

What is the biggest reason that most managers fail to implement a winning sales process and sales management system? I'm reminded of the story of the lumberjack chopping down a tree. It goes something like this: A lumberjack is furiously chopping at a tree with a dull ax. Another lumberjack asks, "Why don't you sharpen your ax?" The lumberjack growls, "Can't you see I'm busy chopping down this tree?" Like the lumberjack, too many managers don't follow through because they're busy and everything seems to be working.

If you're a sales manager who's achieving your revenue goals, consistently forecasting accurately, and you have all Eagle salespeople, then you probably don't need to change. On the other hand, if all three of these criteria for successful sales management aren't where they need to be, then give the Solution Selling sales process and sales management system a try.

CHAPTER SIXTEEN

Creating and Sustaining High-Performance Sales Cultures

Creating and sustaining a high-performance sales culture is essential in achieving success in today's highly competitive and global business economy. This chapter focuses on the leadership role that executives must fulfill to establish and maintain a high-performance sales culture. Societal cultures do not form overnight. They evolve over time. The same is true of sales cultures. It's crucial that executives realize how important decisions they make—or don't make—affect their sales cultures.

THE HIGH-PERFORMANCE SALES CULTURE

Creating a sales culture requires both vision and executive leadership. The vision should contain at least four elements that are consistent across all high-performance sales cultures (HPSC): sales process, sales management system, sales automation, and integration with marketing (see Figure 16.1).

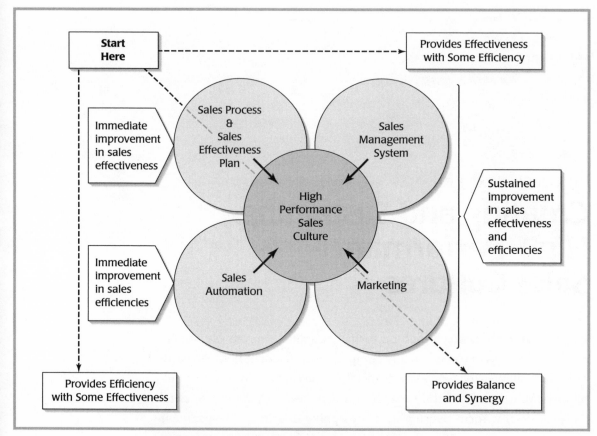

Figure 16.1 The High-Performance Sales Culture

1. *Sales Process*. This element focuses on improving each individual salesperson's performance by establishing a common base of best practices for everyone in the sales organization, from top to bottom (the sales executive, sales manager, and salesperson). These best practices include sales execution, opportunity planning, account planning, and territory planning.

2. *Sales Management System*. With a sales process in place, this element gives sales managers information about key opportunities and overall selling health, allowing them to identify and correct both individual and systematic selling problems (analysis and coaching).

3. *Sales Automation.* With a sales process and an integrated sales management system operating, sales force automation can improve individual salesperson efficiency in capturing and reporting key sales information. This element makes sure that high-quality sales information is available and accessible to salespeople, managers, and executives.

4. *Marketing.* As the fourth element, marketing must be integrated with the overall selling effort to ensure adequate lead streams and coverage and to improve sales effectiveness by linking products and services to customer business problems. Marketing can help salespeople become business consultants (through specific product update and availability messaging, advertising and promotional collateral, and job aids [brand-driven Pain Chains, Pain Sheets, References Stories, and Value Propositions] in the context of the sales process).

Optimally, executives integrate all four elements into one successful operation and achieve their HPSC. Still, how do you get there? After all, you can't get each of the four elements all working simultaneously from the beginning—as I said, cultures evolve over time.

THREE OPTIONS FOR EXECUTIVES

If you look at the HPSC model in Figure 16.1, you'll see that the executive has three options: (1) improve efficiency, (2) improve effectiveness, or (3) achieve a balance between efficiency and effectiveness. Each option leads to different results. Let's look at each option separately.

Option 1: Improve Efficiency

In this option, an executive chooses to implement a sales process complemented by some form of sales force automation (SFA) or customer relationship management (CRM) system. This approach focuses on reducing the cost of sales transactions. This is the option that is chosen most often, but—and beware—it typically has a low level of success.

There are several reasons why. First, sales force automation that is not integrated with the sales management system seldom integrates with the business's sales process. Second, the chosen sales process may be inadequate, which compounds the problem. Third, both conditions can exist together—an inadequate sales process that is poorly integrated with sales force automation.

Option 2: Improve Effectiveness

Executives who select this approach implement sales process and reinforce it with a sales management system. Option 2 focuses on increasing revenue. This effort requires a consistent disciplined approach over an extended period of time (for example, six to twelve months or longer).

For a number of organizations, Option 2 works better than Option 1, because executives are able to integrate their sales process (hopefully, a highly effective one) with their sales management system—and drive results without the expense or distraction that automation projects often bring.

However, some negatives lurk in this option. It is not a complete fix. Unless customer relationship management can be integrated with it, there will be huge gaps in the timely identification, analysis, and reporting of sales pipeline opportunities. Furthermore, sales management reporting will tend to be impaired by incomplete and disparate data and late reporting.

Option 3: Balance of Efficiency and Effectiveness

This is a long-term option. It will take time to get each of the four elements going. Here, executives choose to develop and integrate the sales process, the sales management system, and sales force automation with marketing (note the diagonal line in Figure 16.1).

The far-seeing executive who acts on this option usually achieves a balance of efficiency and effectiveness. This approach, which provides the benefits of the previous two options, requires that all the elements in the HPSC model be highly synchronized.

A Caution There is no one correct path, because every business is different. Clearly, the first option provides reductions in sales costs (with some effectiveness); the second option provides increases in revenue (with some efficiency); and the third option provides both sustained effectiveness and efficiency.

I strongly suggest that you focus first on your sales process combined with a sales management system and then have sales automation support these two key processes. Don't compromise the way you do business just to conform to some inflexible automation system. The good news about many CRM and SFA systems today is that they are flexible. Many packages have user-defined work flow engines that allow you to integrate your sales process and sales management system into the software. This is very important. Automation should support the process, not the other way around.

SALES PROCESS CHARACTERISTICS

Keep in mind that a proper sales process must have three characteristics. It must be repeatable, predictable, and scalable. In addition, salespeople and managers are more likely to use a sales process if it's easy to use and is reinforced through sales tools or job aids. If a sales process is too complicated, salespeople and managers won't use it. This is why some CRM systems are fraught with so many problems. It often becomes a garbage in/garbage out situation, where the only thing companies are automating is chaos.

Being *repeatable* means a company can use the same process over and over to achieve consistent results. Sales management should reward salespeople for consistency in making their numbers versus the big spikes in revenue, typically at month or quarter end.

Being *predictable* implies the use of Milestones to help the sales manager know where salespeople are in specific opportunities and know their pipelines. This knowledge helps to answer questions such as "Will I make my numbers this year, this quarter?" or "Is my pipeline balanced?"

Being *scalable* is important because sales organizations expand and contract according to economic cycles, product changes, marketing promotions, and changes in the size of a business. Moreover, the same sales processes should apply to any size organization, whether there is one salesperson or ten thousand.

Failure of Traditional Approaches

It never ceases to amaze me how often I hear executives say, "Sales is a mystery. Why can't sales be managed like all the other departments?" I tell them that sales can be managed—with a sales process. They say, "We've tried that. We put all our salespeople through sales training, and it didn't make any difference."

Here's what I find really happened behind the scenes. They held a one-day sales training event, but it didn't stick. There's a big difference in implementing an HPSC that includes a sales process as its cornerstone as opposed to a sales training event.

For many years, we've heard sales managers complain about the shortcomings of traditional sales training. Recently, Sales Performance International conducted a survey of 113 corporate sales executives to identify and analyze their complaints. We wanted to hear from these executives about the problems they were having with traditional training methods. Not only did we get a strong response, but we also gained some profound insights into how to help sales executives establish and maintain an HPSC.

One of the biggest misconceptions about creating an HPSC is that training is the key driver in sales performance improvement. As illustrated in Figure 16.2, the most important element in implementation is not the training event, but change management.

When considering the importance of change management, three key drivers enable successful HPSC implementations:

1. Design
2. Training
3. Implementation

1. *Design.* Make sure you design a tailored implementation that encompasses all the elements of an HPSC. Ideally, all four elements

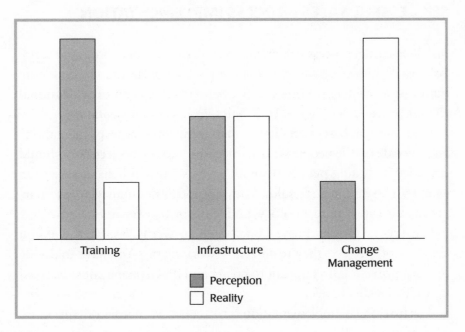

Figure 16.2 Perception Versus Reality

(sales process, sales management system, sales force automation, and marketing) are involved if you want to achieve an HPSC.

2. *Training.* Practice, practice, practice. Practice makes perfect. Training should involve salespeople, managers, executives, marketing, and anyone else in the company who interfaces with customers (for example, in technology markets, product and services technicians are frequently involved). Don't waste your valuable investment.

3. *Implementation.* Support your HPSC rollout. Let it be known that this is what the executives want. Measure it, and remember that people tend to do what they're measured on.

There are sound sales processes, such as the new Solution Selling, that can help you overcome your problems with traditional sales training, but only if you appreciate the scale of change necessary and are committed to making it happen.

SUCCESSFUL SALES PROCESS IMPLEMENTATION

Installing a sales process will impact your organization in profound ways. As a result, implementation of a sales process must be managed as more than just a training event—it must be managed as an organizational change process. (See Figure 16.3, Sales Process Implementation.)

How can you best effect change management in the implementation? First, decide on the people who are necessary to the project. You should consider including people from all areas who will help to effect the change. This can include sales, sales support, sales management, marketing, information technology, and sponsoring executives.

Is everyone already busy? Usually the answer is yes. How will you get them off projects they're currently working on? You have to decide on your priorities. If you want to create an HPSC, people must be freed up to lead such change.

The first step in implementation is to analyze your sales organization. This analysis will help you see the potential barriers to implementa-

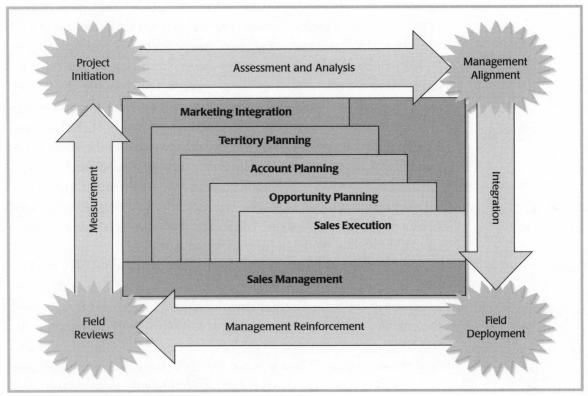

Figure 16.3 Sales Process Implementation

tion, and it will help you discover what is needed to avoid these barriers. If you're completely transforming your sales function, your analysis will probably be quite extensive. On the other hand, if you're only interested in incrementally improving your control of the sales process, a simple review of your organization may be all that is required.

The findings of your analysis will provide the agenda for the executive and management alignment that must take place in your development of an HPSC. Executives need to understand the objectives of the sales process improvement project, the potential barriers to success, the recommended actions to address those barriers, the specific role and actions expected of each manager during the project, and, most important, the specific metrics of success that the management team will use to judge the success or failure of the project.

To eliminate potential barriers to success, I recommend that you integrate the new process with existing systems. For example, it's important to align the new sales process with your CRM systems, measurement and reward systems, hiring practices, and other aspects of the business. During the deployment phase, you can ensure maximum cultural compatibility by tailoring your implementation program content.

Concurrent with the integration phase, or shortly thereafter, you should then deploy the new sales process. Typically, this is accomplished through traditional training workshops, but it may also include e-learning or other media, depending on the needs of your organization.

After implementing the new sales process, you should plan to reinforce the process by coaching managers on how to sustain the new processes in the field. This may involve sales management training and the introduction of automated tools or CRM software, as required. To further improve adoption of the new process, I recommend periodic field review sessions. These sessions help field sales managers to observe and model effective coaching behavior, enabling them to sustain your new HPSC process in your organization.

Finally, you should measure the impact of the project, using the metrics originally identified during the management alignment phase. This will enable your executive team to determine the success of the implementation and make appropriate adjustments.

ESTABLISHING HPSC AS A VALUE SYSTEM

Creating an HPSC requires more than just conducting sales training, hiring the best salespeople that money can buy, and managing the implementation of sales process and supporting automation tools.

Developing and creating an HPSC must be part of the value system that your company is based on—a value system that is so important that it guides your behaviors, decisions, and actions.

The only reason business exists is because of customers. Therefore, customers should be the focal point of everything your business does. This customer-focused philosophy must be the foundation for your value system and sales culture. After all, the source of sustainable value for most companies today is their ability to attract and retain profitable customers. The reason we create and sustain an HPSC is to do just that.

Executives who attempt to create HPSCs for short-term gains are misguided. If you're not careful, you will create a culture that is temporary and jerry-rigged. Naturally, this type of sales culture will not last because it lacks a solid foundation—it has no value system.

To sustain an HPSC, it must first be grounded in something other than short-term gain or greed. I see it all the time—companies want change, so they bring in new executives who promise a better future. Many of these new executives, in order to make a name for themselves, attempt to kick-start the company with a new business model, complete with a dazzling new sales plan full of aggressive goals and programs. Frequently you'll hear them say, "We must be aggressive in the marketplace, and we must create a sales team that won't take no for an answer."

Then they bring in the so-called best and highest-paid sales talent they can find. They train them, along with the holdovers from the former regime, in the latest techniques on "how to close business," all the while thinking that this is the way to create an HPSC. Does this sound familiar? Where's the focal point? What type of culture, if any, is being built?

Don't be misled by short-term thinking. Remember your customers. Make the establishment of an HPSC more than just an objective for this quarter. Make it the heart of your sales organization, a part of your company's value system. Then your customers will remember you not only for what products or services you offer but also by how well you provide them. Your sales organization will become as important a differentiator as any other aspect of your business. And that is a sustainable competitive advantage that's hard to beat.

Creating an HPSC leads to effective and lasting change. In the end, it will continually reaffirm the potential of your business because it leads to higher levels of customer satisfaction, increased productivity, integrated work environments, and more profitable enterprises. Look at the marketplace around you. The competition and constant pressure for results is not going away. You have to compete and win day after day. With the right changes—implemented changes—you can realize high performance.

Value Justification Example

The following value justification is an example constructed around the fictitious company referenced throughout this book, Titan Games, Inc. (TGI). A short review of TGI follows.

TGI's CURRENT ENVIRONMENT

TGI is a twenty-year-old organization that manufactures and distributes educational and recreational games and toys throughout the world. TGI has suffered a decline in overall profits—its primary critical business issue. Three primary reasons are identified for this problem of declining profits: (1) the VP Sales is unable to meet new account revenue targets (2) there are increasing credit write-offs and (3) operational costs are rising. All this affects and concerns the VP Finance, who has watched profits decline for two consecutive quarters. He needs the VP Sales to turn this bad news around.

New account revenues were supposed to contribute 20 percent of TGI's overall sales revenues. Only half of that goal will be realized. The VP Sales feels his salespeople spend too much time servicing existing customers instead of selling to new ones. Further, rising operational costs are mostly attributed to TGI's growing customer service staff. They are needed to handle an increasing volume of customer calls for help. Also, credit write-offs are partially due to shipping games and toys to delinquent, bad-pay accounts. So what follows is an analysis of the important components necessary for creating a good value justification.

VALUE JUSTIFICATION ELEMENTS

1. What elements of the customer's business will be impacted and measured?
2. Who is responsible for the changes within the impacted areas?
3. How much impact and value is possible over what period of time?
4. What capabilities will be needed?
5. When will the investment pay for itself?

1. What Elements of the Customer's Business Will Be Impacted and Measured?

Increased profit	From additional sales revenue
Increased revenue	From new account sales and current account sales
Reduced cost	From reduction in the amount of credit write-offs
Avoided cost	From the traditional hiring of one CSR per quarter

2. Who Is Responsible for the Changes Within the Impacted Areas?

Additional sales revenue from new accounts	VP Sales
Additional sales revenue from current accounts	VP Sales
Reduced cost associated with credit write-offs	VP Finance
Avoided cost associated with hiring CSRs	VP Finance

3. How Much Impact and Value Is Possible and over What Period of Time?

This part of value justification illustrates how much quantifiable value each element in your solution can hope to realize. See Figure A.1 for a detailed view of the benefits.

Increased revenue	5% more selling time per salespeople	= $4M
	Average 1 new account per rep	= $3M
	Broadcast of personalized promotions	= $2M
	Prompt customers for referrals	= $2M
Reduced cost	50% credit write-off reduction	= $400K
Avoided cost	Avoid hiring 1 CSR pre quarter	= $130K

These figures represent the possible value over a one-year period

4. What Capabilities Will Be Needed?

Articulation of the Corporate Buying Vision. See Figure A.2 for a detailed view of the customer investment required to obtain these capabilities.

For Steve Jones:

- IF salespeople spent more time prospecting into new accounts instead of taking repeat order from existing clients, and
- IF salespeople spent more time prospecting into new accounts instead of responding to frequently asked questions by the customer, and
- IF prospects could be made aware of all promotions, and
- IF every customer would be asked for referrals in exchange for discounts,

THEN Steve Jones (VP Sales) could meet his new account revenue targets, also . . .

Detailed View of Value Justification Benefits

Summary of Customer Benefits

Increased profit from increased revenue
  From increased selling time
  $2M quota × 50 reps with 5% more selling time = $5M, of which the customer
  feels $4M is a conservative estimate × profit margin (32%) = $1.28M   **$1.28M**

From new customers
  15% more selling time = minimal acquisition of one new customer × $75K
  in average revenue per new customer × 50 salespeople = $3.75M, of which the
  customer feels $3M is a conservative estimate × profit margin (32%) = $0.96M   **$0.96M**

From increased promotion results
  $10M revenue goal of promotions last year minus the actual achievement
  ($6M) = $4M of which 50% of the shortfall has been attributed to customers
  being unaware of promotions = $2M × profit margin (32%) = $0.64M   **$0.64M**

From increased customer referrals
  Only 10% of customers were asked for referrals, Referrals = $1M, customer
  feels they could double the referral % and associated
  revenue = $2M × profit margin (32%) = $0.64M   **$0.64M**

Total profit increase from revenue increase   **$3.52M**

Avoided costs
  Savings from not hiring CSRs
  4 CSRs added each year (one per quarter) × average burdened cost of a
  CSR ($52K) = $13K per CSR per quarter (Q1 = $13K,
  Q2 = $26K, Q3 = $39K, $130K Q4 = $52K) = $130K   **$130K**

Reduced bad debts
  Annual report confirms bad debt write off for last year = $800K, expectation is
  that at least same debt will occur, frequency of shipping to delinquent
  accounts = 50% of debt. Customer says that all of the delinquent account debt
  can be recovered with capability = $400K   **$400K**

Sources: Revenue figures provided by VP Sales
           Cost figures and profit margin provided by VP Finance

Figure A.1 Detailed View of Value Justification Benefits

Summary of Customer Investment

One-time investment

Professional implementation services ($250K due in Q1, $250K due in Q2)	$500,000.00[1]
Hardware equipment (servers) ($250K due in Q1)	250,000.00[3]
Software ($120K due in Q1)	120,000.00[2]
Training ($21K due in Q1, $21K due in Q2)	42,000.00[4]
Total one-time investment	**$912,000.00**

Ongoing investment

Network ($20K quarterly)	$80,000.00[1, 2, 3]
Maintenance on hardware/software at 18% annually ($250K + $120K × 0.18 = $66,667)	66,667.00[1, 2, 3]
Part-time Web staff ($10K quarterly)	40,000.00[4]
Total ongoing investment	**$186,667.00**
Total first-year investment	**$1,098,667.00**

Source:
[1] Our corporate book value and quantity discount
[2] E-comm Software, Inc. (book price)
[3] Hardware corporation (book price)
[4] VP Finance

Figure A.2 Detailed View of Value Justification Investment

For Jim Smith:

- IF Steve Jones could meet his new account revenue targets, and
- IF customers could utilize frequently asked questions menus instead of calling customer service, and
- If delinquent customers were connected to accounting during their order process

THEN Jim Smith (VP Finance) could meet his profitability goals

For Susan Brown:

- If Jim Smith (VP Finance) can meet his profit goals

THEN Susan Brown (CEO) feels that she can better meet her earnings per share target.

5. When Will the Investment Pay for Itself?

Whether buyers "see" the value of your solution depends on whether it falls within a time period they find acceptable. For example, if they see themselves realizing an agreed-on return on investment soon enough for them to solve their problem, then that can create a compelling reason to take action. If, however, their perceived value happens too far out into the future, they may be discouraged and make a "no decision" or choose to invest the funds elsewhere.

Benefits of cost reduction can be seen immediately in the first quarter due to the avoidance of hiring additional customer service representatives. Because the revenue benefits will "ramp up" fully after one year, only partial benefits should be expected in the second and third quarters, with full benefits being recognized in the fourth quarter. The breakeven point, where return outweighs investment, will be achieved early in the fourth quarter.

So, when the investment will pay for itself becomes an important understanding for you and your buyer to mutually agree on.

Value Justification

Figure A.3 is a summary spreadsheet that answers three primary questions that buyers will have: (1) What is the first year net return? (2)

	Q1	Q2	Q3	Q4
Benefits				
Increased profits				
Revenue × profit percentage (32%)	0	293,333	586,667	880,000
Reduced costs				
Alerted to credit issues ($400K)	0	33,333	66,667	100,000
Avoided costs				
Utilization of FAQ menu ($130K)	13,000	26,000	39,000	52,000
Quarterly (benefits) total	13,000	352,666	692,334	1,032,000
(Quarterly) cumulative value (total)	13,000	365,666	1,058,000	2,090,000
Investments				
(Total) one-time investment	(641,000)	(271,000)	0	0
(Total) ongoing investment	(96,667)	(30,000)	(30,000)	(30,000)
Quarterly (investment) total	(737,667)	(301,000)	(30,000)	(30,000)
Quarterly (cumulative) investment	(737,667)	(1,038,667)	(1,068,667)	(1,098,667)
Net value				
Quarterly total	(724,667)	51,666	662,334	1,002,000
Cumulative total	(724,667)	(673,001)	(10,667)	991,333

Notes:
First-year net return: (Cumulative Q4 value – Cumulative Q4 investment) = approx. $991 K
Breakeven point: return outweighs investment in the beginning of Q4
ROI (first-year): (Cumulative Q4 total/Cumulative Q4 investment) = 90.172

Figure A.3 Value Justification (ROI)—Example

Week of	Event	Us	TGI	Billable
May 10	Kickoff meeting–finalize success criteria	X	X	
May 17	Begin design enhancements to e-commerce software package	X		$250K
June 7	Create customer interfaces from the online order entry system to accounting and inventory systems	X	X	$250K
June 12	Run pilot		X	
June 19	Review pilot results with management team	X	X	
June 24	Finalize the field sales/customer cut-over plan	X	X	
August 1–28	Field sales cut-over: 90% of sales staff		X	
October 1–November 10	Consultants accompany TGI representatives to teach customers how to place their orders online	X	X	$450K
December 31, March 31, June 30, and September 30	Perform customer satisfaction and success criteria review	X	X	

Plan approved by CIO (person responsible for implementation)

Figure A.4 Implementation Plan–Example

What is their investment's breakeven point? (3) What is their return on investment (ROI)? For this sample summary, we have not taken into account more involved elements of value analysis such as discounted cash flow, internal rates of return, and so on. This sample summary is intended to focus primarily on the comparison of benefits against investment over a given time period. *Note*: revenue and cost benefits do not all show maximum return until Q4.

The First Year Net Return TGI's first year cumulative net return of $2.1 million on their cumulative investment of $1.1 million is about $991 thousand.

There is an annual $991 thousand net return. TGI gets back its investment of $1.1 million by the beginning of the fourth quarter.

Return on Investment (ROI) TGI should realize a one-year ROI of 90.2 percent on their investment in the solution.

IMPLEMENTATION PLANS AND VALUE

Note: The Implementation Plan provides the customer with a visual bridge of how they are going to transition from the current state of business to the desired status. In Figure A.4 you will see what the post-purchase part of an evaluation looks like. This includes ongoing (mutual) Success Criteria to be measured (see Figure A.5).

	Baseline	Q1	Q2	Q3	Q4
Annual average # of new accounts per rep[1]	10				
Web site orders placed per customer[1]	0%				
Number of referrals per quarter[1]	7.5				
Credit write-offs per quarter[2]	$200K				
Number of customer service reps[2]	18				

[1] VP Sales
[2] VP Finance

Figure A.5 Success Criteria—Example

Solution Selling: A Scalable Approach

Solution Selling was designed to be scalable and to address both complex, difficult sales cycles as well as less complex, shorter sales cycles. When the subject of the shorter or less complex sales comes up, I'm usually asked two questions: Does Solution Selling apply? If so, how is it used?

The concepts and principles apply to both and it's because Solution Selling is based on human nature and how people buy; not all sales situations are created equal, however. Not all selling situations require an entire sales team to navigate every step of the sales process while using every job aid and technique of Solution Selling—that wouldn't be practical.

Keep in mind that one of the cornerstones of the Solution Selling sales process is to align your selling activities with the buyer's psychological buying phases. You may want to refer to Figure 2.4 in Chapter Two ("Buyers' Concerns Shift over Time"). The buyer has concerns that need to be addressed as they change or shift over time. *Over time* is the key phrase. In a less complex sale, the buyer may go through these phases in thirty minutes instead of thirty days. The job aids, activities, and approaches that we use in the more complex sale might need to be altered, simplified, or ignored. (See Figure B.1.)

It may also only be necessary to focus on a subset of the entire sales process as it relates to specific job functions—that is to say, a particular job function may only execute a few of the process steps. Salespeople

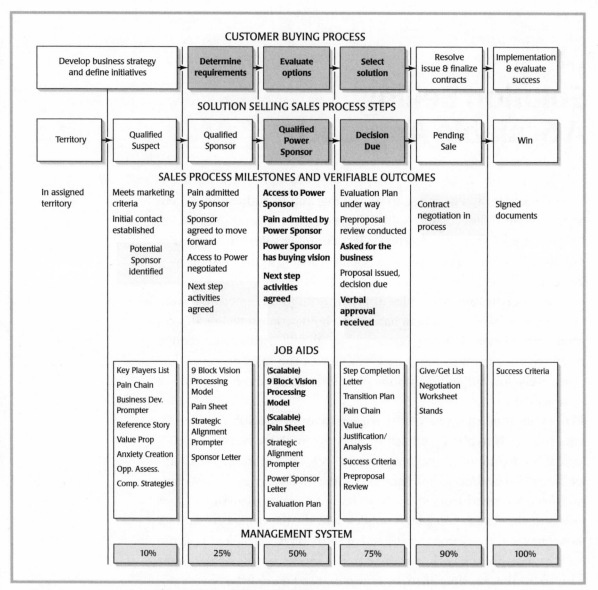

Figure B.1 Scalable Sales Process

who are executing only a few of the steps or who simply have a less complex sale can narrow their focus on specifics of Solution Selling.

The most important skill you can bring to a less complex sale is your need development competency. You simply adapt your questioning to fit the situation. The qualification process is scaled down, too. There's minimal qualification of the buying process (project management); it may be a one-call close. You still need to qualify how your buyer wants to close (get delivery instructions, clarify purchase order procedures, and so on).

A salesperson engaging in smaller sales situations or transactional sales is a likely candidate for a streamlined version of Solution Selling. If this is the case, the use of the entire 9 Block Vision Processing Model may be overkill. The impact column (Explore Impact) may become nonexistent. Because the confirming questions (especially R3 and I3) tend to sound redundant in short conversations, I recommend not using them. Since we use the Pain Sheet within the Vision Processing Model, your entire conversation will probably only use two columns—(Diagnose Reasons and Visualize Capabilities [R1, C1]) and two rows—(Open Questions and Control Questions [R2, C2]).

Let's review how you can apply the Solution Selling principles to a transactional sale. Scale the 9 Block Vision Processing Model to correspond with your sale's complexity. Narrow your focus on boxes R1, R2, C1, and C2. Pain Sheets can help you focus in this kind of a sale. For example, for the questioning sequence, use a two-column version of your Pain Sheet—Diagnose Reasons (R1, R2) and Visualize Capabilities (C1, C2). In fact, I recommend that in your precall planning you prepare two-column Pain Sheets. That will make the sales easier.

TELEMARKETING

Solution Selling applies also to telemarketing. If a telemarketer is engaged in fielding inbound calls (where prospects and customers are calling in for product information, terms, and conditions), I suggest

Figure B.2 Scalable
Job Aids

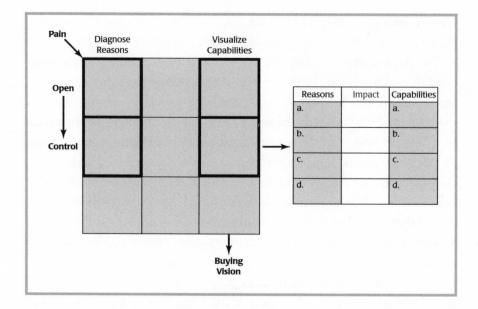

using the same philosophical approach. Again, use a streamlined approach; scale your selling activities according to the situation.

Understand the Caller's Current Vision

For example, if a prospect calls in asking for voice mail, the salesperson should ask an Open Visualize Capabilities (C1) question: "How do you see yourself using voice mail?" Taking time to understand the prospect's vision before the salesperson talks about his or her product makes it a more "problemcentric" call. Remember the principle *diagnose before you prescribe*. Imagine how this differentiates a salesperson from his or her competitors. To continue with my example, the prospect might answer, "When I leave the house, and I get a call concerning any of my children's activities, like soccer or Scouts, I want to make sure I get the message."

Diagnose How The Prospect Operates Today

Ask Diagnose Reasons questions (R1, R2), such as "How are you getting these messages today?" With this question, the salesperson attempts to understand the specific problem the prospect is seeking to solve. The prospect might respond, "The coach or the Scout leader has to call me at home, not at work. Sometimes my children get home first. They take the call, but forget to give me the message. I have a cell phone, but I don't want to give that number to everyone."

Even if the salesperson doesn't extend the vision further and begins talking about the offering, the prospect already feels that the telemarketer is taking time to focus on his or her situation. This is better than diving straight into product discussions.

Extend or Re-engineer the Buyer's Original Vision

The salesperson can try to further develop the prospect's existing vision using a capability, or C2 question. It works best to ask this in a capability format (when, who, what); for example, "Would it help you if, when you left the house, you could dial your cell phone number into the phone so that when a call comes in, it's routed to your cell phone? This way those lost calls might be avoided." The salesperson is simply selling a capability the prospect wants. The salesperson may then propose an additional feature, such as call forwarding. This would be an add-on to the buyer's original vision of voice mail.

As you can see, need development (Vision Creation and Vision Re-engineering) is the key and sometimes the only skill exercised in less complex, one-call sales. That is why the questions asked by the salesperson are so vitally important.

Afterword

Now that you've read all about Solution Selling and what it takes to increase sales and establish a high-performance sales culture, it's all up to you to make this a reality in your personal life or organization. To do this well, you will need courage and resiliency, but the potential rewards are worth the investment.

I recently had lunch with the retired chairman of Bank of America, Hugh McColl, whom I consider one of the great visionaries and leaders in the financial service industry. Hugh recognized that the financial industry was changing and instead of ignoring change, as most others did, he embraced it and found opportunity. And as a result, he helped grow Bank of America's business by more than fifty times to $610 billion in assets and more than 142,000 employees in twenty-one states. By embracing change, Bank of America has become one of the world's great success stories.

To succeed in business and in life, you do have to take some risks. Embracing a sales process like Solution Selling or introducing it into your business carries some risk of failure, if you don't sustain the changes the process requires. More than 500,000 sales professionals worldwide have overcome that risk, and are using Solution Selling every day. You have the opportunity now to make a real difference to yourself or organization by implementing Solution Selling, thus making a difference to your customers, to your business, and in your own life.

After embracing it personally or introducing the Solution Selling process into your organization, be prepared to encounter some resistance, and don't be discouraged. If we allow naysayers to dominate, we'll never do anything. The job of leadership is to articulate a vision that people can understand so they can follow. Be a leader by explaining the value of adopting the Solution Selling process. In fact, you can use Solution Selling to create that vision in the minds and hearts of your people.

I have a philosophy that I can achieve anything in life as long as I help others achieve what is important to them. I have also learned that if you want people to follow you, then you have to look after them, and you have to think about them. Helping your people with a proven process for serving customers and winning more business is a great way to demonstrate your commitment to their success.

In addition, by adopting Solution Selling, you are really giving your people a greater opportunity for victory, and for sharing that success with your organization. There's nothing like winning to create a sense of optimism, to feel that any obstacle can be overcome.

The potential rewards of embracing the principles of Solution Selling have been described at great length in this book. But let me describe one additional benefit which may not be so obvious. By using a proven process to win more sales, you are providing increased value to your customers, which allow you to create more wealth, and as a result, enjoy more freedom for yourself, for your family, and for everyone in your organization.

In this book, I have described how to create and sustain a high-performance sales culture that keeps the customer in the center of attention. Nothing is more important to achieving success in today's business environment. But, as I said before, the choice to make it happen is all up to you.

I wish you courage in your efforts to implement Solution Selling and optimism in realizing the freedom that comes from the success of you and your people.

Index

About the Author

Keith M. Eades is the founder and president of Sales Performance International (SPI) and Solution Selling, Inc. He and his associates have trained more than 500,000 sales and sales management professionals on the principles of Solution Selling. His clients include the world's top selling organizations, such as IBM, Microsoft, AT&T, and Bank of America.